Praise for
The Doom Loop

"This important and sobering book delves into the root causes of a perilous period for the global economy. Eswar Prasad, one of the United States' top economists, clearly and elegantly explains how the post–World War II international order has been undermined in a destructive feedback loop of financial and debt crises, populist domestic politics, and dramatic geopolitical shifts. Despite the bleak picture, Prasad's deep analysis offers critical insights into how we can escape our current predicament, the doom loop, of his title."

—Fiona Hill, author of *There Is Nothing for You Here*

"In *The Doom Loop*, Eswar Prasad explains why the foundational institutions that underpinned global prosperity in the latter half of the twentieth century are now faltering, and why no obvious alternatives have emerged to stabilize the world that America built. With his signature clarity and insight, Prasad excoriates Western powers and the institutions they created, arguing their failure to adapt has deepened today's crises. *The Doom Loop* is essential reading for anyone seeking to understand the forces shaping the unraveling global order—and the urgent choices ahead as we attempt to forge a new one."

—Raghuram Rajan, author of *Fault Lines*

THE
DOOM LOOP

Also by Eswar S. Prasad

The Future of Money: How the Digital Revolution Is Transforming Currencies and Finance

Gaining Currency: The Rise of the Renminbi

The Dollar Trap: How the U.S. Dollar Tightened Its Grip on Global Finance

THE
DOOM LOOP

Why the World Economic Order
Is Spiraling into Disorder

ESWAR S. PRASAD

BASIC

VENTURE

New York

Basic Venture
Hachette Book Group
1290 Avenue of the Americas, New York, NY 10104
www.basic-venture.com

Printed in the United States of America

First Edition: February 2026

Published by Basic Venture, an imprint of Hachette Book Group, Inc. The Basic Venture name and logo is a registered trademark of the Hachette Book Group.

The Hachette Speakers Bureau provides a wide range of authors for speaking events. To find out more, go to hachettespeakersbureau.com or email HachetteSpeakers@hbgusa.com.

Basic Venture books may be purchased in bulk for business, educational, or promotional use. For more information, please contact your local bookseller or the Hachette Book Group Special Markets Department at special.markets@hbgusa.com.

The publisher is not responsible for websites (or their content) that are not owned by the publisher.

Library of Congress Control Number: 2025936167

ISBNs: 9781541705937 (hardcover), 9781541705944 (ebook)

LSC-C

Printing 1, 2025

To Basia
My love, my light, my life
Zawsze i na zawsze

Contents

Disorder

The gods love what is secret and abhor what is obvious.
—Roberto Calasso, *Ardor*

In 1991, two years after the Berlin Wall crumbled, the Soviet Union disintegrated and the United States became the world's undisputed economic and military superpower. At that time, America accounted for about one-quarter of world gross domestic product. Its closest economic rival, Japan, captured a one-seventh share but had little military power to speak of. Over the next decade, the United States became even more dominant. By the year 2000, its share of world GDP rose to nearly one-third, while Japan's share was the same as in 1990 and China accounted for barely one twenty-fifth. It seemed as though US hegemony was becoming more deeply entrenched, with its market-oriented liberal democracy setting the standard for the rest of the world. US dominance was enhanced by its partnership with other rich industrial nations that shared similar values. Collectively, the seven largest industrial economies at the time—Canada, France, Germany, Italy, Japan, the United Kingdom, and the United States—produced nearly two-thirds of world GDP in 2000.

In recorded human history, no civilization or empire has maintained its supremacy indefinitely. The Roman, Byzantine, and Ottoman Empires, and more recently the British Empire, were once all-powerful and controlled vast swaths of territory. Each of them eventually withered away, brought down by some combination of external competition and internal rot. Perhaps US hegemony should not be measured by the same yardstick used to judge previous regimes. Over the past century, at least prior to Donald Trump's second term as US president, the United States has had no serious ambitions to annex and directly control territory outside its borders.

US command over the global economic and financial order and the country's aggressive advocacy of free-market liberal democracy across the globe, including by force in some cases, is still reminiscent of an aspiring empire. If history proves a reliable guide, American dominance will one day meet the same fate as that of empires of yore, even if that day lies in the distant future. To its detractors, American power already seems diminished as it struggles to sustain democracy and free markets within its own borders.

Prognostications regarding US dominance and rivals who could usurp its primacy represent only a part of the bigger picture, though. Instead, we must consider the broader implications of the forces reshaping the world order—implications that extend beyond the mere distribution of economic and military power to fundamental questions about which economic and political models may prevail.

These issues are coming to the fore amid momentous changes. Some of the changes are hugely positive—an increase in living standards around the world, longer human life spans thanks to medical advances and better nutrition, and the rise of new economic powers such as China and India, which has lifted millions out of poverty. Others, such as climate change and rapidly aging populations, are portents of tougher times ahead, some aspects of which already stand at our doorsteps. Internecine warfare, the expansionary tendencies of some autocrats, competition between rival forms of political and economic organization, and the warping of democracy worldwide are affecting all our lives. New technologies and innovations, including artificial intelligence (AI) and social media, are bringing us closer together and simultaneously tearing us apart. Each of these changes has ramifications for economies, societies, cultures, and, of greatest relevance for this book, the global economic and financial order.

Looking back, the beginning of this millennium will be seen as an important inflection point. In that year, dramatic changes that had been brewing for a while picked up pace. Some of them would shake up the world order, while others, such as the creation of a monetary union in Europe, would fail to deliver fully on their promises. The biggest shifter would prove to be the opening up of China, which was admitted into the World Trade Organization (WTO) in 2001. That gave Chinese exports access to international markets, kicking off a period of supercharged economic growth that has reshaped the world economy.

Today, the composition of the world economy has changed markedly since the beginning of the millennium. The US share of global GDP has fallen back to 26 percent, while China's share has soared to 17 percent, leaving other countries in the dust (global GDP is the sum of each country's annual GDP measured in US dollars at market exchange rates). The era of US economic dominance is hardly at an end, but the period since 2000 has not been favorable to America's close allies. Japan's economy has shrunk to 4 percent of world GDP, close to India's share. The combined share of world GDP of what used to be the seven largest industrial economies, which constitute the Group of 7 or G7, has fallen to barely 44 percent, a 20 percentage point decline since 2000, with Canada and Italy now bringing up the rear of the top ten economies.

My tribe of economists believes that competition is a positive force in practically every realm, certainly better than the alternative of unchecked monopoly power. Competition spurs efficiency, discipline, and innovation. Uber's technology for matching people seeking rides with those willing to offer them was remarkable, but it is competition that has kept the company on its toes. Uber's competition with Lyft in the United States and with other ride-sharing apps in various countries keeps prices down for riders and forces those companies to continually innovate and manage costs. Apple and Microsoft have to do the same in their incessant battle for market share, while at the other end of the spectrum Google's dominance in search and other services arguably gives it undue power that is not in the best interests of consumers.

Now, it is true that basic precepts of microeconomics do not always apply to the complex world of geopolitics. However, the underlying logic—that power cemented in the hands of only one or a few is less beneficial to society than a system where power is shared among many—is the animating force behind the democratic principles the West holds dear. A unipolar world is not without its advantages, though. A hegemon willing to exercise leadership and use its heft to maintain a rules-based system can be conducive to stability. For much of the post–World War II era, the United States willingly took on that role, but its muscular approach to maintaining order earned legitimate criticism. Indeed, the United States itself, particularly under the Trump administration, appears to have lost its appetite for this role.

Shifting from a unipolar world, in which the United States and its Western allies dominate in every sphere of global competition and influence, to one where new powers such as China and India assert their presence should offer opportunities for greater stability, as countries deploy their power in constructive ways for fear of losing influence. That, at least, is the theory. Reality is proving to be rather different.

Intensifying competition in the marketplace for global power is fomenting destabilization and tribalism as the world lurches toward a new order in which instability seems typical. Some might find comfort in the hope that this turmoil is simply the result of the world's adapting to a reconfiguration of economic and financial power and that eventually things will settle into a new and more stable equilibrium. This is not the case, though. In fact, I contend that the forces that should be pushing the world toward balance are deepening the rifts and inciting disorder rather than fostering stability.

Global trade and financial capital flows, driven by private businesses seeking profit and investors searching for better returns, once helped create bridges even between countries that were geopolitical rivals. American firms, for instance, invested heavily in China while building up their global supply chains. China benefited from the technology these firms brought with them. The firms were thus in a position to advocate with both governments for policies that would help to maintain good relations between the two sides.

Amid rising bilateral tensions and growing hostility from the Chinese government, American companies have begun retreating from China. The tensions cut both ways, with Chinese firms that operate in the United States now facing greater scrutiny. The social media app TikTok, created by the Chinese company Byte-Dance, found that even its user base of over half the American population did not insulate it from the threat of a ban on national security grounds. Legions of distressed teenagers and social media influencers do not, unfortunately, carry as much weight in geopolitical matters as business interests.

Moreover, it is not just American and Chinese companies that are shifting their behavior in the face of the rising hostility they face in each other's countries. Worldwide trade in intermediate goods, final consumer products, and even technology is being reshaped as firms look to run their supply chains through friendlier countries that have established better relations with their home countries. Flows of financial capital are similarly reorienting in line with geopolitical fissures, deepening rather than bridging over those fractures.

These developments are shredding the script about how the mutual benefits from economic integration offset or even outweigh the intrinsically competitive structure of geopolitical influence, in which one country's gains are another's losses. That script worked well for a while. Globalization, the expansion of international trade and financial flows that gathered momentum in the mid-1980s, delivered many benefits. Countries saw a future of common prosperity, with improving living standards not only supporting a shift toward open and democratic societies but also giving political leaders reason to tamp down geopolitical tensions that could damage economic and financial integration. China looked as though it was gradually but surely being co-opted into the liberal democratic order, led along by the promise of growing affluence.

Now, however, the feedback loop between economics, domestic politics, and geopolitics is spiraling out of control and becoming destructive on every front, turning into a doom loop. It has become apparent that the benefits of globalization have been distributed unevenly, resulting in debt-fueled financial crises in developing countries and wiping out manufacturing firms in some industries in advanced economies. The ensuing populist backlash has put in power leaders who have undermined democratic institutions and are hostile to globalization. International trade has been portrayed by these populists as a phenomenon in which one country gains only at the expense of others rather than enabling common prosperity. And the system of rules that underpinned the post–World War II world order is at risk of decay or, worse, irrelevance.

Thus, the prospects of a multipolar world are creating new dangers rather than quelling old ones. This is where we begin our exploration of the shape a new world order might take, the forces that will determine its contours, the perils that lie ahead, and some reasons for hope. This book will guide us through the twists and turns of this perilous journey, with some unexpected outcomes along the route. (That route is laid out by chapter below.) Forces that should promote stability, I argue, have become perverted into instruments of instability. Rather than just a transitory phase en route to a calmer and more orderly system, we find ourselves in a deeply troubled new world in which destabilization has become the norm.

Dimensions of Power

Dramatic changes have been underway since 2000 in the global composition of national incomes. The group of countries referred to as "emerging markets"—mostly middle-income countries such as Brazil, China, and India that have opened up their economies to international trade and financial flows—have risen significantly in economic power. These countries now account for a growing share of global GDP and other measures of economic activity such as world trading volume. Greater balance in economic power surely ought to have a stabilizing effect, with economic outcomes in any one country no longer having an outsize impact on others. More evenly balanced competition should also generate greater efficiency, increasing the size of the worldwide pie and making everyone better off.

Multiple factors, though, are throwing off this balance. Despite their rapidly expanding sizes, emerging-market economies remain relatively poor. On its present trajectory, India will become the third-largest economy in the world by 2030. But with its massive population, India's per capita income will barely equal one twenty-fifth that of the United States. The gulf in per capita incomes between emerging-market and richer, more advanced economies affects their respective approaches to matters of global concern, making cooperation more elusive.

Take combating climate change, an issue on which there ought to be a clear commonality of interests. China, the United States, and India, in that order, are the three largest emitters of greenhouse gases. The United States is a far richer country and, on a per capita basis, has much higher emissions than the other two. Moreover, on this basis, India's emissions remain well below those of the top ten emitters. This discrepancy generates tension in apportioning the blame for both carbon emissions and other drivers of human-induced climate change, as well as the costs of alleviating them. Climate change mitigation measures, such as reducing industrial and automobile emissions, are seen as costly, creating an inescapable trade-off with economic growth. Poorer economies feel it is unfair for them to shoulder the burden of this trade-off and limit their growth. The sad irony is that these economies tend to suffer the most from the destructive effects of phenomena such as floods and hurricanes that are exacerbated by climate change.

What about military power, once the key determinant of a country's eminence in world affairs? US military expenditures exceed those of the next nine economies (ranked by the size of those expenditures) combined. While still lagging the United States, China's military capabilities are growing along with its willingness to use those capabilities to aggressively expand its regional sphere of influence. The deterrence effects that two major military powers have on each other are being undercut by fraying ties between them in other areas. The once widely held view that countries that are deeply connected through trade are less likely to go to war with each other suggests that weakening trade linkages across the globe—US-China trade in particular—may bode ill for a peaceful world order.

Moreover, while conventional military prowess remains important, nuclear weapons have given small countries that possess even a handful of them outsize capacity for destabilization. Military power can substitute for weaknesses in other areas and elevate the status of rogue states, whose threats then need to be taken seriously, as North Korea's belligerent behavior has shown.

In short, a less concentrated distribution of "hard power," measured by GDP and military muscle, has not exactly been conducive to greater harmony between nations. Meanwhile, the tussle for "soft power"—influence that goes beyond a country's money and arms—has shifted in ways that do not promote stability either. The United States' diminishing interest in providing global leadership has given China an opening to augment this alternative dimension of its power. China's attempts to accrete soft power through economic engagement as well as support of regimes shunned by the West have won it numerous friends and geopolitical allies in Africa, Asia, and Latin America. The worm is, however, turning. Many countries are now pushing back against China, blaming it for their debt burdens and for seeking to influence their domestic politics. Rather than benefiting from greater competition for soft power, a large majority of countries have been harmed by the disengagement of one superpower and the less-than-constructive engagement of the other.

Currency Competition

Financial power, which is often linked to the prominence of a country's currency, has changed surprisingly little in one respect and in unexpected ways in another. The US dollar's preeminence in the global financial system has persisted, notwithstanding American policy stumbles and political dysfunction and despite pushback from rivals frustrated with the United States for wielding dollar dominance as a geopolitical weapon.

Meanwhile, ostensible competitors of the dollar such as the euro and the Chinese renminbi (RMB) are proving too fragile to mount a serious challenge, while other traditional powerhouse currencies such as the Japanese yen and the British pound sterling have taken a beating in recent years. These currencies, along with the upstart currencies of smaller economies such as Australia and Canada and those of emerging powers such as India, are now trading places in an increasingly fragmented second tier.

This is one area in which the usual (economist's) conception of competition as fostering better outcomes is turned on its head. The unrivaled status of the dollar could paradoxically prove a source of stability amid destabilizing competition between other currencies and particularly at times of severe stress in financial markets, when the entire world's trust in the dollar can keep a bad situation from turning worse. But the dollar's dominance comes with its own costs, exposing the rest of the world to financial turbulence caused by the vagaries of US economic policies and politics.

Globalization: Cohesion or Disarray?

The grand hope of globalization—greater trade and financial integration across national borders binding countries together in a mesh of shared interests, building harmony, and fostering progress toward a world united by shared values—has been dashed. Instead, integration has taken a turn toward fragmentation that closely parallels geopolitical rifts, deepening the fault lines between groups of countries that perceive others as rivals rather than as participants in a cooperative endeavor that benefits everyone. The positive-sum game of economics, where all countries can benefit from freer trade in goods and resources, is being recast by unscrupulous politicians as one where a country can benefit only at the expense of another, and as an excuse for the failures of those politicians' policies. Thus, economic forces are no longer countering the inevitability of the zero-sum game of geopolitics.

The aggressive jockeying between China and the United States exemplifies this shift. The two superpowers are explicitly engaged in competition for economic and geopolitical supremacy, with free and open trade falling victim to this competition. With no countervailing forces that can maintain a healthy balance, superpower competition is especially treacherous and destined to intensify, with every action and provocation deepening the rift. As large as these two countries are, though, this story is not just about their rivalry.

Globalization had a hand in sowing disarray around the world. Its devastating effects on jobs in some industries, and the decimation of entire industries in a few cases, have played an important role in bringing many once-vibrant democracies to the precipice of anarchy. The American Rust Belt might have faced a gradual decline in the best of circumstances, owing to technological shifts and the US economy's reorientation away from traditional smoke-stack manufacturing to services and high-tech industries. But imports from China and other low-wage countries accelerated that process, creating a class of marginalized workers, eroding support for free trade, and rewarding political appeals to resentment. Benefits from the freer flows of goods, services, and financial capital have been less noticed, let alone welcomed, by voters. Harnessing globalization's potential to improve economic outcomes and lives while allaying its destructive effects will be even more challenging with countries at loggerheads.

The urge to diversify economic (and, as we will see later, geopolitical) relationships has become a common theme underlying ongoing realignments of trade and financial flows. Businesses are taking the lead, shifting away from linear, cost-efficient supply chains that wind through multiple countries toward a new approach that promises greater diversification in their supply chains and in the markets for their products and services. American corporations, for instance, are limiting new investments in China while increasing investments in production facilities within the United States itself, as well as in Mexico, India, and other friendlier countries. Such actions in principle make these companies less vulnerable to risks associated with climate change, political instability, and cross-national tensions. This strategy comes at a cost, but one that businesses seem willing to pay to mitigate uncertainty. In another paradox, this very behavior risks worsening geopolitical tensions by diminishing the once-powerful counterbalancing force of strong economic ties.

Rules of the Game

Corporations and countries do seem to agree on one principle: that a set of fair and transparent rules governing cross-border commerce, financial flows, and even international relations is highly desirable. Beyond that general proposition, though, we see discord at every stage. Rules designed to promote evenhanded and orderly competition can make all countries better off, but the very question of who writes the rules and who enforces them is inevitably fraught and sets off contests over influence.

The legitimacy and effectiveness of multilateral institutions are now under threat. The WTO, the arbiter and enforcer of global trade rules, has tried to be evenhanded, not shying away from taking even the United States to task for violating those rules. But the view that it has been lax in applying the same standards to serial violators like China culminated in the Trump administration's disengagement of the United States from the organization and its threat to withdraw altogether. The WTO is hindered by the perception that its rules are formulated and enforced in ways that kowtow to economic and financial power rather than embodying principles of fairness.

Fairness no doubt lies in the eye of the beholder, but the perception of unfairness has serious effects. Emerging-market economies view the rules regulating international commerce, which have been devised largely by the advanced economies, as stacked against them. China, in particular, has been frustrated that its voting power at multilateral financial institutions such as the International Monetary Fund and World Bank lags behind its economic size because the traditional economic powers, particularly Europe and Japan, have been loath to cede their own influence. China has therefore taken to setting up its own institutions, such as the Asian Infrastructure Investment Bank, where it largely runs the show. It has also attempted to draw other emerging markets more tightly into its embrace through organizations such as the New Development Bank, which was set up in tandem with Brazil, India, Russia, and South Africa. The five founding members are in principle on equal footing, but there is little doubt that China dominates in all matters of consequence.

Competition between institutions can be healthy if it causes each of them to aspire to higher standards in governance and transparency and in maintaining legitimacy across a broad membership. Instead, though, it is creating a patchwork of rules and regulations that will ultimately hinder the free flow of goods, services, and money that underpins globalization. This turns the array of new and old international institutions into forums for destructive competition and, possibly, the eventual erosion of standards, rather than into sources of order and stability. The Trump administration's contempt for and open hostility toward multilateral institutions, many of which the United States was instrumental in setting up, have added to this ferment.

Middle Powers and Alliances

The fracturing of globalization and international governance has deepened geopolitical rifts, creating a predicament for established and rising middle powers. Ranging from large countries like Brazil, India, and Indonesia to smaller ones such as Chile, South Africa, and Vietnam, these countries typically lack independent power bases but have a common interest in enhancing the stability of the world order, for they are perilously exposed to global turbulence. Their behavior, in the face of a set of unsavory choices, is likely to prove detrimental to that stability.

With the United States and China engaged in a battle for global domination, there is no obvious alternative pole to which middle-power countries that depend on alliances with larger countries can tie their fortunes. The available choices therefore vary only in their degree of bleakness. For all its protestations about maintaining a strong presence in the Asian region, for instance, the United States has hardly been a reliable and trustworthy ally. This was exemplified by the last-minute US withdrawal from the Trans-Pacific Partnership, a trade agreement that had been actively promoted by the United States itself to counter China's expanding influence on the rules governing trade in the region. Such mercurial American behavior, which predates Trump but has certainly been amplified by his administration, has put many countries, especially those at China's doorstep, in a quandary.

Countries that have established strong economic or security-related relationships with both China and the United States are now being pushed to choose sides, a decidedly awkward and uncomfortable prospect. Some countries that seem to be deliberately balancing on the narrow ridge between the two sides risk falling into one valley or the other in a manner not entirely of their own choosing. Countries such as Singapore, South Korea, and Vietnam cannot easily escape their tight trade and financial links with China. Yet, while wary of being drawn deeper into China's economic and political embrace, they seem reluctant to push back too hard against the region's dominant power, particularly since neither Japan, once the leading economy in the region, nor the United States can be counted on to serve as an effective or reliable counterbalance.

The theme of diversification, which is becoming pervasive in business operations, is also apparent in the behavior of many countries that are choosing to diversify their loyalties rather than allying themselves too closely to any one global power. This strategy undermines the advantages gained by developing close alliances that can provide economic and security benefits. On the other hand, the rewards gained by tying a country's fortunes to that of any single power can be outstripped if the benefactor ends up on the losing end of global competition for economic and geopolitical power. This sets up what is often an impossible balancing act for small countries in particular, which depend on others for their economic and political survival.

The balancing act is complicated even for countries that have the luxury of size or wealth, but some of them are finding a new path. Issue-based alliances that flex with changing circumstances are likely to become pervasive, with countries finding common ground with others on specific issues and at particular times but without forming broader alliances that cover all the bases. India, for instance, has shifted back and forth between serving as an independent voice for developing economies, allying itself with other major emerging-market economies, and trying to build a stronger and more stable relationship with the United States. These objectives are not necessarily inconsistent but come into conflict when circumstances such as the Russian invasion of Ukraine force India's hand. In this case, India put its economic interests first and allied itself with Russia and China, refusing to participate in US-led financial sanctions on Russia or limit purchases of Russian oil.

Alliances that are based on hard-nosed short-term considerations rather than a shared set of values are unlikely to promote a more stable world through cooperation. Such transactional relationships, with countries often seeing their interests as not necessarily compatible with the broader global good and unwilling to compromise when promoting narrowly defined goals, can instead breed instability. When each issue is viewed as deserving resolution on its own merits, reaching compromise through grand bargains becomes challenging.

New Technologies: Panacea or Peril?

Technology and innovation are indispensable for achieving economic progress in a world with finite resources. They not only improve the quality of human existence but can also level the playing field, distributing economic power more evenly within and between countries.

New financial technologies built on digital platforms, collectively referred to as fintech, have transformed lives in many less developed countries. Consumers, businesses, and even street vendors now have access to fast, convenient, and secure digital payments. Fintech is also bringing countries closer together by improving international payments, reducing frictions in the flow of money across national borders. Some of these technologies, which are cheap and easily scalable, are giving middle- and even low-income economies the capacity to compete on a level footing with richer economies. China and India, for instance, have leap-frogged the United States in making low-cost and efficient digital payments widely and easily accessible.

These changes are not just about making payments more efficient. Mobile phone–based banking, which runs on basic flip phones and is readily accessible even to the illiterate and innumerate in low-middle-income and low-income countries like Kenya and Somalia, connects a country's citizens to its financial system, giving them opportunities to better manage savings, credit, and risk. This in turn gives them a stronger interest in seeing reforms enacted that are needed to fuel economic progress, helping to turn around the narrative that any reforms benefit only the rich while leaving the poor to suffer the dislocations caused by those reforms. Thus, technology can indirectly help make a better case even for globalization and build support for the reforms needed to make it work well for entire populations.

And yet, for all its promise, the darker side of technology is rearing its head in disturbing ways. Every new technology that can serve the broader public good can be used as easily in a damaging manner. Digital currencies, especially cryptocurrencies such as Bitcoin, have become havens for rampant speculation and illicit commerce. AI has unleashed powerful forces that will be difficult to control, deepening the alienation of those already marginalized by exclusion from economic opportunities. Social media, which was intended to bring us all together and eliminate physical distance as a barrier, has become an instrument for sowing and amplifying discord.

Technology by itself does not ensure international cooperation, which requires a sense of common purpose and shared interests rather than just closer connections. Moreover, human rapacity and the power of new technologies in the hands of individuals or even countries with malign intentions can cause enormous damage. These add up to a potent, toxic combination for destabilizing individual countries and the world order by undermining national and international institutions.

Visions for the World

There was once a widely held belief that liberal democracy and market-oriented capitalism went hand in hand, reinforcing and strengthening each other, and that this combination would eventually dominate the world. This optimistic view was probably most pervasive in countries that already operated liberal market-oriented democracies and that happened also to control the major global sources of information. There were certainly good reasons to accept this narrative, with the fall of the Soviet Union bolstering it and making it seem like an inevitable outcome. Recent history, though, has not been kind to this vision.

The messiness of democracy, particularly when it runs off the rails and puts (phony) populists in power, has hardly been helpful in building the case that it is the ideal form of political organization. Figures such as Jair Bolsonaro in Brazil, Boris Johnson in the United Kingdom, Viktor Orbán in Hungary, and Donald Trump in the United States rose to power through democratic elections. With its mechanisms that rely on norms and decency proving no match for such demagogues, who shamelessly pander to tribal instincts and thrive on breaking norms, democracy has not looked this fragile in nearly a century.

China has aggressively pushed its own vision of the ideal economic and political structure, which manifests in tight state control over the economy and society. This vision certainly resonates well in many countries where it is far easier for the political and economic elites to maintain control over the reins of power and dismiss any notion of accountability to the broader public.

And yet, communist economies such as China have to a significant degree relied on private enterprise, market mechanisms, and competition to achieve their economic objectives. The most important legacy left by Deng Xiaoping, who served as China's paramount leader from 1978 to 1989, was the set of reforms that ended the collectivization of agriculture and allowed private enterprise to flourish, in addition to opening up the economy to foreign trade and investment. Even Chinese President Xi Jinping, clearly a firm believer in the virtues of a state-dominated command economy, seems to recognize that private enterprise has become too important to China's prosperity to quash altogether. Meanwhile, governments in countries that extol the virtues of competition and free markets, including the United States, have become increasingly interventionist in their own economies and financial systems.

This convergence, which is admittedly modest and at odds with increasingly sharp rhetorical differences between the two competing visions, is hardly something to celebrate. It is instead the result of deeper rifts in views of the system of rules and institutions underpinning the global order and its ability to deliver fair and equitable benefits. If dysfunctional rules and institutions render free markets unable to deliver broadly beneficial outcomes within and between countries, then governments will step in, perhaps to an intrusive extent. And this will not only hurt economic progress but also undercut cooperation. More extensive state intervention, for instance, makes it harder for private businesses to foster economic connections across countries that in turn serve as a counterweight against other factors pulling countries apart.

Reclaiming Order from Disorder

Economic, political, and geopolitical forces have become entangled in a doom loop, with factors that ought to promote stability instead being twisted around and fueling disarray. To counter the forces of disorder, which are feeding off each other, the world needs true leaders—political leaders who are able to better align their countries' long-term interests with those of the global community and who are able to inspire their citizens to recognize that prioritizing short-term parochial interests over all else serves no one well. The world also needs a better way of devising and enforcing rules that are evenhanded and promote the common welfare. The political systems we now have, alas, are turning into refuges for those intent on perpetuating their own power rather than serving the public good.

The real challenge is to develop more effective institutions, at both the national and global levels, with which to harness all the good that humanity is capable of. This brings us to the central paradox we now face. Robust institutions, which design and administer rules that are fair and transparent, can help countries and their leaders circumvent human prejudices, narrow interests, and short-termism. But we need to rely on our better nature to create such institutions, keep them in healthy functioning order, and rejuvenate them when they weaken. As institutions fray, visionary leaders will find it harder to emerge and gain power while demagogues and false populists become entrenched in the power structure even as they twist it to their own ends.

Instability and chaos are becoming the status quo in the new world order. Breaking out of the doom loop that characterizes this order will require an extraordinary level of engagement from all of us, as citizens not just of our countries but of the world. But we must first understand the forces at play and how they are becoming perverted from constructive into destructive forces. Only through this understanding can we begin to find ways to effect the positive change that is essential to rebuilding and reinforcing national as well as global institutions. The difficult task ahead is to fortify institutions such that they promote prosperity and stability for all. We must confront these challenges head on rather than turning away. The stakes are simply too high.

1

Dimensions of Power

The course of history—whether you like it or not—has made you the leaders of the world. Your country can no longer think provincially. Your political leaders can no longer think only of their own states, of their parties, of petty arrangements which may or may not lead to promotion. You must think about the whole world, and when the new political crisis in the world will arise...the main decisions will fall anyway on the shoulders of the United States of America.

—Aleksandr Solzhenitsyn,
"Words of Warning to America"

A scene from the television series *Game of Thrones* shows Lord Petyr Baelish (Littlefinger) and Queen Regent Cersei Lannister in a tense conversation. The conniving Littlefinger, having risen from humble beginnings to occupy an influential position in the court through various machinations, makes it known that he is aware of the royal family's many dark secrets. He observes to Cersei that prominent families such as hers often forget an important truth. With his usual patronizing air, he proceeds to enlighten Cersei, proclaiming, "Knowledge is power." Cersei reflects on this for a moment, then orders her guards, "Seize him. Cut his throat." As Littlefinger struggles in panic with a knife at his throat, she interjects, "Stop. Wait. I've changed my mind. Let him go." With a wry smile, Cersei reminds the shaken Littlefinger of a greater truth: "Power is power."

On the world stage, power comes mainly from economic size, as measured by GDP, which represents the value of all the goods and services produced by a country in, say, a year. Historically, economic, financial, and geopolitical power have gone hand in hand, although the potency of these elements and how countries rank along each of the dimensions often diverge. With the dissolution of the Soviet Empire in 1991, the United States became the world's dominant power by almost any measure (except that Russia had more nuclear warheads). America accounted for a quarter of global GDP in 1990, much higher than the 14 percent share of the second-largest economy, and even that belonged to its geopolitical ally Japan. Over the next decade, the economic rivals of the United States fell further behind, cementing its dominance. By 2000, US GDP was more than double that of Japan, which was still the world's second-largest economy, and more than eight times that of China.

The United States remains a colossus, although a slightly shrunken one since then, with its share of global GDP falling back to 26 percent in 2024 from 30 percent in 2000. China's dramatic rise is of course *the* economic story of this millennium. China's GDP of $18 trillion in 2024 amounted to 17 percent of global GDP, up from 4 percent in 2000. Cumulatively, China has added even more to global GDP than the United States since the financial crisis of 2007–2009. After the COVID pandemic, however, China's economy stumbled, while the US economy held up much better than others. Still, even if China does not revert to the remarkably high growth rates it experienced in recent decades, its economic size makes it a formidable rival to the United States.

Although the United States and China are the main characters, this story encompasses more than just those two countries. India and other emerging-market economies are advancing rapidly up the list of countries ranked by GDP, while many of the traditional economic powers—including Germany, Japan, and the United Kingdom—wane.

The economic center of gravity is clearly shifting from the West to the East, reflecting a more even distribution of GDP and other measures of economic prominence such as trade. As a military power, China is catching up with the West, and it has also cultivated soft power, as indicated by its greater influence on the policies of other countries through adroit use of its economic might. These developments should promote a more balanced and steady world. After all, a world dominated by just one unrivaled hegemon carries the risk of subjecting all countries to the whims and whimsies of the hegemon's unchecked power, no matter how benevolent it might ostensibly be.

There are additional forces that ought to foster a broader balance in the future. Western countries and even China face declining and rapidly aging populations, as a result of which their labor forces are shrinking and dragging down growth. By contrast, a number of other countries—India, Indonesia, Nigeria, many others in Africa—have younger and still growing populations, which in principle bodes well for their economic futures. Some of these countries also hold vast pools of natural resources, another ace in their pockets—if played well.

Several factors are, however, disrupting this balance. The economies of many emerging-market countries are expanding rapidly, but they remain relatively poor, with per capita incomes still far below those in advanced countries. China's GDP makes it the second-largest economy, but its per capita GDP lags at only one-sixth that of rich economies such as the United States. Per capita incomes in India and other middle-income economies are even lower. This disparity reflects the broader divide between the advanced economies—rich but (with the exception of the United States) sluggish—and the emerging-market economies, which are large and growing rapidly but still not wealthy. It shapes how the two groups of countries view their relative contributions to problems such as human-induced climate change and their responsibilities for addressing them.

China, the United States, India, and the European Union, in that order, now rank as the four largest emitters of greenhouse gases. Yet on a per capita basis, the United States has undisputably claimed the top spot in this group. On that basis, China emits about half the volume of greenhouse gases the United States does, while India emits merely about one-seventh what the United States does. The historical context is relevant for this comparison as well. Whereas China's emissions per capita now exceed those of the European Union, the total emissions of the United States and the European Union together eclipsed those of China and India combined until 2008.

In other words, setting aside the past two decades, the rich economies have contributed disproportionately to greenhouse gas emissions due to their unrestrained industrial activity and wanton consumption. Since these countries can marshal abundant financial resources, there is presumably a moral imperative for them to shoulder the costs of the disruptive climate change consequences of their emissions. And yet it is now the middle-income economies that are being asked to restrain their industrial development—or at least to reduce their environmental impact, which is of course a costly undertaking. The common problem of climate change, and especially the tricky question regarding which countries should do more to address it or whether affected countries should be compensated, looks very different when viewed through these distinct lenses—per capita versus total emissions; historical versus current emissions—each of which is arguably as valid as the next. As a result, discussions regarding which countries should do more to implement climate change mitigation measures and who should bear the lion's share of the costs often end in stalemates.

Thus, notwithstanding the broad agreement on objectives, the conflicting perspectives of these groups of countries have brought progress to a standstill, with little agreement on strategies or time-frames for taking action even on such pressing problems. These divisions are now being exacerbated by divergences in assessments of the underlying causes and of the need to spend resources on measures to mitigate climate change. Such discord adds to the challenges of collective action on matters of global consequence. The outcome of the November 2024 United Nations Climate Summit is emblematic of these challenges. Countries could not even bring themselves to repeat the previous summit's call to transition away from fossil fuels and were able to agree on only a modest contribution from advanced countries to meet developing countries' financing needs for cutting emissions and to address the mounting costs of climate change.

In this chapter, we will parse the evolution of various elements of power and the interplay between them: economic power, military muscle, cultural and institutional power. We'll also explore how countries wield that power, and how shifts in the balance of power are destabilizing the world order. Let us start by looking at the distribution of economic might. Even that, it turns out, is a complicated task.

Economic Power

Making international comparisons of economic power based on GDP can be tricky. Counting up and comparing the kilograms of rice and numbers of cars produced by various countries might seem easy enough. But how does one take into consideration that the prices paid for these goods are expressed in terms of each country's own currency, making cross-country comparisons difficult? Things become even trickier when appraising the value of haircuts, cultural activities, and government services. To enable cross-country comparisons, the value of a country's output of goods and services must be calculated in monetary terms and then expressed in a common currency. Sounds simple, but the best way to do this in practice is a matter of much debate.

National statistical agencies report their countries' GDPs in their respective domestic currencies; those values can be converted into a common currency (the US dollar) using market exchange rates. By this measure, as we have seen, China's economy is about two-thirds the size of the US economy. By another measure, however, China's economy is already larger than that of the United States. This alternative comparison is based on purchasing power parity (PPP) exchange rates, which account for variations in purchasing power across countries.

A basket of goods and services costing the equivalent of $500 in China (when converted from dollars into Chinese RMB at market exchange rates) might cost twice that amount—roughly $1,000—in the United States. Reflecting such adjustments, at the end of 2024 one RMB was worth 14 cents at the market exchange rate, but its local purchasing power was the equivalent of 28 cents based on the PPP exchange rate. Differences in purchasing power matter even within a country that has a single currency. An inhabitant of rural North Dakota with an annual income of $50,000 would live a much larger life than an inhabitant of New York City with twice or even three times that income, especially given the differences between the two areas in housing costs but also in the prices of haircuts and other services.

Using PPP exchange rates instead of market exchange rates makes a big difference. By this measure, China's GDP overtook US GDP in 2016. This appears dramatic but is worth interpreting with caution. PPP exchange rates are relevant for measuring the domestic purchasing power of national incomes but are less relevant when comparing international economic power. An American tourist in Tokyo with $1,000 in her wallet would have greater spending power than a Chinese tourist visiting the same city with the equivalent of $500 in her wallet, even though those amounts would give them the same degree of purchasing power back in their home countries. The principle carries through if we consider foreign travel by the North Dakotan and the New Yorker, even if their purchasing power–adjusted incomes at home were identical.

Assuming they allocated similar proportions of their annual incomes to vacation travel (an admittedly dubious assumption given the many temptations a New Yorker faces for other expenditures), a foray to a Caribbean vacation destination would leave the North Dakotan at a disadvantage relative to the New Yorker.

To compare the relative economic well-being of Chinese and American households, PPP exchange rates are indeed the relevant measure, and they yield a sizable difference when used in place of market exchange rates. Per capita income in China is about one-sixth that in the United States based on market exchange rates. The gap narrows if one uses PPP exchange rates, with China's per capita income amounting to just under one-third that of the United States. Similarly, India's per capita income is the equivalent of 3 percent of US per capita income at market exchange rates but 13 percent of US per capita income based on PPP exchange rates.

Much has been made of the fact that, using PPP exchange rates, China's economy not only surpassed that of the United States in 2016 but, by 2024, was 30 percent larger. When comparing international financial power, though, market exchange rates are the relevant measure. These exchange rates do of course move around from month to month, day to day, and even minute to minute, just like stock prices. An exchange rate between two currencies is the price at which they can be traded for each other and is affected by a variety of factors in both countries and even outside them. PPP exchange rates are by construction stable because the daunting exercise of constructing price indexes that are comparable across countries takes place once a year, with benchmarking of these indexes to take account of changing consumption patterns occurring even less frequently—only once every few years. This contrived stability does not render PPP exchange rates superior to market exchange rates. The upshot is that, rather than taking too literally year-to-year fluctuations in GDPs based on market exchange rates, one should be judicious and use longer-term trends to evaluate shifts in international economic power.

While the rise in China's economic might and the decline in that of the United States since 2000 attract the most attention, there are other significant shifts underway. One of the more dramatic changes involves low- and middle-income economies (as measured by per capita incomes), which increased their share of global GDP from about 21 percent in 2000 to 42 percent in 2024. This surge largely reflects growth in the emerging-market economies, a set of countries that have opened up to international trade and financial flows (although not fully in all cases) and by now have solidified their middle-income status.

China is certainly the star of this group, with sustained rapid growth, but others, including Brazil and India, have also grown rapidly, although more unevenly than China. China, India, and Brazil now rank among the top economies worldwide. Unless Japan and Germany can shake off their economic malaise, and even if they do manage to eke out modest growth rates, India has a realistic prospect of becoming the world's third-largest economy before the end of this decade.

Some of these shifts reflect changes in market exchange rates. From 2000 to the end of 2024, China's RMB went up by 13 percent in value relative to the US dollar, while the Japanese yen's value fell by about 40 percent relative to the dollar. These are sizable changes but still play only a modest role in the large shifts in GDP shares discussed above. If one were to use PPP exchange rates rather than market exchange rates to compare national GDP figures, the increases in the global GDP shares of the emerging-market countries and the corresponding declines in the shares of the rich countries would look yet more dramatic.

It is not just GDP but also shares in global trade and manufacturing that corroborate the shifting power balances in the world economy. In 2000, China accounted for 4 percent of global exports of goods. By 2020, its share had risen about fourfold, to 15 percent. Over this period, the combined share of global exports of the G7 advanced economies fell from 45 percent to 30 percent.

Emerging markets and other developing countries are exporting much more robustly—in addition, they now conduct much of their trade with other countries in this group. In the 1970s and 1980s, these countries relied on the much richer advanced economies to absorb their exports. How things have changed, thanks to the rapid growth and burgeoning middle classes of developing economies, which have turned them into important export destinations for advanced economies. Japan and South Korea now send more of their exports to China (including Hong Kong) than to any other country. China is also one of the top export destinations for Germany, and China's voracious appetite for commodities to feed its industrial machine also makes it a key market for commodity exporters such as Australia and Canada.

The global structure of industrial production, once the key metric of economic power, has also shifted massively. The collective share of the old industrial powers, the G7 countries, fell from two-thirds of global manufacturing in 1990 to one-third in 2024, about the same as China's share. In 2024, China's share of global manufacturing output was double that of the United States, five times that of Japan, and seven times that of Germany. Again, this is a story in which China is most prominent, but it also features a bevy of other emerging-market economies that have experienced rapid industrial growth, surpassing traditional manufacturing hubs. The United Kingdom's manufacturing output is now overshadowed by those of India, Mexico, and Russia, with Brazil and Indonesia nipping at the UK's heels.

Human beings constitute one of the most important of a country's resources. It is not just the number of humans but also (and perhaps more significantly) their knowledge and skills, usually measured in terms of formal educational attainment or number of years of schooling, that determines a country's "human capital" and in turn affects its growth prospects. When it comes to population growth, there is a stark divide between richer and poorer countries that will have a bearing on future shifts in economic power.

It is a well-documented empirical regularity that richer societies exhibit lower fertility rates than poorer ones (and richer people within a given society generally exhibit lower fertility rates than those who are less well off). In most rich countries, fertility rates—the average number of children a woman is likely to bear during her lifetime—have fallen below the replacement rate of 2.1 that is the threshold for maintaining a stable population.

In some countries, such as Italy and Japan, the fertility rate hovers around 1.3, much lower than the replacement rate and indicating a rapidly shrinking population. Even some middle-income countries face demographic problems. China's population began declining before reaching high-income status, a result of the one-child policy that was put into effect in 1980 and that certainly delivered on its intended objective of controlling population growth. By the time the policy was reversed in 2016, with the government encouraging its citizens to bear more children, the force of rising incomes, which almost always pushes fertility rates down, was in direct conflict with the government's new objective.

Most countries are also faced with graying populations, as reflected in rising ratios of the elderly to the working-age population. This ratio, referred to as the old-age dependency ratio, is of course a happy consequence of the increasing life spans that result from better nutrition and health care, and wealthier countries typically benefit from having better health care systems. But when fewer people in the population are of typical working age, a heavier burden falls on working-age persons to support the elderly. In 1960, every person in the United States receiving a retirement or disability check was supported by about 5.1 workers. Over the years, this ratio has steadily declined, and by 2022, the number of workers supporting each beneficiary had dropped to just 2.8.

This combination of dwindling and aging populations means shrinking labor forces. Japan's working-age population (typically defined as those fifteen to sixty-four years of age) peaked at eighty-seven million in the mid-1990s and has fallen steadily since then, down to seventy-four million in 2024, a 15 percent decline. Again, it is not just rich countries but those in the middle-income group that face similar issues. China's labor force, for instance, has declined gradually over the past decade.

Immigration can be a powerful force in determining which countries suffer less from deteriorating demographic profiles. This in part explains why the United States faces a less dire demographic situation than most other advanced economies. Net immigration accounted for about two-fifths of US population growth (about twenty million people) from 2010 to 2019. Countries like China and Japan that are relatively closed to immigration do not have this avenue to offset the shrinking and aging of their populations. In fact, China has had a net negative migration rate since the 1970s, meaning that more people leave than enter the country.

Immigration of course comes with its own problems, especially the difficulties with cultural and other forms of assimilation that can lead to societal and political tensions. Waves of immigrants fleeing war, poverty, and natural disasters in Africa and the Middle East have altered the political discourse in many European countries, with right-wing parties opposed to immigration gaining ground and mainstream parties adopting more hard-line stances on the issue. German Chancellor Angela Merkel's welcoming stance toward immigrants and her decision to allow over a million asylum seekers to enter Germany in 2015 created a backlash that, by 2025, resulted in the head of her own party vowing to crack down on illegal immigration and increase deportations if he became chancellor. Even in the United States, which has benefited from inward migration that has brought not just more labor but also enormous talent and brainpower, Trump has succeeded in demonizing immigrants. Restrictions on both legal and illegal immigration could limit the advantages the United States has long enjoyed and cause its demographic profile to start resembling that of other advanced economies.

The big "winners" in the demographic realignments are countries that continue to experience population and labor-force growth. Most countries with low per capita incomes are expected to experience more rapid labor-force growth over the next three decades. By contrast, for most rich countries—those with annual per capita incomes above $20,000 in 2023—labor-force growth rates are projected to be minimal or, in a majority of cases, negative. Among middle-income countries, India and Indonesia have an edge because of their growing and still relatively young populations.

Large and growing populations, once seen as a liability, are now viewed as a source of strength—but they could just as easily turn out to be time bombs if their rising aspirations are not fulfilled. A growing workforce by itself will not help a country's economy. Labor-force participants need to receive the right sort of education and training that equips them for the types of skills that are in demand. And the economy needs to generate jobs that can productively employ those participants.

Shifting attitudes toward globalization could make it harder for countries whose populations are young and growing to take advantage of this "demographic dividend." Rising trade protectionism will stifle the growth of developing countries and leave young workers bereft of prospects for economic advancement, especially through relatively high-paying manufacturing jobs. This combination of expanding workforces and limited job growth has ramifications for the structures of societies and political systems, for not only can frustrated youth cause domestic turmoil, but when they emigrate in search of economic opportunities, they can export that turmoil to other countries.

Natural resources represent a potent source of power. Control of a large share of easily extractable oil deposits has enriched the Middle East, giving countries like Saudi Arabia enormous clout in global affairs. Africa has extensive natural resources, but many countries on the continent are beset by corrupt governments, insufficient expertise, and lack of domestic funding, with the result that foreign corporations that are willing to offer funding as well as technical equipment and know-how eagerly exploit these resources. Most of the profits have been cornered by these corporations along with the political and economic elites in each country, with only crumbs left for the rest of the population.

The distribution of natural resources has implications for global institutions and for tackling issues associated with negative externalities, where a particular country's policies and pursuit of its own interests can have negative consequences for the rest of the world. For instance, Saudi Arabia has consistently pushed international financial institutions such as the World Bank to downplay the effects of fossil fuel emissions on climate change, arguing that such issues fall outside the mandate of institutions that should focus on trade, finance, and development aid.

Natural resources are finite, though, and the power they confer on a country is not immutable. Technological developments can change a country's fortunes dramatically, either by generating greater demand for a particular mineral or other raw material or, in some cases, having the opposite effect of squelching demand or expanding alternative sources of supply. For instance, new techniques for extracting natural gas and other fossil fuels have made the United States, which was a major oil importer as recently as the late 2010s, largely energy independent, although it still remains vulnerable to changes in worldwide energy prices.

The advancement of technology does not always reduce demand for natural resources; in some cases it even increases demand. That is the case with demand for rare earth minerals, seventeen metallic elements that are, in small quantities, essential components of a broad range of high-tech products such as cell phones, computers, televisions, electric vehicles, and industrial goods. Even semiconductor chips, which power the creation of cryptocurrencies and underpin AI technologies, need rare earth minerals.

China harbors nearly half of the world's reserves of rare earth minerals. Brazil and India hold sizable reserves, and so do the United States and Greenland. But it is in the mining and processing of these elements—activities that have significant adverse environmental impacts, releasing toxic chemicals and endangering workers' health—that China has become dominant. This gives China a stranglehold over the supply of these minerals, which the rest of the world craves. The United States, for instance, relies entirely on imports for twelve critical minerals.

The recognition that such dominance gives China a major weapon against its economic and geopolitical rivals has led other countries to reduce this dependency through a combination of diversification of countries these minerals are sourced from, substitution where possible, innovation that reduces the need for them, and recycling. When China and Japan engaged in a trade spat in 2010, China restricted shipments of rare earth minerals to Japan. This spurred Japan to adopt strategies to reduce its dependence on rare earth imports from China from 90 percent to 60 percent. The reality, though, is that China still remains—for the foreseeable future—a critical global supplier of rare earths, giving it substantial if rather transitory power.

This situation presents an opportunity for other countries endowed with rare earth minerals. Many poor countries in Africa are rich in deposits of these and other minerals such as chromium, cobalt, platinum, uranium, and even diamonds and gold, all of which could become important sources of revenue.

An abundance of rare earths and other natural resources is not always a blessing, however. Take the Democratic Republic of Congo (DRC), one of the most resource-rich countries in the world. Its untapped deposits of raw minerals are estimated to be worth more than $24 trillion, a wealth of resources that has become a curse for the country. With the government poorly run and doing a dreadful job of managing its resources, illicit trade in these minerals has created a calamity for the common citizens of the DRC, who have been subject to environmental degradation, social and political upheaval, human rights abuses, and violence. To make things worse, the economic benefits accruing to common citizens have been scarce, as the economic and political elites have plundered the country, often in cahoots with foreign mining firms.

The phenomenon wherein resource-rich countries experience low growth, economic and political instability, and high rates of internal conflict because of the mismanagement of those resources has come to be dubbed the "resource curse." That poignant irony is heightened when neighboring countries without such resources prove more stable and even deliver higher GDP growth. As Kenneth Kaunda, the first president of Zambia, said in reflecting on the plight of his and other countries in Africa that have been torn apart by the ostensible boon of abundant natural resources, "We are in part to blame, but this is the curse of being born with a copper spoon in our mouths."

Not all examples are quite as bleak. Guyana, a small country in South America that was once one of the poorest in the Western Hemisphere, enjoyed the prospect of a bonanza from discoveries of significant offshore oil fields during the most recent decade. Guyana is now one of the fastest-growing economies in the world, which has translated into rapid job growth, improved

35

infrastructure, and even the nation's first Starbucks. Still, it was a foreign company, ExxonMobil, that made the discoveries and that, along with its partners, has reaped many of the benefits. Much of the Guyanese population remains stuck with meager wages, high inflation, and environmental concerns, while all the natural bounties have only amplified social unrest and political turmoil.

Thus, it is not just a country's abundance of natural resources but, often more importantly, its capacity to extract and utilize them effectively that helps shape the balance of power. The distribution of natural resources often drives instability. First, it grants outsize power to countries that use control of essential resources as a weapon against rivals. Second, it fuels domestic instability in countries suffering from the resource curse, marked by endemic corruption and weak political institutions.

The bottom line is that a more even distribution of various components of economic power among countries has not clearly fostered greater international cooperation, instead often fueling disharmony.

Military Muscle

Queen Regent Cersei's contention that power is power has shaped policies in countries of all sizes and political stripes. The capacity to defend its own borders and even those of its allies is a key attribute of any country's global power. Size matters when it comes to assessing military expenditures, for a country needs to be able to deploy forces not just on its own borders but across the region in which it is located and even farther afield.

Military expenditures are difficult to isolate, with the line between defense and purely civilian projects hazy at best. For instance, expenditures on cybersecurity and nuclear energy research benefit both the civilian population and the military; the classification of these expenditures in the United States depends on which agency undertakes them. In some countries, military expenditures are not widely advertised, as they could raise questions about the power and influence of the military or about a leader's priorities. There is greater transparency in countries where national legislatures must approve government expenditures. In any event, the cross-country comparisons below need to be taken with a generous cupful of salt.

US military expenditures amounted to some $916 billion in 2023. This was greater than the sum of the comparable expenditures of the next nine countries combined when ranked by the size of their military expenditures (expressed in US dollars at market exchange rates). Based on this metric, the world still seems unipolar. When comparing military expenditures, however, PPP exchange rates are more relevant than market exchange rates. Chinese soldiers are paid in RMB, and the costs to the country's armed forces of building and maintaining tanks, aircraft, and warships are largely based on RMB-denominated costs. For 2024, China's defense budget was set at RMB 1.7 trillion, which would amount to about $230 billion at market exchange rates (as of December 2024) but roughly $470 billion at PPP exchange rates. Even at market exchange rates, over the past two decades China has been steadily closing the gap with the United States in military expenditures.

Besides the United States, the military budgets of other major economic powers such as Germany and Japan have been restrained since the end of World War II, due initially to international pressure and then owing to domestic political dynamics. Trump's antipathy toward America's North Atlantic Treaty Organization (NATO) obligations is causing European countries to increase their military expenditures, for they can no longer rely on the bloc's collective defense obligations being honored by its most significant military power. Diversion of resources from other public expenditures will only poison domestic politics in these countries, some of which are already financially strapped, while addressing security concerns only to a limited extent against an aggressor like Russia.

China, India, Russia, and Saudi Arabia now rank in the top ten in terms of estimated military expenditures. This does not necessarily mean that the emerging-market economies constitute a military bloc that rivals the West—some of the expenditures are dedicated to fortifying their shared borders against one another. India's military expenditures are to a large extent driven by concerns over Chinese aggression on the country's northeast border.

The nature of a country's military expenditures carries implications for whether they engender further instability or, through deterrence effects, stability. Nuclear weapons, which enable a country to devastate an enemy's population centers, provide significant mutual deterrence effects. The nuclear warheads in the arsenals of China, Russia, and the United States can together incinerate practically all the world's major cities many times over, which in principle deters these countries from inciting nuclear war against each other. Simply counting up nuclear warheads, however, is by itself of not much help in evaluating this aspect of military power.

Nuclear weapons can substantially alter a country's bargaining position even if its conventional armed forces are lacking in heft. A country's first few nuclear warheads with effective long-range delivery systems enhance its power more than additions to an already-large stockpile of such weapons. A few small rogue states, such as North Korea, or those with highly unstable governments, such as Pakistan, maintain modest stockpiles of nuclear warheads that could nevertheless inflict enormous damage on their rivals. Iran could one day join this list of countries wracked by economic mismanagement and poverty yet boasting outsize destructive power. Adding such countries, which have less to lose and more to gain from actually using nuclear devices, to an already volatile mix of major nuclear powers substantially raises the risks to regional as well as global stability.

While the very existence of a country's nuclear weapons capability can shift the balance of power, recent wars, even those involving nuclear powers, have been fought using conventional forces alone. The greater balance in military expenditures, though, raises rather than reduces the risks of cross-border conflicts using conventional weapons, particularly as China strives to expand its sphere of influence in regions where the United States has for a long time had no rival. A more assertive India, which shares contentious borders with China and Pakistan, adds to these concerns.

The Ukraine war resulting from Russia's aggression and the open conflict between Israel and its neighbors triggered by Hamas's attacks on Israel have resulted in enormous loss of human life and destruction of civilian infrastructure. Although these wars have remained relatively contained geographically, the conflicting interests of the major economic and military powers have kept them simmering and unresolved for a long period. The prolonged stalemate in the Ukraine war in particular shows how conflict and devastation can easily become normalized in a world without a single hegemon, and how a more evenly balanced distribution of hard power does not by itself necessarily conduce to peace and harmony.

Intangible Power

Counting up automobiles, refrigerators, working-age people, mineral deposits, tanks, and nuclear warheads, and comparing these numbers to the corresponding numbers in other countries is actually the easy part in evaluating a country's relative global power. Many of a country's intangible attributes, including institutions, culture, and language, are as important, if not more so.

In their book *Why Nations Fail*, Daron Acemoglu and James Robinson draw on a vast trove of academic research to make the compelling case that high-quality political, economic, and legal institutions are indispensable to economic success. A number of countries rich in natural and other resources have proven to be economic failures on account of their weak institutions, leaving the vast majority of their citizens mired in poverty. By contrast, good institutions have lifted per capita incomes in countries like Singapore, which is endowed with few natural resources, beyond those of its neighbors and even those of many Western countries. So what exactly are the ingredients that make up this special sauce?

The range of institutions that foster success is broad. It starts with a government that is responsive to the needs of and accountable to a country's citizens. Such a government is typically characterized by a system of checks and balances that regulate relations between its branches. In the United States, for instance, the executive, legislative, and judicial branches can and do restrain each other's power, although this precept is certainly being put to the test in the Trump era. Open and transparent liberal democracies are typically seen as embodying the form of political organization that best delivers on these aims.

The rule of law is a crucial piece of the institutional architecture. It means in particular that, although a central government appoints the judiciary and creates laws, it must apply those laws impartially and follow them consistently itself. Government officials and even leaders must be subservient to the same laws that govern the broader society. At a more prosaic level, a judicial system that rapidly and effectively protects contractual and property rights is essential to the smooth operation of a market economy.

One institution that has become more important in practically every country is the central bank. Central banks are responsible for keeping inflation low and also for ensuring the stability of a country's banking and financial systems. In recent years, effective and agile central banks have become indispensable for well-functioning economies, especially in the face of traumatic events such as the Great Recession of 2008–2009 and the COVID-induced recession of 2020. In less well-developed economies, they are often seen as the one institution that functions relatively well and operates on sound principles, at least when compared with other institutions.

Thus, central banks have become, as some have put it, the only game in town. Their technocratic reputation, and the fact that they can help in offsetting episodic failures of fiscal and other government policies, has helped reinforce their autonomy from political interference, although that autonomy still hangs by a thread in many cases. Even in large democracies such as Brazil and India, the heads of central banks have faced enormous pressure from governments to do their bidding and have been shunted aside when seen as insufficiently pliable. An independent and effective central bank, in addition to a competent set of financial regulators, is vital for maintaining the confidence and trust of both domestic and foreign investors in a country's currency and financial markets.

There is a strong positive correlation between the quality of a country's institutions and its economic progress. Whether this is a causal relationship cannot be easily established. Do more effective institutions promote growth, or does economic progress breed good institutions? Perhaps the equation runs both ways. A large body of academic research strongly suggests that there is in fact a causal relationship: Better institutions promote economic prosperity. There is, however, one elephant in the room—or, on closer inspection, what turns out to be a panda—that cannot be ignored.

China stands out as a glaring exception to the proposition that the institutions described above are essential to economic success. This powerful country does not feature a democratic government, the rule of law, or an independent central bank. Chinese officials and academics will tell you that the country hews assiduously to the rule of law, but that is only in the narrow sense that the courts ostensibly enforce property and contractual rights. And even that extent of legal order exists within certain well-defined limits. China's judicial system explicitly defers to the Communist Party of China, with challenges to any level of government either discouraged or outright prohibited. The People's Bank of China, the central bank, is not autonomous even in its operational decision-making, with all significant policy decisions having to be ratified by the State Council, an organ of the government that is composed of high-level party officials. So China lags on practically every element of the institutional framework that is closely associated with economic success.

While the Communist Party of China controls all levels of government in China, promotions within the party—except for promotions to the Politburo, the top policymaking body—have long been regarded as mostly meritocratic. Chinese citizens do not have the opportunity to vote freely for their representatives at any level, but officials are still seen as accountable in the sense that their promotions depend on their ability to maintain stability in their fiefdoms, which in turn is predicated on economic progress and efficient governance. Whether these are adequate substitutes for an institutionalized system of checks and balances is debatable. Foreign businesses and investors, above all, are keenly aware that they are subject to the whims of government officials and cannot count on the fair application of rules and regulations.

The absence of a strong institutional framework, at least based on conventional metrics, has not blunted China's economic progress. As we will see in later chapters, though, it could constrain China's ability to turn its economic might into broader influence or even financial power on a global scale. For instance, China's narrow interpretation of the rule of law and the lack of independence of its central bank are likely to make it difficult to earn the trust of foreign investors, limiting the RMB's prominence in international finance. Institutional weaknesses can also generate more immediate consequences, as they affect the nimbleness of governments.

An important aspect of power that is harder to quantify but crucial in a volatile world is the agility and flexibility of a country's government and institutions, including encouragement of or at least tolerance of a free press and broader freedom of expression for a country's citizens. The world is a risky place, and countries that are able to effectively plan for and manage risk enjoy better outcomes. Renowned political scientist (and my colleague at Cornell University) Peter Katzenstein has argued that an important element of global clout is "protean power," which, in the context of this book's themes, refers to a country's capacity to cope not just with risk but with uncertainty. Uncertainty is distinct from calculable risk (such as the probability your house will burn down or, more pleasantly, that you will live past one hundred years of age, which could be a risk to your finances). Uncertainty encompasses developments that are unforeseeable or difficult to calculate reasonable probabilities for based on historical patterns. The capacity to respond with agility and speed in the face of uncertainty has implications for a country's domestic fortunes and for global power.

Consider, for example, the near-total lockdowns imposed by the Chinese government in response to the COVID pandemic, which originated in China in late 2019 and quickly spread globally. While the lockdowns limited Chinese fatalities during the initial stages of the pandemic, they came at a huge economic cost. The success in limiting human loss was soon offset by the prolonged lockdown, as the government seemed unwilling to admit that a once-effective policy had turned detrimental, with mounting economic and social costs. The government also seemed unable to respond effectively to changing circumstances, with any criticism of the official policy, either online or in public protests, squelched harshly by the authorities. Still, the pushback from Chinese citizenry proved harder to contain over time as their pain grew.

Eventually, and very abruptly, China's lockdown was lifted in late 2022 with little notice and with scant preparation for the rapid surge in infections that inevitably followed. Fatalities spiked greatly (although official statistics suggest otherwise). Such drastic policy turnarounds point to the rigidities of an institutional structure in which power is highly centralized and few avenues enable common citizens to express their views freely. Open channels for citizens to convey their opinions might have prompted an earlier and smoother adjustment of policies. In a world beset by escalating risks and uncertainty, a rigid government and institutional framework can exact substantial costs. It can even undermine the confidence of citizens in their government's ability to effectively navigate periods of uncertainty, even as dire uncertainty on multiple fronts becomes the norm worldwide.

In the 1970s, when I was a young boy in Madras (now Chennai) who had no opportunity to travel abroad, my view of the world outside India was shaped largely by the weekly sheaf of magazines that my family received from a subscription service. A bloke on a bicycle would deliver five of the latest magazines every weekend (and take back the previous week's magazines, which would then be recirculated multiple times down the line to households with cheaper subscription plans). We could choose up to three "foreign" magazines. I devoured the ones we chose—*Life* (sadly now defunct), *Reader's Digest*, and *Time*—becoming convinced that the United States was the land of milk and honey, with untold riches, untrammeled personal freedoms, and the world's finest, most generous, and most beautiful people. We could not afford a television until much later (and I never touched a computer before coming to the United States), so magazines pretty much defined the world for me and my friends.

Cultural power is important, for it can shape thinking and public opinion and, by extension, affect policy. The global dominance of Hollywood movies and American pop music probably contributed to the country's image abroad as the epitome of all that is good and prosperous. Similarly, the aura of French films and culture, alongside colonial legacies that maintained the language's importance in many parts of Africa, allowed a relatively small country to exercise outsize influence, even if indirectly. Now that is all changing. Easy access to domestic and foreign media through the smartphone has proliferated in every corner of the world. Illusions of unsurpassed US supremacy have been washed away, although Hollywood and American culture still command worldwide attention.

We are now experiencing phenomena like the Korean wave, with TV shows such as *Squid Game* permeating households around the world (including mine). And who hasn't heard of the K-pop group BTS, which is estimated to have added more than $3 billion annually to the South Korean economy and helped lift the country's profile. South Korea's cultural content exports amounted to $12.5 billion in 2021, although the country's influence has mainly been in specific sectors such as cosmetics, fashion, and music. Cultural power has clearly become more widely dispersed, and at least along this dimension the world is unarguably better off when power is not concentrated.

Culture is tied up with language, and in this case size does matter. Native speakers of Mandarin, who number roughly 1 billion, outnumber those of any other language (followed by Spanish, English, and Hindi, in that order). But the number of nonnative speakers of English, estimated roughly at more than 1.1 billion, puts it well ahead of all others as the most widely spoken language in the world, with about 1.5 billion total speakers. More importantly, English remains the language of international commerce and diplomacy. The effects are subtle. The ways in which words and emotions, and even dry technical concepts, are expressed often differs by language and can affect outcomes of negotiations. The common understanding of certain issues is shaped by the language that intermediates that commonality.

The Vienna Convention on the Law of Treaties establishes that international treaties authenticated in multiple languages should be equally authoritative in each language. Nevertheless, bodies like the WTO often treat English text as the "master" text, implying that the English meanings of such ambiguous terms as "shall," as opposed to the meanings of similar French or Spanish words, prevail. Adoption of English as a lingua franca has even been shown to reduce impediments to cross-country trade based on language barriers, promoting trade volumes for countries where English is not a widely spoken language. Thus, there are strong incentives for individuals worldwide to attain proficiency in English, which invariably comes with exposure to and the possibility of being influenced in subtle ways by broader American culture. For middle-class Indians, education in "English-medium" schools has long been seen as an essential step on the pathway to success.

There is also the practical matter that English-language newspapers and magazines such as *The Economist, Financial Times, The New York Times*, and *The Wall Street Journal* are highly influential because they tend to be read by influential people in business and government around the world. Investors everywhere generally view these publications as trustworthy, giving them sway in international finance as well. In recent research, my coauthors and I found that institutional investors (such as mutual funds and pension funds) rely on local media narratives in their home countries drawn from domestic English-language media when making decisions about how much money to invest in Chinese equity markets and in which sectors.

In short, the convergence in economic might between emerging-market countries and advanced countries has not been accompanied by a corresponding convergence in key elements of intangible power, especially in areas such as institutional frameworks and cultural influence. If anything, this persistent imbalance generates resentment in countries lacking on these dimensions, instigating their attempts to reshape the field of battle in other ways. For instance, information has become a valuable commodity, and controlling it is a key aspect of the struggle for a dimension of power that the late Harvard University historian Joseph Nye described as "soft power," which we turn to next.

The Exercise of Power

Acquiring power is one thing, but wielding it effectively is equally challenging. In evaluating Queen Regent Cersei's wisdom on the subject of power, one must take into account that, for all the influence she exerts as a scheming and ruthless ruler, she eventually (spoiler alert!) ends up losing her empire and dies buried under a pile of bricks. There is something to be said for the wise use of whatever modicum of power a person or country has: wielding it with restraint for the most part and then deploying it to maximum effect when the timing is right. After all, to slay Goliath, David relied on just a stone, a good sense of timing, and unerring aim.

The notion of American exceptionalism has led to many misadventures that have stirred up hornet's nests and left countries in worse shape than before US intervention. In some cases, these episodes have been the product of good intentions marred by the absence of a clear strategy and by poor execution. In other cases, they have resulted from a clash between American priorities and the best interests of another country and its people.

In the twentieth century the United States intervened both directly and covertly in many Latin American countries, usually to protect its commercial and strategic interests. While recent interventions in various regions of the world have been associated with ostensibly noble objectives involving the overthrow of repressive regimes, one would be hard put to argue that the peoples of

Afghanistan and Iraq are better off today than before American intervention. And yet, with a weak and ineffectual Europe barely able to police matters in its own backyard, it eventually fell to the United States to lead efforts to contain the civilian massacres in Bosnia in the mid-1990s and to push back against Russian aggression in Ukraine. American passivity and failure to act in a timely manner have thus had negative consequences as well. In short, both US interventions and periods of isolationism can be detrimental, in different ways, to the rest of the world.

In his second term, Trump has further roiled an already shaky world order. His administration has torn apart long-standing alliances, breaking with European allies and siding with Russia by accepting its narrative blaming Ukraine for the war it was dragged into by Russian aggression. His interest in acquiring Greenland, which is under the control of Denmark, a NATO member, and his threat to take the territory by force if need be, has undermined a key security alliance. The open admiration that Trump and members of his administration have expressed for strongmen such as Russia's Vladimir Putin and Hungary's Viktor Orbán has rendered the United States a superpower to be feared rather than admired and emulated.

Wariness regarding the United States, in tandem with the shifting distribution of global economic power, suggests that a reconfiguration of both hard and soft power is in the offing. Emerging-market countries generally enjoy only limited sway in world affairs, however, as they grapple with their own economic problems and with political systems that emphasize domestic issues. In many cases, their civil servants are not accustomed to thinking strategically about how best to cultivate influence abroad. There are of course exceptions. China and India have both sharpened the ways in which they project themselves on the world stage, including by building or shoring up regional alliances.

It fell upon David to dispose of Goliath by himself, but allies can usually play a useful role in expanding the effects of one's power. Scholars at the Lowy Institute, a think tank in Australia, have concocted various measures of global power. Based on these measures, they describe Japan as "a quintessential smart power, making efficient use of limited resources to wield broad-based diplomatic, economic and cultural influence in the [Asian] region." They also point to countries such as Australia, Singapore, and South Korea as having influence that exceeds their raw power, primarily because they are "highly networked" and make a determined effort to work collaboratively with other countries to pursue collective interests. Leaders in these countries know that they have to work with others to have any impact, and they have made a virtue of that reality.

In later chapters of this book, we examine the evolution and effectiveness of various alliances, each of which can multiply a country's power but also features its own power dynamics. First, however, it is worth considering China's concerted effort to develop its soft power in tandem with its rising economic prowess.

History is replete with examples of countries that have punched above or below their (GDP) weight, depending on how effectively they deploy their resources to maximum economic and geopolitical effect. China's approach is an object lesson in opportunistic influence building and learning by doing, with course corrections as it has absorbed and learned from its mistakes.

In the 2000s, China began using its rising financial clout to broaden its spheres of economic and political influence, offering investments, aid, and various forms of financial support to other economies. The recipients of this largesse were its neighbors in Asia, as well as a number of countries in Africa and Latin America endowed with large stocks of the natural resources that China craved for its manufacturing machine. By 2010, China had become a $6 trillion economy, its growth trajectory seemed secure, and the government recognized that it needed to adopt a more systematic approach. Officials in Beijing began putting together an ambitious set of plans to deploy China's financial might to better effect.

In the fall of 2013, President Xi Jinping proposed two major economic initiatives—the Silk Road Economic Belt and the 21st Century Maritime Silk Road. The two have come to be referred to jointly, and in an unfortunately clunky combination, as the Belt and Road Initiative (BRI). It covers, but is not limited to, the area along the ancient Silk Road—a patchwork of roads, trails, and paths that once facilitated economic and cultural exchange across Eurasia. The BRI focuses on tying together China, Central Asia, Russia, and the Baltics; linking China with the Persian Gulf and the Mediterranean Sea through Central Asia and West Asia; and connecting China with Southeast Asia, South Asia, and the Indian Ocean. The BRI is thus envisioned as covering the continents of Asia, Europe, and Africa, connecting a large and disparate group of economies, from the economically vibrant and rich to those that are poor but potentially ripe for economic development.

Part of the financing for the BRI was to come from the Silk Road Fund, set up by the Chinese government in December 2014 with initial funding of $40 billion. The stated objective was "to promote connectivity, and contribute to the realization of the master blueprint and bright future of the Belt and Road Initiative in accordance with a principle of market-orientation, international standards and professional excellence." The postulation about following market principles and meeting or exceeding the best international standards of governance permeates many of the documents. China obviously wanted to make it clear that projects undertaken under the initiative would not foster or tolerate low technical, environmental, or governance standards. In 2023, the Silk Road Fund received about $11 billion more from the Chinese government.

With its high-minded goals of improving infrastructure and promoting trade across the Asian region and beyond, the BRI provides an avenue that enables China to entice foreign banks and international financial institutions to fund projects that will ultimately expand China's economic and political influence. China was clearly hoping to bring in foreign investors to leverage the limited direct financing that it provided to the initiative. Participation by a broader group of investors would not only pull in more funds but also give the initiative a multilateral flavor, all while allowing China to maintain control of the projects and garner greater influence in the region.

China has maintained that it adheres strictly to a principle of noninterference in other countries' internal affairs, especially regarding political matters, and that its aid and investments are provided with "no political strings attached, and never offering blank promises." As President Xi put it at a summit in Johannesburg, "China supports the settlement of African issues by Africans in the African way." Such sentiments are of course music to the ears of the leaders and officials of the countries receiving the funds.

In spite of this lofty rhetoric, however, many observers of the BRI became concerned that China was simply exploiting the countries to which it was giving aid or loans and, even worse, that the money was propping up corrupt regimes, enriching venal officials, and creating a debt burden that would haunt those countries. A contrary view was that China was stepping in where other foreign investors feared to or simply did not care to tread—in countries wracked by political instability or low profit potential. These countries lacked financing for even basic infrastructure projects, without which they had no shot at economic development. If China was willing to step in—and make a buck for its companies that were bold enough to participate in such ventures—where was the fault?

China's overseas financing has increased to nearly $2.5 trillion since 2005, spread over every continent, including Antarctica. Over the past decade, China has undertaken a cumulative investment of about $290 billion in sub-Saharan Africa and $160 billion in South America. China has also given money to countries that have been shut out from borrowing in international financial markets and are unable (or loath) to turn to Western institutions or countries. In Ecuador, for instance, Chinese money has financed dams, roads, highways, bridges, and hospitals. In return China has, by some estimates, locked in nearly 90 percent of Ecuador's oil exports, the revenues from which go largely toward paying off those loans.

During his visit to Pakistan in April 2015, Xi announced $46 billion in financial support for energy and infrastructure projects. This figure would eclipse all the economic- and security-related financial assistance given by the United States to Pakistan since 2002, which amounted to roughly $31 billion. Xi's visit to Africa in December 2015 culminated in a new China-Africa strategic partnership featuring cooperation in areas such as industrialization, agricultural modernization, infrastructure construction, financial services, green development, and public health. China offered $60 billion in funding support in grants, loans, loan write-offs, and capital for various development funds, a hefty sum for the recipient countries on the continent.

China's investments in and aid to Africa, Asia, and Latin America have no doubt strengthened its economic and political ties with countries in those continents. Chinese financial assistance has the attraction of coming with only a few ancillary conditions, unlike funding from institutions like the World Bank, which has many strings attached—pesky conditions about meeting environmental and labor standards, safeguards against corruption, and more. Chinese funding mainly requires the use of Chinese labor, although other terms of the loans can come back to bite the borrowers. The terms often include high interest rates, stringent repayment conditions, and pledges of collateral such as land that has to be handed over to China if the conditions are not met. As a result, such commercial and charitable endeavors have not been viewed favorably in many quarters of the international community—sometimes not even in the recipient countries themselves.

Cut off from other sources of financing, Sri Lanka has relied heavily on Chinese funds, including for building up its infrastructure. One prominent example is the deepwater port in Hambantota, which was intended to take advantage of its location at the southern end of Sri Lanka. China provided financial and technical help for the project, and much of the work was contracted out to a Chinese state-owned company, but the port failed to generate enough business to turn a profit or even to pay off the loan, which had high interest rates attached to it. The heavily indebted island nation was compelled to hand over to China ninety-nine-year leases on the port and on additional land. So, while Sri Lanka accrued few benefits from the deal, Beijing secured a strategic outpost near one of the world's busiest shipping lanes. This sparked violent protests, with a local politician describing the port as having become a "Chinese colony."

Sri Lanka's economic woes are the result of government mismanagement, but Chinese debt made a bad situation worse. The country's leaders once welcomed Chinese support. In 2017, President Maithripala Sirisena noted warmly that "the Chinese government and its people have always helped us and for that I appreciate and thank them[,] and I hope this relationship will only get further strengthened." By 2022, Sri Lanka had soured on its financial relationship with China, which was increasingly seen as predatory. Sri Lankan Minister of Justice Wijeyadasa Rajapakshe wrote a letter to Xi Jinping accusing Beijing of entrapping Sri Lanka in debt to expand its political influence. Rajapakshe stated, "It is manifestly visible that your friendship with us is no more genuine and candid[;] instead you use our relations to achieve your ambition of becoming the world power at the stake of [the] lives of our innocent people."

In 2018, Malaysia stopped taking loans from China due to fears of overextending itself, especially because many of the funded projects were unviable. Prime Minister Mahathir Moha-mad described Forest City, a Chinese-built city that turned into a ghost town, in derisive terms: "This is not Chinese investment but a settlement." A local politician pointedly asked, "Who is the real beneficiary of all this financing? The Malaysians or the Chinese? . . . I am worried that our sovereignty has been sold."

While Chinese economic activities abroad have clearly created an optics problem for its government, it is far less clear whether China's money has yielded a net benefit or caused harm to recip-ient countries. Some studies have found that high levels of Chi-nese aid have had a harmful effect on human rights and economic development across Africa. Other studies have concluded that aid from China is, in fact, oriented toward poorer countries, although with a tilt toward those that have provided foreign policy support to China at international forums. Commercially oriented forms of Chinese state financing are directed mainly to countries with an abundance of natural resources. Chinese investors do seem more willing than their counterparts in Western countries to take chances investing in countries that are politically unstable. Over-all, the academic literature arrives at a mixed evaluation: Chinese money has in some ways played a positive role in Africa's eco-nomic development but with significant risks to and costs in some sectors.

China has adopted a concerted, strategic approach to the pro-cess of binding countries to itself economically and politically. Over time, however, it has become increasingly clear that some elements of this approach have not worked as intended. The much-hyped BRI has underdelivered on many of its promises and generated pushback against China from many countries. Even as Chinese officials have continued to extol the initiative, their am-bitions have ratcheted downward as their plans run head-on into complex economic realities.

That certain countries involved in the initial rounds of the BRI suffer from mismanaged economies, poor public governance, and political instability—factors that undermine infrastructure and other projects—has posed a key challenge to efforts to scale up the initiative. China's bid to leverage its own funds with financing from the private sector and from multilateral institutions has also come up short. China had been hoping to lure in foreign investors, both private and official, whose participation would strengthen the multilateral aspect of the BRI while still allowing it to maintain control and expand its influence. This hope has been realized, at best, only to a very modest extent, due to a mix of concerns about the commercial viability of some projects and the degree of Chinese control. By early 2024, with China's economic woes limiting its financial capabilities, the initiative had shifted its focus from grand, large-scale projects to "small and beautiful" ones, mostly in Southeast Asia.

China has come to recognize that its lending activities do not always yield economic or geopolitical benefits, often (eventually) sparking resentment rather than gratitude from recipient countries. Seeking to limit such damage, by 2021 China had spent roughly $240 billion bailing out twenty-two highly indebted low-income countries, including Sri Lanka. But China remains a significant lender to many developing countries. And for all the rancor over China's debt diplomacy, especially in Western capitals and international institutions, China is still viewed positively by many countries that have benefited from its largesse. A survey of Southeast Asian countries in 2024 revealed that China continues to be seen as their main economic and political-strategic partner, far outpacing the United States along both dimensions.

Seeing an opening as the BRI faltered and countries on the receiving end grew wary, the Biden administration led the G7 countries in creating a new initiative—the Build Back Better World

(B3W) partnership—to help address the infrastructure financing needs of low- and middle-income countries. B3W was launched in June 2021 and, a year later, was rebranded as the Partnership for Global Infrastructure and Investment (PGII). The PGII represented a clear and direct challenge to China's attempts to build influence in the developing world by helping to meet critical infrastructure needs. The Biden administration was keen to put the United States back in the leadership role by allying with the other G7 countries to offset China's rising global economic and political influence and to win back some of the ground the United States had lost under the first Trump administration. To drive home the contrast with the BRI, the initiative was billed as a "values-driven, high-standard, and transparent infrastructure partnership led by major democracies."

To further sharpen the distinction from projects supported by China, a group led by the United States and composed mainly of major advanced economies launched the Blue Dot Network in parallel with the PGII. This network, which went into operation in April 2024, was designed to provide a certification process for high-quality infrastructure projects deemed "environmentally and socially sustainable, resilient, open and transparent, and economically efficient." That was as clear a signal as any that the projects should be deemed worthy of private-sector support, unlike those backed by China.

The PGII set a goal of mobilizing $600 billion by 2027 to fund global infrastructure investments, with the United States accounting for $200 billion of this funding. G7 leaders clearly recognized that, unless they rounded up financing from their own budgets and from the private sector, the initiative would lack credibility, especially in light of China's willingness to open its own pockets. Within a year of the PGII's launch, the United States in fact claimed to have mobilized as much as $30 billion through government and private-sector funds for infrastructure projects across the globe. Funding from other countries was scarcer, hardly a surprise in view of the limited political appetite for launching massive efforts to aid other countries while their own economies were struggling. Still, the PGII represented an attempt to draw clear battle lines with China in the deployment of economic power to attain broader ends.

Trump's reelection in 2024 pulled the rug out from under the PGII initiative. Even though the United States did not immediately terminate its involvement in the partnership, it was clear that no additional financial support would be forthcoming. In a more drastic move, one of Trump's early executive orders after taking office in effect shuttered the US Agency for International Development, which had been responsible for channeling more than $40 billion of humanitarian and development assistance annually to over a hundred countries around the world. In one fell swoop, Trump erased the goodwill that the United States had built up even in far-flung corners of the world through this agency. Not everyone was dismayed, for the agency's funds had also supported prodemocracy and civil society organizations in countries with authoritarian regimes. Leaders of some of those countries celebrated the end of US financial support for organizations that had been thorns in their sides, referring to the organizations as "terrorists" (Nicaragua), "a black box of corruption" (Venezuela), and "the fugitive opposition" (Belarus).

As a result of such American policy actions, and at least in terms of an overt strategy to deploy its financial clout to maximum geopolitical benefit, China seems to have gained an advantage over the United States. But China is not seen as a benign patron, thus leaving developing countries around the world adrift as the global landscape of power shifts under their feet. In any event, low-income developing countries that are in desperate need of funds to promote infrastructure expansion, in addition to meeting their populations' basic needs such as education, health care, and sanitation, now find themselves enmeshed in a great-power competition that is usually to their detriment. Inasmuch as any financial support is tied to the geopolitical ambitions of China on one side and of the United States and its Western allies on the other, not to mention the swings of domestic political sentiment in these potential benefactors, developing countries cannot count on consistent, stable sources of funds. Another distressing consequence of this situation is that anticipated inflows of private capital into these countries, expected to be spurred by official funding, have failed to materialize due to the unreliability of those funding streams.

Balancing Forces Go Rogue

The distribution of economic and military might is shifting, with the dominance and influence of the traditional major powers other than the United States waning, while emerging-market countries accrete more of both. The future course of the world order will be swayed by the evolution of the various elements of power discussed in this chapter but also by how countries play the cards they have been dealt. To draw on one of the many lessons Littlefinger imparts to those he mentors: "There's no justice in this world, not unless we make it."

Consider, for instance, the world population, estimated at about eight billion in 2025 and expected to hit ten billion by 2060, with the growth rate staying positive but gradually declining over that period. As we saw earlier, the populations of some low- and middle-income countries are still increasing, while those of many of the richer economies are declining. Rising populations, once perceived as a problem, are now seen as a possible boon in some countries—if they can turn the situation to their advantage rather than letting it transform into a different kind of scourge. Countries like India and Indonesia could find that their young workforces spawn social and political instability rather than economic progress if well-paying and meaningful jobs remain scarce or if their education systems fail to prepare workers for the challenges posed by a rapidly changing economy. Similarly, natural resources, including precious metals such as gold, can also turn into a bane rather than a blessing if not used well and if all they do is breed corruption and other problems.

The implications of abundant human and natural resources are particularly relevant in Africa, which remains a continent of great yet unfulfilled promise. The instability resulting from the misuse of various types of resources in poorer countries will, through flows of migrants seeking better economic prospects or safety from civil strife, continue to spill over into richer countries.

The broader distribution of military power is, likewise, hardly conducive to peace and stability. Nuclear armaments give even small and poor countries that possess them leverage in global matters, far more than could be accomplished through practically any other means. If the cost is that a country's resources are diverted toward military expenditures and away from education, health, and social support, any empowering effect will only benefit the country's leaders, not its people. In a similar vein, attempts by the two major powers, China and the United States, and their allies to exploit their financial clout for geopolitical objectives are, in many cases, adding to financial problems and domestic strife in low-income countries.

The elements discussed in this chapter are crucial for determining relative economic and geopolitical power. One additional aspect—financial power, and more specifically, the international standing of a country's currency—interacts with the others in important ways. The long-standing dominance of the US dollar in global finance has come to represent both the best and many unsettling aspects of US hegemony. Let us turn next to that story, which has some surprising twists.

2

Currency Competition

Pampa Kampana smiled lovingly. "If one is to tell an important lie," she said, "it's best to hide it among a crowd of unarguable truths."

—Salman Rushdie, *Victory City*

The US dollar is the most easily recognized, broadly accepted, and eagerly desired currency in the world. It is also widely reviled for the power it gives the United States over global affairs. It is not just US rivals but even the country's allies that chafe at their reliance on the dollar, with the French usually being the most aggrieved of the lot. French Finance Minister Bruno Le Maire pleaded for other European countries to reduce their reliance on the dollar and added, "I want Europe to be a sovereign continent, not a vassal." This sentiment seems to encapsulate the worst nightmare for the continent, at least from France's perspective. In a more expansive speech, French President Emmanuel Macron called for Europe to reduce its dependence on the "extraterritoriality of the US dollar," because otherwise, "if the tensions between the two superpowers heat up ... we won't have the time nor the resources to finance our strategic autonomy and we will become vassals." Clearly serfdom is a mortifying prospect. But not just for the French.

Other national leaders have offered stronger words. Brazilian President Luiz Inácio Lula da Silva railed against the dollar in an impassioned speech before a (needless to say) friendly audience in China: "Every night I ask myself why all countries have to base their trade on the dollar. Why can't we do trade based on our own currencies? Who was it that decided that the dollar was the currency after the disappearance of the gold standard?" And Russian President Vladimir Putin harshly—and predictably—accused the US government and its citizens of "living like parasites off the global economy and their monopoly of the dollar." Singapore's Foreign Minister George Yeo was more temperate, simply calling the dollar "a hex on all of us."

Actions, though, speak louder than words. Consider a presidential candidate who refers to his own country's currency as "trash" and, for good measure, adds that it is "worth less than excrement." That candidate, Javier Milei, would go on to an unexpected and resounding victory, capturing the Argentine presidency in November 2023. A key plank of Milei's campaign called for ditching the Argentinian peso, whose value had been pummeled by high inflation. And perhaps replacing it with the currency of a country boasting close economic ties with Argentina, as that would make trade between the two countries easier? Argentina's trade with Brazil, China, and the European Union, its top three trade partners, collectively represents about five times its trade volume with the United States. Yet Milei's currency of choice was not the Brazilian real, the Chinese RMB, or the euro. His vision, instead, was to "dollarize" the Argentinian economy. The plan did not materialize, though it seems to have resonated with Argentinians, who already viewed the dollar as an unofficial national currency, widely used within the country and more trusted than the peso. Milei's admiration for the dollar hardly makes him an exception.

Around the world, the one currency against which everyone, from ordinary citizens to central bankers, measures the value of their own currency is the US dollar. Several countries use the dollar as their de facto national currency, while many others, including prominent players like Saudi Arabia, peg their currency to the US dollar. Numerous countries implicitly or explicitly manage their currencies' value—aiming to limit fluctuations—relative to the US dollar. The dollar is widely recognized and accepted, usually enthusiastically, for payment in practically any corner of the world. In a crunch, I have been able to use dollar bills to pay for cab rides in London, New Delhi, Shanghai, and Singapore when I was short of local currency (and did not have local payment apps installed on my phone). On a recent family trip to Rome, in the land of the euro, the limo driver taking us to our rented apartment, who had requested a cash payment, happily accepted dollars (a generous tip possibly helped).

Perhaps we are on the cusp of change. After all, we saw in the previous chapter that emerging-market economies are rivaling the economic and military brawn of the advanced economies. One would expect currency power to follow a similar trajectory, with the relative importance of various currencies in the international monetary system reflecting the new economic realities on the ground.

And yet, that has not happened. The rising economic might of the emerging-market economies has far outpaced their currencies' clout, which trails that of the advanced economies, even as growth in the latter group of economies falters. China accounts for one-sixth of global GDP, yet its currency remains a modest player in global finance. The emerging-market economies jointly account for roughly one-third of global GDP. Still, currencies like the Indian rupee and the Brazilian real are hardly used outside the countries that issue them.

In today's world economy, a small set of currencies play outsize roles. Even more noteworthy is the concentration of financial power in the hands of one country—the United States. Much of this power comes from the dominance of the US dollar in all aspects of international trade and finance—a dominance that has persevered for nearly a century through financial upheaval and geopolitical realignments. The United States now accounts for only a quarter of global GDP, but the US dollar is still by far the leading currency for invoicing, payments, and all other aspects of cross-border transactions.

It should not be so. The United States, after all, sparked the global financial crisis of 2007–2009 and, in response to all the tribulations its economy has suffered since then, has vastly expanded the supply of US dollars. Its federal government debt is well in excess of a year's worth of national GDP, and the political system is dysfunctional. Most of all, the United States has wielded dollar dominance as a cudgel against its geopolitical rivals, particularly with the threat or actual use of financial sanctions. By all logic, the dollar should have been knocked off its pedestal already. Yet, I will argue, dollar dominance is unlikely to be upended anytime soon. The dollar's role in international finance—and with it, American influence on financial markets everywhere—is likely to remain far greater than America's weight in the world economy.

So what if the dollar's prominence has persisted against all odds? Is that fact of any practical consequence, or does it simply confer bragging rights? There are in fact symbolic as well as practical reasons why the status of a country's currency in international markets matters for economic and geopolitical power. Moreover, the imbalance in currency power could potentially add a destabilizing element to a world where economic and military prowess are becoming less concentrated. Washington's willingness to aggressively—and, in the eyes of its rivals, recklessly—exploit the dollar's stature contributes to global financial instability and is fracturing financial markets in a way that deepens geopolitical fissures.

We need to begin this chapter, though, with a more rudimentary issue, which is how to evaluate a currency's relative importance in global financial markets. Then we will review how and why the dollar remains king and explore why that will not change anytime soon. We will see that, while dollar dominance might prove a saving grace at times of crisis, it is that very dominance which has a destabilizing effect worldwide, for it exposes other countries to the mercurial and often undisciplined economic and financial policies of the United States. Although it seems logical that more evenly balanced currency competition would promote stability, that conventional wisdom collapses in the absence of other currencies backed by strong financial markets and institutions capable of rivaling the dollar. Thus, in a curious twist, the preeminence of the dollar confers upon the United States the power to rescue the world when a crisis erupts, but that power has itself become the source of worldwide turbulence.

Currency Dominance

Money has evolved over time, from being primarily physical (coins and banknotes) to functioning mostly in digital form. In modern economies, it is not just central banks but also commercial banks that create money, through loans and corresponding bank deposits that lubricate economic activity. And of course a raft of payment service providers, from credit card companies to PayPal to Apple Pay, facilitate the use of money in commercial transactions.

The functions of money are often classified into three categories: as a unit of account for denominating transactions, as a medium of exchange for making payments, and as a store of value for shifting resources over time. Whoever creates it and whatever forms it takes, the core functions of money are relevant in the context of a currency's role in domestic as well as international finance.

The US dollar is by far the dominant international currency in all respects—as a unit of account for invoicing cross-border transactions, as a medium of exchange for payments involving multiple currencies, and as a store of value for global investors, especially central banks.

Trade between countries, including virtually all international contracts for commodities like oil, is denominated in dollars to a far greater extent than in any other currency. Even by conservative estimates, more than half of all cross-border trade in goods is denominated in dollars, making it the main invoicing currency.

The dollar is the leading payment currency as well; by some measures, roughly half of international payments are settled in dollars. When China imports iron ore and soybeans from Brazil, or Brazil purchases semiconductor devices and telephones from China, most of that trade is invoiced and paid for in dollars rather than in Brazilian reais or RMB. (The Chinese currency is sometimes referred to as the yuan, which is actually the unit of account of the currency, used to express prices and exchange rates, rather than its formal name.) The dollar is not the only currency that plays a role as a "vehicle currency," facilitating transactions between other pairs of currencies (even when invoices are issued in either of those currencies). The euro accounts for about one-fifth of international payments. However, once you subtract the share of payments made within the eurozone (which are denominated in euros, of course), the euro's share of global payments (and trade invoicing) becomes smaller, while the dollar's share is correspondingly greater (close to 60 percent).

The dollar is the principal global reserve currency; about 57 percent of foreign exchange reserves held by the world's central banks are held in dollar-denominated assets. Foreign exchange reserves, which are in effect a central bank's rainy-day funds, are typically invested in relatively stable currencies that enjoy worldwide acceptance. Reserves can help ensure a steady stream of imports, even when a country's domestic currency is falling in value and foreign exporters are loath to accept it as payment. Reserves can also be used to pay back foreign investors, making them less likely to dump their investments for fear that the country might be unable to repay them. The US Federal Reserve—the Fed— holds barely any foreign exchange reserves. As the creator of dollars, which are enthusiastically accepted worldwide, it doesn't need to! Foreign exchange reserves need to be kept in assets that are perceived as safe and are also liquid, which means they can be easily disposed of in large quantities at short notice. The size and liquidity of US government bond markets has for a number of years made the dollar the reserve currency of choice.

The dollar is also a key funding currency in global debt markets. When firms or governments in developing countries borrow in foreign currencies, usually because foreign investors lack confidence in the value of those countries' domestic currencies, they tend to do so in dollars. About two-thirds of debt securities issued by corporations outside their home countries are denominated in dollars.

These features reinforce each other. Foreign central bank demand for US Treasury securities helps finance US government borrowing. Stronger demand for its debt means that the US government has to pay a lower interest rate on that debt. This keeps US interest rates lower than they would otherwise be, making it attractive for foreign governments, corporations, and financial institutions to borrow in dollars. The widespread use of dollars in international trade gives developing countries an incentive to hold reserves in dollars to facilitate a steady stream of imports even when foreign finance dries up. Additionally, the pervasiveness of the dollar makes shifting away from it harder.

The Fed's willingness to support the world's demand for dollars has bolstered the currency's prominence. To meet a surge in demand for dollars during the global financial crisis, the Fed gave a small, select group of major central banks access to dollar swap lines, which meant they could borrow dollars from the Fed using their own currencies as collateral. Even the Bank of England and the European Central Bank had to borrow dollars on behalf of their commercial banks and corporations, which had taken out cheap dollar loans and needed dollars to pay back those loans. The extensive use of these swap lines highlights the continued reliance of other reserve currency economies on dollar funding.

During the COVID-induced global recession, the Fed put in place a broader program giving most countries access to dollar financing using their holdings of US Treasury securities (which are denominated in dollars) as collateral. This canny move allowed the Fed to provide a large group of countries, including those such as India that had previously been unable to secure swap lines, access to dollars at minimal risk to itself. The Fed's apparent magnanimity gives central banks around the world a stronger incentive to hold their reserves in dollars, pulling them even more firmly into the clutches of the dollar.

We've established that the dollar is the dominant international currency. Does this have any practical consequences for the United States and the rest of the world? Well, other countries chafe at dollar dominance because it confers many advantages on the United States, although there are some costs as well. For the rest of the world, there are mostly only downsides.

A Mixed Blessing

Christmas is a season of joy and an important time of year for retailers in many countries. In the United States, some retailers earn a disproportionately high share of their annual sales revenues between Thanksgiving and Christmas. Shopkeepers have to order their wares months in advance, not knowing how strong demand will be or whether their products will be in or out of fashion by the time they hit the shelves. For exporters and importers of goods and services, there is another variable to contend with: the exchange rate of their domestic currency relative to other currencies.

An exporter whose revenues are denominated in a foreign currency must convert those revenues, when she receives them, into her domestic currency to pay her workers and suppliers. The exchange rate between the domestic and foreign currencies could change between the time she sends an invoice to her customer and receives payment. If the domestic currency were to depreciate, meaning that one unit of the foreign currency was worth more units of the domestic currency, she would receive a larger amount of domestic currency than she had anticipated, nicely fattening her profits. But if the domestic currency appreciated, meaning that one unit of the foreign currency was worth fewer units of the domestic currency, her profits might disappear.

Importers face similar risk regarding whether they will have to pay less or more of their domestic currencies to obtain their goods at an agreed-upon foreign currency price. If a domestic currency depreciated before goods were delivered and payment had to be made, the bill for the goods would be higher. Passing on the higher price to consumers would be difficult, especially in the face of competition from locally manufactured goods.

What if a country's international trade were to be invoiced in its own currency, with payments also settled in that currency? This would eliminate a major source of risk for the country's importers and exporters. That is the lucky circumstance for the United States, as global trade is priced in its currency. American importers might not know whether the clothes they stocked up on for Christmas will be in vogue with customers, but at least they won't have to worry about the added risk of exchange rate fluctuations.

There are other ways to mitigate such risk. Long-term contracts and foreign exchange hedging markets can, at some cost, help reduce risk by locking in prices at a particular exchange rate. Hedging exchange rate risk is in effect a way to offload the risk of unfavorable exchange rate movements onto speculators who are willing to take on that gamble—for a price, of course. US exporters and importers typically don't have to worry much about this risk or the costs of mitigating it.

A dominant currency is not always a boon. Greater demand for a currency usually reflects confidence in a country's policies and the strength of its economy, which can drive its exchange rate higher than it would otherwise be. Appreciation in the exchange rate of a country's currency usually makes imports cheaper. Dollar appreciation is good for American consumers but makes it harder for domestic manufacturers to compete with foreign counterparts. Exchange rate appreciation also makes a country's exports more expensive in foreign markets. An American exporter of soybeans might charge the same number of dollars per bushel, but a Chinese importer now has to pay more in yuan, perhaps leading the importer to prefer Brazilian soybeans instead. Thus, a stronger exchange rate can reduce demand for a country's exports and, by extension, curb job growth in sectors that compete with foreign manufacturers in both domestic and worldwide markets.

This has led some countries to actively discourage the world from becoming too enamored with their currencies. From the late 1960s through the early 1980s, West Germany attempted to restrict purchases of deutsche mark–denominated assets by foreign investors because it was far from enthusiastic about having its currency become a major reserve currency for precisely this reason. The Japanese showed a similar reluctance to having the yen regarded as a major global currency.

Both countries maintained large manufacturing sectors and relied on exports to boost growth. They recognized that greater demand for their currencies could drive up their exchange rates, reducing the international competitiveness of their manufacturing industries and hindering exports and job growth. Despite the efforts of the two countries' governments, the share of the deutsche mark in global foreign exchange reserves rose from 6 percent in the mid-1970s to 16 percent at the end of the 1980s, while the share of the Japanese yen rose from barely 1 percent to about 8 percent. The shares would likely have risen even further if the countries had welcomed foreign money rather than discouraging it.

A well-regarded currency carries other risks. Living beyond one's means is well and good until one day, perhaps inevitably, financing dries up and the party ends. This proposition is true not just for individuals but for countries as well. Over the preceding five decades, the dollar's strength has allowed the United States to buy more goods and services from other countries than it sells to them, with this difference—the trade deficit—being financed by borrowing from the rest of the world. If the United States continues borrowing from the rest of the world to finance its purchases, it could become increasingly vulnerable to a shift in sentiment that causes foreign investors to want to switch out of dollar assets. Falling confidence in the dollar would force the US government to pay higher interest rates on the debt that it issues to finance its budget deficits, soaking up a greater proportion of tax revenues. This could also cause the dollar's value to plunge relative to other currencies, raising the price of imports and necessitating belt-tightening by American consumers.

That this has not happened despite decades of large US trade deficits is surprising. What is even more surprising, as we will see later in this chapter, is that there are several reasons the day when the United States is held to account for its spendthrift ways, if it ever arrives, might be well off in the distant future.

Much of the world regards the dollar's dominance as undesirable, with good reason. The intermediation of so much international trade and finance through the dollar leaves other countries, especially smaller and developing ones, at the mercy of the dollar and the whims of US policies. Fluctuations in the dollar's value and actions taken by the Fed affect other economies, occasionally in damaging ways. For instance, when the Fed cuts interest rates to prop up the US economy, money often flows out of US financial markets into fast-growing emerging markets in search of better returns, causing their exchange rates to appreciate and hurting their exports. On the flip side, when the dollar appreciates against other currencies, perhaps because the Fed has raised interest rates to control inflation at home, capital tends to flow out of those economies and into dollar assets, deflating those countries' stock markets. To the chagrin of policymakers around the world, the Fed takes account mainly of domestic factors when making its policy decisions. It pays heed to foreign developments only insofar as they affect the US economy. For the most part, it ignores the effects of its policies on other countries, as doing so is not part of its official mandate.

The dollar remains by far the world's deepest and most liquid financing currency, making it easy to raise large amounts of dollar funding (bank loans and debt securities denominated in dollars) relatively cheaply. The temptation of cheap dollar funding has been difficult for foreign governments and corporations to resist, particularly as it is available easily and abundantly. For their part, investors worldwide are usually eager to provide dollar funding because the dollar's traditional strength and the Fed's apparent willingness to provide dollars in copious quantities in times of stress reduce the risks of such lending. When US interest rates are low, investors and global banks find it tempting to lend to non-US corporations and governments to secure better yields. But because such lending is carried out in dollars, the risks associated with exchange rate fluctuations fall entirely on the borrowing corporations and countries. Thus, while the dollar's prominence is hardly the root cause of indebtedness, it certainly creates perverse incentives for both lenders and borrowers, often leading to debt distress for poor countries that overborrow and struggle to repay.

All things considered, the world seems eager to reduce its dependence on the dollar. Even most Americans might view its dominance as a mixed blessing with many downsides. So why hasn't the dollar tumbled from its exalted perch atop all other currencies?

The Perplexing Persistence of Dollar Dominance

The value of a currency depends on the confidence people place in it. Sensible monetary and fiscal policies are essential for underpinning a currency's stability. Yet the present state of the US economy, banking system, and policymaking process hardly inspires confidence across the rest of the world. Meanwhile, broader shifts are also underway in global finance, carrying both economic and geopolitical implications.

When a government spends lavishly and takes in less in taxes and other revenues, it must borrow (by issuing debt securities) to finance the gap between expenditures and revenues. Spending on education, health care, bridges, and roads is worthwhile, especially because it can increase an economy's future output and help it function more smoothly. Special periods like the COVID pandemic might justify a sharp upsurge in government spending. Governments also spend in wasteful ways, such as by providing subsidies that favor their preferred constituencies, including, in some countries, bloated and inefficient state-owned enterprises.

This sets up an inescapable fiscal policy tension for governments of all stripes, although the challenge is even greater in democracies: Most citizens want more government spending but also dislike paying taxes. Issuing debt is an easy way out, but that debt becomes harder to finance as it swells, imposing other costs as well. In a country like India, nearly half the central government's tax revenues go toward paying interest on the public debt, squeezing out other expenditures. The debt burden grows more crushing if debt expands more rapidly than an economy's output. Cutting expenditures or raising taxes to repay debt is painful. It is far easier for a government to order its central bank to print more money that can be used to pay off the debt. This of course has its own cost—it increases inflation. For all these reasons, and also because high levels of public debt affect confidence in a government's policies, they tend to impede growth and damage the value and standing of a country's currency.

One of the greatest concerns over the dollar's prospects is the sheer level of US government debt. Gross federal public debt at the end of 2024 stood at $36 trillion, roughly 125 percent of annual GDP. Still, Washington seems reluctant to address the annual deficits that continue to add to the debt.

Perhaps the dollar's special status means that the usual constraints on fiscal policy do not apply. Advocates of the so-called modern monetary theory have argued that the United States should take full advantage of the singular power it has to print large sums of money to finance government expenditures. This proposition is as tempting (who wouldn't want lavish and unrestrained spending with no consequences?) as it is dangerous, because it risks legitimizing ever-rising budget deficits. For all the opprobrium from economists—MMT is neither modern nor a theory, let alone a coherent monetary theory—it is striking that the United States has, in effect, followed this approach for many decades. This hardly means the US economy is exempt from the basic laws of economics—the surge in government expenditures and corresponding deficits in response to the pandemic-induced recession did contribute to a spike in inflation in 2022—but it is clearly on a much longer leash than other economies.

Rating agencies pass judgment on the relative safety of debt securities based on a variety of financial indicators associated with the issuer. These ratings provide a useful guide to investors, as they help in assessing the prospective returns on and riskiness of those securities. Government securities are typically considered safer than those issued by corporations, although the bonds issued by some countries, including Argentina, Bolivia, Mozambique, and Pakistan, to name a few, are certainly worthy of junk status— meaning they are highly likely to default.

In August 2011, one of the three major global rating agencies, Standard and Poor's, reduced the US government's credit rating by a notch, from AAA to AA+, marking the first time the world's safest issuer of debt was downgraded. This was a stunning move, for the very prospect of a default on US government debt had long been considered unthinkable. A default would shake faith in the US government, undercut the perception of the safety of US government debt, and create mayhem in markets for a wide range of financial securities whose values are benchmarked against those of US Treasury securities.

In short, a US government debt default would be a cataclysmic event with unpredictable but probably dramatic fallout for US and global financial markets. Such a scenario became no longer unthinkable, however, because the Republican Party realized that the threat of forcing a default would provide leverage in negotiations to advance their policy priorities. After all, faced with this threat, the Democrats would surely cave in to Republican demands for fear of otherwise setting off turmoil in US financial markets. Inconceivable as it might seem that politicians would want to turn full faith and confidence in US government debt into a bargaining chip, courting financial disaster in the process, that is now the reality.

So far, the prospect of havoc from a debt default has prompted the United States to pull back from the brink each time. But the risk that a small group of politicians might decide that these consequences have been overstated, coupled with the ever-rising debt, has led to further downgrades. In August 2023, another major rating agency, Fitch, downgraded the US government's long-term debt rating from AAA to AA+.

It is extraordinary for what is widely perceived as the safest asset in the world to be rated as less than perfectly safe. What is even more extraordinary is the effect the downgrades have had.

Usually, a downgrade of a government or corporate security prompts investors to unload it, causing its price to fall. This, in turn, means investors demand a higher interest rate to compensate for the increased risk (since a bond's price moves inversely with its interest rate). A downgrade of a government's debt would thus raise the cost of borrowing to finance its deficits, adding to its interest expenditures and worsening its fiscal position. The country's currency also usually takes a beating when this happens. This is why governments (and corporations) fear the rating agencies and the effects of their downgrades.

So what happened to US interest rates after the downgrades? And what of the US dollar, which should also have taken a hit as foreign investors turned to government securities issued by other countries? In a word, nothing. In the days and weeks after the downgrades, the US dollar *strengthened* against most other currencies. One could argue that this was because the ratings downgrades simply ratified what financial market participants already knew and had priced in, meaning the downgrades offered no new information. Nonetheless, it is remarkable that, unlike any other country, the United States can brush off downgrades of its government bond ratings with barely any consequence.

While the United States has repeatedly pulled back from the edge of fiscal and financial precipices, it is hard to imagine that such near doomsdays wouldn't eventually erode confidence in the US economy, financial system, and currency. Each downgrade conveys little new information, but it still reinforces the perception that the dollar's global dominance rests on a fragile foundation. Indeed, when Moody's, the third major rating agency, lowered the US government's credit rating in May 2025, long-term interest rates rose and the dollar fell, but only moderately and briefly.

Central bank independence is one of the key pillars underpinning a trusted currency. Because central banks are led by unelected technocrats whose decisions affect the economic well-being of a country's citizens, it is a fair question why elected representatives shouldn't have more direct influence over a central bank's decisions on interest rates and other aspects of monetary policy. It has come to be widely recognized, though, that leaving a central bank alone in its technical decision-making renders it most effective. Otherwise, the prospect that a central bank could have its arm twisted by political masters to print money as a means of funding government budget deficits can lead to galloping inflation.

Another pillar supporting a global currency is the rule of law, which is especially important for both domestic and foreign investors. Investors need confidence that a country's laws will be interpreted consistently and fairly, even if they might not like the laws, and that the government has to abide by the laws once it has created them. A third pillar is a set of robust checks and balances to ensure that no arm of government can undertake policies that are destructive to a country's interests. An open and democratic system of government is helpful in this context, as a government that performs poorly can be voted out.

All the traditional reserve currency economies (including the eurozone, Japan, and the United Kingdom) boast such an institutional framework. In the United States, though, each of these pillars came under attack during the first Trump administration. Unhappy with the Fed's policy decisions on interest rates, Trump excoriated the institution as "pathetic," filled with "boneheads," and an "enemy" of the country. His nominees for the Fed's board of governors, which is responsible for the Fed's policy decisions and oversees its work, included a political hack or two and economists who favored gutting the Fed's regulation of banks. One nominee, Judy Shelton, was a longtime Fed critic with unconventional ideas (to put it mildly) who had advocated for reverting to the failed experiment of tying the dollar's value to the price of gold. Her nomination missed Senate approval by the narrowest of margins, with two Republican senators unable to vote because they were quarantining after being exposed to the coronavirus.

Thus did the guarantor of the dollar's stable value, the Fed, come to have its independence and credibility threatened by the president of the United States, ostensibly the protector of the country's institutions. Not only was the central bank's independence threatened, but a president willing to openly flout laws exposed the limits of the judicial system. And Congress proved unwilling to challenge even Trump's most egregious behavior, raising questions about the effectiveness of checks and balances.

These patterns were reinforced in Trump's second term, with both houses of Congress in the control of the Republican Party and with the US Supreme Court dominated by conservative judges, three of whom had been appointed by Trump in his first term. Trump has made it clear that his selection of appointees to the Fed's board will put more weight on personal loyalty to him and his policies than on technical competence. Moreover, his administration has undercut the rule of law and further enervated checks and balances.

The apparent shakiness of the American institutional framework should, by all logic, cause the pedestal on which the US dollar has long been perched to wobble. But it is not just Republican administrations and weaker domestic institutions that ought to be contributing to such wobbling. Technology could play a role, too.

The dollar's role as an international payment currency is likely to be affected by new payment systems. One prominent example is China's Cross-Border Interbank Payment System (CIPS), which enables direct links with other countries' payment systems. India, Russia, and other emerging-market countries are developing their own payment systems that can be connected to CIPS.

New payment systems render it easier to conduct transactions between pairs of emerging-market currencies. China and India, for instance, will no longer need to exchange their respective currencies for US dollars to conduct trade. The use of dollars has long been the norm because it is so much easier and cheaper to conduct trade in that currency, as dollars are plentiful and easy for banks to move across countries. For instance, an Indian importer of Chinese telephones would change rupees into dollars and pay the Chinese exporter in dollars; then the exporter would exchange the dollars for RMB. Exchanging rupees directly for RMB will soon become cheaper and simpler.

Such developments could eventually chip away at the dollar's dominance as an international payment currency by simplifying direct transactions between currencies and reducing the need for the dollar as an intermediary. At the same time, these changes could undermine the roles of other international currencies, such as the euro and the yen, thus weakening the dollar's closest rivals even further.

The United States has wielded the dollar's dominance as a powerful geopolitical tool, often by imposing financial sanctions on its adversaries. The dollar-centric global financial system gives US sanctions particular bite because they affect any country or firm that has dealings with a US-based bank or even a secondary relationship with such institutions. This situation also entangles countries that may not agree with US policies but are forced to follow its lead for fear that their own banks could be cut off from transactions that involve the dollar.

In addition to the denomination and settlement of a majority of cross-border trade transactions in dollars, there is another choke point in the international financial system. The messaging system that connects commercial banks in different countries, enabling global payments, is managed by SWIFT (the Society for Worldwide Interbank Financial Telecommunication). Headquartered in Belgium and owned by the banks that use its services, SWIFT is in principle nonpartisan and apolitical. But with US banks playing a major role in global finance, the organization is vulnerable to American pressure, especially when other Western economies join in. This can result in specific institutions being cut off from the messaging system, and when applied broadly, it can cripple an entire country's access to international finance.

The US Treasury has deployed these tools in sanctions imposed on the central banks and political figures of many nations it considers rogue, including Iran, North Korea, Syria, and Venezuela.

Russia's annexation of Crimea in 2014, followed by its invasion of Ukraine in 2022, have made it the most significant target of financial sanctions imposed by the United States and its Western allies. Russia was cut off from the international payment system when most of its major banks lost access to SWIFT. Selective sanctions were also imposed on a few individuals and firms in other countries—including China, Türkiye (the new name for Turkey), and the United Arab Emirates—that were deemed to have helped Russia evade payment restrictions.

Financial sanctions had in the past affected mainly cross-border payments. But now even foreign exchange reserves have become the target of sanctions. Thanks to its massive oil export revenues, in the early 2000s Russia had accumulated a war chest of foreign exchange reserves—held mostly in dollars, euros, pounds sterling, and RMB—precisely to protect the ruble's value during economic or geopolitical turmoil. The freezing of the Russian central bank's accounts in Western financial capitals in response to Russia's invasion of Ukraine effectively sealed a big portion of this war chest.

China certainly helped soften the blow that US and other Western countries' sanctions dealt to Russia's economy and its financial system. China did this by offering various forms of financial support to Russia, but the support was in the form of RMB that could be used primarily for imports from China itself. Access to RMB funding is of little help in preserving the ruble's value against the major reserve currencies such as the dollar and the euro. Because the RMB is not yet a fully convertible currency, which means the Chinese government restricts how much of it is available and how freely it can be transacted outside the country, its use in global foreign exchange markets is inherently limited.

While it might help Russia evade sanctions, China's relatively modest footprint in global financial markets and the vulnerability of Chinese firms and financial institutions to secondary sanctions limit the viability of this escape route. For an economy such as

Russia that still relies a great deal on export revenues and on international trade more broadly, losing access to global finance is a painful blow that China can only partially mitigate.

Russia, China, and other US rivals are certainly motivated to reduce their dependence on the dollar-centric financial system, including by creating direct payment channels using their own currencies and developing mutually compatible payment messaging systems to bypass SWIFT, which now monopolizes messaging for all transactions between banks internationally. China's CIPS already has messaging capabilities that could sideline SWIFT. The dollar-dominated global financial system and American influence over SWIFT have long given US financial sanctions substantial traction. The efficacy of such sanctions will inevitably erode over time.

Restrictions on transactions involving Russia's central bank that effectively froze the country's foreign exchange reserves could just as easily be applied by the United States and its allies against other countries. This should encourage not just Russia but other countries, particularly US rivals, to shift their reserves out of dollars and into the currencies of friendlier countries like China. But, as Russia has discovered, the limited worldwide acceptability of RMB-denominated reserves means that, at crunch time, they are of limited help in preventing the collapse of its own currency. Still, the restrictions on Russia's access to the Western-dominated global financial system will undoubtedly drive it into a deeper economic embrace with China.

US government officials are not blind to the risks of using financial sanctions too aggressively. As former US Treasury Secretary Janet Yellen put it, "There is a risk when we use financial sanctions that are linked to the role of the dollar that over time it could undermine the hegemony of the dollar." Yellen also pointed out, however, that the dollar's widespread use as a global currency was because it was "not easy for other countries to find an alternative with the same properties," and "we haven't seen any other country that has the basic infrastructure, institutional infrastructure, that would enable its currency to serve a role like this." It is of course not ideal if a currency's stature hinges on a lack of alternatives rather than its own merits.

Even if the United States were a paragon of sound macroeconomic policies, well-functioning government, and robust institutions, the dollar ought to become less dominant over time. Financial markets around the world, including in some emerging-market economies, are becoming more developed, creating a broader pool of assets for central banks to use in parking their foreign exchange reserves. From a diversification perspective, it makes little sense for any central bank to hold more than half its investment portfolio in a single asset or single currency. The high degree of concentration in dollar-denominated reserves—the equivalent of an investor's devoting more than half her portfolio to one company's shares—is risky. When it comes to reserves, the risk is both economic and geopolitical, as we saw in the case of Russia.

Emerging-market central banks hold nearly $6 trillion in foreign exchange reserves (as of late 2024), with China accounting for about half this total. Managers of those reserve funds, particularly China's central bank, are certainly eager to diversify away from investments in countries and currencies perceived as being on the other side of deepening geopolitical fissures. The difficult reality reserve managers face, however, is that the supply of financial assets that are easy to buy and sell cheaply and in large quantities, and are backed up by strong central banks and regulatory frameworks, primarily comes from large, advanced economies. And even in this small group, the US dollar continues to stand above the rest.

In a world where logic held greater sway, concerns about the dollar's safety, stability, and long-term value would increase borrowing costs for the US government and make it harder to finance large budget and trade deficits. Many of the problems discussed earlier, such as high and rising levels of US public debt, mean that the United States is in fact increasing its share of the supply of "safe assets," which investors around the world are happy to lap up. In yet another irony, it is precisely US fiscal recklessness that enables its bond markets to tower over the rest, with the market value of outstanding US government bonds exceeding those of the euro area, Japan, and the United Kingdom combined. China's government bond market is large, but its bonds lack some key characteristics—such as easy access and tradability for foreign investors—that are typical of those in advanced economies.

Still, this picture seems discordant. American politics and policies are undercutting the foundations of the dollar. Moreover, there is clear enthusiasm for ending its dominance and a deep-seated desire among both American rivals and allies to find alternatives. In the international marketplace, only a handful of major currencies still matter. So why haven't any of them assumed the mantle?

Feeble Alternatives

After its creation in 1999, the euro was seen as the main rival, if not the successor, to the dollar. The euro area's GDP matched that of the United States, and its financial markets and institutions were seen as robust. Within a few years of its creation, the euro's share of global foreign exchange reserve holdings had risen by about 7 percentage points, the dollar's share had fallen by a corresponding amount, and the writing seemed to be on the wall for the dollar. Prognostications were rife that it was just a matter of time before the euro overtook the dollar, with the only question being how long it would take. As with many projections of present trends into the future, the prognostications proved wildly off the mark.

The euro's share of global foreign exchange reserves peaked at 28 percent in 2009 but had fallen back to 20 percent by 2024. The global financial crisis, followed by the eurozone debt crisis, put paid to the euro's rise. It became apparent that the zone's financial markets were not fully unified, creating hindrances even to moving money across banks within the zone. The United States, by contrast, has one financial system, making it much easier to conduct dollar-based transactions, as moving money between US banks is straightforward. Moreover, the supply of eurozone government bonds that could be considered safe assets is smaller than suggested by the overall size of the government bond markets of the member countries. The illusion that a Greek or Italian government bond is similar to a bund (a German government bond) and carries the same level of risk is no longer tenable. The eurozone continues to be riven by economic malaise and political dissension, with centrifugal forces constantly straining at its unifying fabric. So the euro's prospects as a serious rival to the dollar have faded.

Surely the second-largest economy in the world should have a currency that matches its heft on the global economic stage. Spurred by this ambition, in 2010 the Chinese government and central bank initiated a project to promote the "internationalization" of the RMB. The government committed to reducing restrictions on financial flows into and out of the country, limiting its control of the RMB's exchange rate relative to the dollar, and giving foreign investors easier access to China's equity and bond markets. These promises paid off.

In October 2015, the International Monetary Fund (IMF) officially designated the RMB an elite reserve currency by announcing that, within one year, it would be included in the small "basket" of currencies that determine the value of the IMF's own currency unit, the special drawing rights. The SDR is a composite currency created out of thin air by the IMF and distributed to all its member countries. From 1999 to 2015, the SDR basket included the dollar, the euro, the Japanese yen, and the British pound sterling. The RMB's addition to this basket was a symbolically momentous event both for China and the international financial system, the first time an emerging-market currency was put on par with major advanced-economy currencies.

Meanwhile, China's central bank, the People's Bank of China, signed agreements with a number of central banks around the world providing them with easy access to each other's currencies—much like the Fed's currency swap arrangements. The Fed limits its arrangements to a handful of select central banks, but the People's Bank of China was far more inclusive, signing agreements with more than thirty counterparts, including the central banks of many developing countries. The point was to encourage those central banks to view the RMB as a viable international currency that would be readily available to them in time of need.

All of this ought to have transformed the RMB into a world-class currency. From 2010 to 2015, the RMB indeed made significant progress on the path to becoming an international currency. Within this very short span, it went from accounting for virtually no cross-border payments to being used in nearly 3 percent of such payments. Perhaps not an impressive number, but with the dollar and euro dominating global payments, even this modest share meant the RMB had become the fourth or fifth most important payment currency in a remarkably short period. As is typical, predictions placing the RMB on an unstoppable linear path to shattering the dollar's dominance began bubbling up.

Then reality hit, and the RMB's rise stalled. In August 2015, the People's Bank of China set off turmoil in currency markets by devaluing the RMB by about 2 percent relative to the dollar, a move meant to support the country's exports at a time when the domestic economy was weak. The timing was particularly inopportune as the Chinese economy was stalling and the government was in the midst of an anticorruption campaign. With wealthy

Chinese worried about the safety of their fortunes and with foreign investors souring on the country's stock markets, money fled the country. The government curbed capital outflows and still ended up spending about a trillion dollars of its sizable foreign exchange reserves (which, at their peak, amounted to $4 trillion) to support the RMB and prevent it from collapsing in value against the dollar.

These events reflected China's violations of its commitments to reduce restrictions on cross-border financial flows and to allow market forces free rein in determining the exchange rate of the RMB. Despite this turmoil, the IMF went ahead with its decision to include the RMB in the SDR basket, effective October 2016, to honor an agreement it had made with the Chinese government. But the rise of the RMB had fizzled by then, and the illusion that it was one of the elite global currencies had been shattered.

The RMB may one day resume its rise. Reflecting China's clout as a major trading partner for many countries and its large role in global goods trade, the RMB is likely to make further progress as an invoicing and payment currency. Access to RMB is useful for countries that have formed strong trade and financial linkages with China, and such access could become increasingly attractive as the RMB gradually rises in stature as an international currency. The RMB's share in emerging-market economies' reserve holdings will grow, driven by efforts to diversify those holdings and by geopolitical tensions, although this increase will be constrained by China's capital controls and weak institutional framework.

None of this will make the RMB's rise, which will remain modest, a game changer in global finance. The RMB's role as an international payment currency will also be limited by the Chinese government's unwillingness to fully free up cross-border financial flows and to allow the currency's value to be determined by market forces. Despite the IMF's imprimatur, the RMB will not become a significant reserve currency until China allows its financial markets to develop more freely and subjects those markets to effective regulations that enable foreign investors, both official and private, to easily acquire and trade high-quality RMB-denominated assets. The currency's role in global finance will ultimately be determined by the degree of commitment on the part of Xi Jinping's government to economic and financial market reforms.

Even changes in China's economic and financial policies will not elevate the RMB to the status of a "safe haven" currency that could threaten the dollar's status as the dominant global reserve currency. To become a safe haven currency, one that foreign investors turn to for safety during financial upheaval, China would also need to engender the trust of foreign investors. This would require a more open and transparent form of government, with checks and balances, the rule of law, and a trusted and independent central bank. Xi's government has made it abundantly clear, in both word and deed, that broader legal, political, and institutional reforms are off the table. Even under the most optimistic scenarios, the RMB is a long way from playing a major, let alone dominant, role in global finance.

Barry Eichengreen of the University of California, Berkeley, has highlighted the rise, during the 2010s and early 2020s, in the shares of smaller and nontraditional currencies in global foreign exchange reserve portfolios. Collectively, their share of global foreign exchange reserves was about 11 percent in 2025 compared with 2 percent in 2000. The shares of such currencies as the Australian and Canadian dollars, the Swedish krona, the South Korean won, and the Singapore dollar have all risen. The Australian and Canadian dollars, the leaders of this motley pack, each now accounts for 2–3 percent of global payments and reserves.

None of these currencies amounts to much by itself, though, and the increase in their collective shares of cross-border payments and reserves merely points to a desperate worldwide desire for currency diversification. These changes, along with a greater role for the RMB, could result in a realignment of the relative positions of certain global currencies. Ironically, while the US dollar's position as the dominant international currency may erode modestly as part of this realignment, the larger effects appear to be on the second-tier currencies such as the yen and the pound sterling. The importance of these once powerful currencies has declined in recent years, both in international payments and in foreign exchange reserves.

Occasional proposals to combine the financial firepower of multiple countries to create a stronger currency are attractive but ultimately unrealistic. China, Brazil, and Russia—three of the five countries that comprise the BRICS group—would dearly love to disengage from the US dollar. Even India and South Africa, the other two countries in the group, would no doubt prefer a world in which they are less vulnerable to the whimsies of Fed policies. So this group of countries has talked up the possibility of creating a common currency, based on the notion that their collective economic might and prominence in global trade should give such a currency immediate traction if they agreed to use it among themselves.

The alliterative appeal of such a currency—whose value would be based on the rand, the real, the renminbi, the ruble, and the rupee (the currencies of the five countries)—is undeniable. Questions about who would issue and manage the currency might prove too challenging, though, for a group with some common aims but little mutual trust. A BRICS currency will, in any event, remain a mirage until the countries involved can strengthen their financial markets and regulatory structures, and, most importantly, enhance their institutional frameworks by broadening the rule of law and establishing truly independent central banks.

Gold has long been an alluring asset (I, too, recently acquired a smidgen—for a tooth filling). Its limited supply has resulted in an article of faith among many investors and even some central banks that it will hold its value well over the longer term. Gold has certainly been around as a store of value for centuries if not millennia, far predating any of the fiat currencies (official currencies issued by national central banks) now in circulation.

Similarly, the cryptocurrency Bitcoin is scarce in supply, and proponents view that as the underpinning of its value as a financial asset. A specific preprogrammed number of Bitcoins is created roughly every ten minutes, and this number is programmed to decline over time, ultimately capping the number of Bitcoins at twenty-one million. Bitcoin has no intrinsic worth, as it has not proven to be a trusted medium of exchange for transactions because of its volatile value. Nevertheless, this original cryptocurrency has instead become what it was never intended to be—a financial asset.

Neither gold nor Bitcoin is a viable alternative to the dollar as a payment or invoicing currency, due to their unstable values and limited supply. Their suitability as reserve assets is constrained by these same limitations, as well as their lack of liquidity. Imagine what would happen if a central bank tried to sell tens of billions of dollars' worth of gold or Bitcoin in a short period. Prices would tank, and the seller would soon be selling into a sinking market.

Perhaps one way to keep the dollar at the center of global finance while erasing some of the undesirable side effects of its dominance is to link its value to that of gold. The idea of backing dollars with something that is scarce and whose supply cannot easily be expanded seems an appealing way of maintaining a stable value for the dollar and limiting inflation. Pinning the value of the dollar to what is in effect a purely speculative financial asset, however, is hardly a sensible path to durable monetary and financial stability.

There is a good reason why the backing of the dollar and other major currencies by gold was abandoned many decades ago: It severely constrains monetary policy and restricts exchange rate fluctuations, depriving countries of tools and mechanisms to stabilize their economies in response to changing circumstances. Adherence to the gold standard contributed to the Great Depression of the 1930s by limiting the increase of money supply that could have stimulated growth. Reverting to a gold standard remains a misguided and dangerous idea in the worlds of modern money and finance, where such constraints on central banks can severely limit their capacity to guide economic activity and maintain financial stability by using interest rates to influence the extent of credit creation.

Hope springs eternal, and some of those eager for a switch out of the dollar have pinned theirs on the IMF's SDR. The IMF itself emphasizes that the SDR is not a typical currency. It cannot, for instance, be used directly in transactions. You, dear reader, and I could not deposit SDRs in our accounts that we could then use to treat each other to a fine meal. Neither could a retailer use it to pay for imports. The IMF describes the SDR as "a potential claim on the freely usable currencies of IMF members." In simpler terms, SDRs can be used as collateral by national governments to borrow real money, such as dollars and euros, that they can use to purchase imports or pay off creditors. Inasmuch as the IMF is a trusted institution, surely as trusted as any major central bank, and can create as many SDRs as its members will allow it to, this seems a simple and obvious solution for a globally accepted currency that can supplant the dollar. The IMF would just credit countries' accounts at the institution with newly minted SDRs.

In fact, however, emerging-market policymakers are wary that IMF money might come with strings of one sort or another attached (even if not explicitly), such as requiring them to undertake painful economic reforms or agree to meet certain labor and environmental standards. Moreover, with voting power at the institution largely in the hands of Western economies, countries that exist on the other side of the geopolitical divide can hardly count on unfettered access to money from the IMF, even if it sits in their own accounts at the institution.

There are also economic reasons why the IMF cannot supply large quantities of SDRs without affecting their value relative to real currencies. Every central bank, even one that has operational independence when making monetary policy decisions, is protected by the taxing authority of the national government that stands behind it. That authority takes the form of the government's insisting that tax obligations be paid using only money issued by the country's central bank. This requirement generally helps protect the relevance and value of central bank money (unless the government spends recklessly and runs large budget deficits). The IMF has no such backing; it relies on the goodwill of its member countries, including the United States, to provide their currencies in exchange for SDRs when needed. And the system of checks and balances that anchor the values of major fiat currencies is absent, so the SDR could face a crisis of trust during difficult times. Thus, for all its virtues, the SDR is not destined to become a rival to the dollar.

Why the Dollar Will Remain Dominant

It is becoming ever harder to view the United States as a well-functioning, dynamic economy with a deep and sound financial system, backed by a robust policymaking process with checks and balances. For all the country's strengths, its economic and financial woes and the degree of dysfunction in its policymaking process will ultimately take a toll on US economic and geopolitical leadership. Still, the absence of any viable alternatives that could seriously rival the dollar will put off its day of reckoning well into the future. In fact, and much to the world's consternation, many forces are driving *increasing* concentration of the dollar's power and growing fragmentation in the power of other currencies. This currency bipolarity, with one dominant renegade currency on one side and a plethora of other currencies with their own shortcomings on the other, seems a recipe for instability. Could change be imminent?

Dollar doomsayers invariably point to the cautionary tale of how quickly the dollar replaced the pound sterling as the dominant reserve currency soon after World War II (or a couple of decades earlier, according to some scholars). The implication is that this could just as easily—and just as quickly—happen to the dollar. But times are different. Unlike in past episodes of shifting currency dominance, the United States has no serious rival that can match its combined economic and financial market size. And although its institutions have frayed, those of other major economies are in worse shape.

There are other quirks that make any drastic change in global currency markets unlikely. As we saw earlier, America has lived beyond its means for the past five decades, running large trade deficits that are financed by borrowing from abroad, thereby increasing its indebtedness to the rest of the world. In the early 2000s, expectations were rampant that the rest of the world would tire of lending to the United States and that the dollar would collapse. Curiously, the turmoil unleashed by the global financial crisis instead led central banks and other investors around the world to seek safety in the dollar, the currency of the very country that precipitated the crisis!

Foreign investors, motivated by the quest for safety as well as good returns, hold far more value in US financial assets than American investors hold in the rest of the world. By 2014, US foreign liabilities were $32 trillion, and US foreign assets amounted to $25 trillion, rendering the United States a net debtor to the tune of $7 trillion. In theory, this should have given the rest of the world power over the dollar: If foreign central banks and other investors had pulled money out of the dollar, the currency would have collapsed.

In my 2014 book, *The Dollar Trap*, I highlighted one crucial point (drawing on the work of numerous scholars of international finance). US liabilities to the rest of the world are denominated in dollars, while its assets are denominated mostly in foreign currencies. So what would happen if the world turned away from the dollar, sending its value plummeting relative to other currencies?

If the world did try to shun the dollar, from the US perspective the value of US liabilities to foreigners would not be affected; they would still be worth the same number of dollars (and of course it is the Fed that prints those dollars, making it even easier to repay dollar debts). But US-owned foreign assets would now have a higher value in dollars because each unit of foreign currency would be worth more dollars. For example, if an American investor held a million dollars' worth of RMB-denominated Chinese equities, and the US dollar depreciated by 10 percent against the RMB, then that investor would gain $100,000. Conversely, foreigners would take a beating on the value of their dollar assets when converting back to their home currencies. The Chinese central bank's holdings in US Treasury securities, for instance, would be worth fewer RMB. So, in effect, a plunge in the value of the dollar would be a huge financial gift from the rest of the world to the United States!

Recognizing the perilous position they have put themselves in, countries around the world should obviously have reduced their exposure to the dollar trap. Quite the opposite. By the end of 2024, America's foreign liabilities and assets were $62 trillion and $36 trillion, respectively, almost quadrupling the US net debtor position to $26 trillion over the preceding decade. The United States now has the rest of the world in an even tighter chokehold!

A stark rendition of the shifting balance of financial power, in a direction that favors rather than weakens the dollar's position, can be seen in the determination of the value of the IMF's SDR. The weights of currencies in the SDR basket are based on a formula that takes account of a country's GDP, its share of world trade, and the share of global foreign exchange reserves held in that currency. The weights sum to one hundred.

When the IMF added the RMB to the SDR basket in 2016, the formula assigned the RMB a weight of 10.9 percent. That 10.9 percent had to come out of the shares of the other four currencies. Virtually all of it came from the other three major reserve currencies, with the US dollar's share barely affected. The euro was the biggest loser, with its weight shrinking from 37 percent to 31 percent.

The IMF updates the weights roughly every five years to reflect changes in the variables that go into the formula. The latest revision, which took place in 2022, bumped up the weight of the RMB to 12.3 percent as the Chinese economy had continued its progress, despite the hit from the COVID pandemic. Interestingly, for all the talk of American decline, the hard facts on the ground resulted in the US dollar's weight *increasing* by nearly 2 percent. Again, the other three currencies lost additional ground, with the euro's weight shrinking further, to 29 percent.

This outcome is as clear an indication as any of one of the most remarkable enigmas in international finance. Despite everything the United States has done that should have driven the world away from the dollar—especially its questionable financial policies and institutional erosion—it remains far and away the dominant economic and financial power.

Rickety Currency Configurations

The US dollar is a bundle of desires, resentments, and paradoxes, all rolled into one currency. While the dollar still reigns supreme, changes are afoot that should, in a more rational world, threaten its dominance. As the analysis in this chapter has shown, those factors are playing out in ways that have unexpected consequences. Indeed, other traditional major currencies have faced even greater erosion in their status as payment and reserve currencies. The euro has stumbled and the RMB has stalled, leaving no realistic alternatives to the dollar's status as the dominant global reserve currency. America's size and dynamism relative to other countries and the weak institutional frameworks of competitors like China still give the United States an edge on the global stage. Many of the forces discussed in this chapter will simply reshuffle the relative importance of other currencies while the dollar retains its primacy, even if that supremacy is knocked down a notch or two.

Competition between purveyors of once prominent currencies seeking to maintain their relevance and upstart currencies establishing footholds in global finance, at least as regionally important currencies, could fragment the global monetary system. China, India, and many other emerging-market countries are encouraging their neighbors and trading partners to use their currencies for trade and other transactions. The ensuing competition between currencies that are not anchored by strong economies and financial systems has the potential to hinder cross-border transactions and destabilize capital flows because such currencies are vulnerable to sharp swings in business and investor confidence.

Now the world is tiring of US economic and political dysfunctionality, financial fragilities, and heavy-handed global engagement. The prospect of the dollar's meeting its comeuppance from some quarter or another is tantalizing for those who despise the power the currency's dominance confers on the United States, not to mention the worldwide financial turbulence often stirred up by US policies. But if the dollar was knocked off its pedestal, that might still be cause for worry.

Consider a reprise of the global financial crisis. In that moment of great peril, the dominance of the dollar and the willingness of the Fed to provide essentially unlimited quantities of funding to US and global financial markets kept a bad situation from worsening. Even other major central banks relied on access to dollars to stabilize their own financial systems. The fact that there was one reliable, widely known, and easily available currency, and that it was issued by a central bank that was trusted the world over, meant the world could coordinate its faith in one currency. In the Trump era, the Fed may struggle to take every possible step to help other countries avert financial catastrophe, as such actions might not align with Trump's narrowly defined view of America's interests. Yet the situation could be even more dire if the dollar were to lose its primacy.

A world in which multiple currencies, issued by central banks endowed with varying degrees of trust from domestic and international investors, competed on relatively equal terms could experience chaos. If financial markets were melting down, investors who were trying to figure out which currency was the safest could add volatility, especially at a moment when timely and reliable information was difficult to come by. Sharp swings of investor funds into and out of various currencies would become more likely, and therefore more destabilizing, in a world where technology makes it easier to move money around instantaneously. In short, a world marked by fiercer currency competition might be stable in normal times, but fragility would arise during financial panics, possibly fomenting instability as investors switched between currencies without a single anchor to tie themselves to.

This is hardly an uplifting story of American exceptionalism; rather it is a melancholy one of frailties in the rest of the world that allow the United States, and especially its currency, to tower over others despite all its weaknesses and its propensity to create financial havoc in far-flung corners of the world. To reduce dollar dominance, other countries would have to further develop their financial markets, improve their monetary and fiscal policies, and strengthen their institutions. That is a tall order, especially in countries beset by other problems such as shrinking labor forces, unstable politics, and government policies that sap economic dynamism. Given this state of affairs, the end of dollar dominance would be destabilizing as well, just in a different way and under different circumstances.

All told, the dollar's preeminence spells destabilization from every angle, exposing other countries to turbulence but simultaneously stoking fear that moving away from the dollar, especially if it were to happen abruptly, could unleash far greater turmoil. A true doom loop if ever there was one.

Let us turn next to what should be a more heartening story: the rise of globalization, creating a system that ought to bind the world more closely together. Unfortunately, this will also turn out to be a discouraging story in some ways, although less bleak than some doomsayers would have it, and for reasons other than those commonly assumed.

3

Globalization: Cohesion or Disarray?

He never knew, to our frustration,
A dactyl from an anapest.
Theocritus and Homer bored him,
But reading Adam Smith restored him,
And economics he knew well;
Which is to say that he could tell
The ways in which a state progresses—
The actual things that make it thrive,
And why for gold it need not strive,
When *basic products* it possesses.
His father never understood
And mortgaged all the land he could.
                    —Alexander Pushkin, *Eugene Onegin*

In August 2020, a few months before the November elections that would temporarily oust him from the White House, President Donald Trump summarized his rejection of globalization, asserting that it had "made the financial elites who donate to politicians very wealthy, but it's left millions and millions of our workers with nothing but poverty and heartache—and our towns and cities with empty factories and plants.... We have rejected globalism and embraced patriotism." A few months later, at the World Economic Forum's Davos Summit in January 2021, Chinese President Xi Jinping made the case *for* globalization, arguing that it was a natural outcome of scientific and technological advancement and that it would boost global productivity while also providing an impetus to global growth. He added that China would "push for an economic globalization that is more open, inclusive, balanced and beneficial to all."

By the fall of 2024, these diametrically opposed positions had become more deeply entrenched. One of Trump's signature promises on the campaign trail ahead of his second term in office was a pledge to impose a broad swath of tariffs on US trading partners, with particularly high tariffs on US imports from China. He referred to "tariffs" as the "most beautiful word in the dictionary" and described actual tariffs as the "greatest thing ever invented." Meanwhile, Xi pushed back even harder in a speech soon after Trump's reelection, arguing that unilateralism and protectionism should be rejected in favor of globalization.

Trump's threats were no empty bluster; soon after taking office in 2025 for his second term, his administration followed through with tariffs on imports from China and many other countries. Retaliatory tariffs by those countries soon followed. Trump's second presidency thus set off a new wave of protectionism around the world, reinforcing fears that the current era of globalization is drawing to an end. China took the opposite tack. In a speech delivered soon after Trump's inauguration, Chinese Vice Premier Ding Xuexiang channeled Xi in describing globalization as "an overwhelming trend of history" that had "demonstrated strong resilience and dynamism."

This juxtaposition might seem remarkable—the leader of the country long seen as the bastion of free trade and globalization repudiating it while the leaders of the Communist Party of China extol its virtues. The shifting geopolitical and domestic political winds that led us to this point have in truth been building for a long time. And Xi Jinping's lofty rhetoric notwithstanding, China's approach to globalization has hardly been a full-on embrace if that would mean wholly opening up its own economy.

Rather than writing an obituary for globalization, though, we must reflect on what it actually means, where it went astray, and how it might be transforming to reflect new realities. The changing nature of globalization appears less a benign evolution than a radical shift from a force that promotes cooperation to one that fuels conflict.

Not too long ago, globalization was seen as a powerful force bringing the world closer together and promoting a shared interest in economic prosperity and stability. Proponents of globalization argued that it would connect countries integrally through flows of goods, services, financial capital, natural resources, and people. These flows would also act as conduits for transfers of knowledge, ideas, and technology across national borders. In short, it would be a win-win proposition that stood to benefit all countries by allowing them to trade freely in goods and services, access global capital markets for financing and better investment returns, and move toward greater common prosperity. Globalization would bridge divides between countries, enmeshing advanced and developing economies in a web of mutually beneficial economic and financial linkages.

In response to these promises, trade and financial flows between countries began expanding rapidly around the mid-1980s as governments dismantled barriers restricting them. Technological developments helped boost trade, with transportation costs falling rapidly. Even the advent of standardized shipping containers, which streamlined the logistical aspects of cross-border trade, played a role. It was no longer far-fetched to contemplate the notion of a unified global marketplace for goods and services, with each country able to specialize in whatever it was relatively better at producing, thereby increasing world output and creating more resources, with only their equitable distribution remaining to be resolved. Governments, especially in developing economies, that had been worried about losing control over money flowing across their borders began to see benefits in the freer flow of capital.

There was a broad consensus that shared economic interests would ultimately triumph and even help smooth over geopolitical frictions. Commercial interests, especially businesses keen to build global supply chains and sell their products and services worldwide, would serve as the glue binding the world closer together.

This narrative held up well for most of two decades through the mid-2000s, even though not everything went according to plan. Tensions rose as globalization's benefits were not shared equally within or between countries. Even as emerging-market countries benefited from access to foreign capital and foreign markets for their exports, some were ravaged by volatile capital flows and the fickleness of international investors. During the 1980s and 1990s, countries such as Indonesia, Malaysia, Mexico, and Thailand faced painful debt and currency crises as international investors who had financed borrowing by these countries' corporations and governments abruptly turned their backs and refused to roll over the loans or provide new financing. The ensuing economic calamity resulted in the toppling of governments in many of these countries.

Domestic political repercussions from the less favorable side effects of globalization have not been limited to emerging-market economies. Widening economic inequality, often attributed to free trade, roiled many advanced economies and has had far-reaching political consequences. Populist politicians have implicated free trade and other aspects of globalization as responsible for the economic woes and social alienation among their constituents.

Still, it was widely believed that globalization would forge ahead, and that with some policy tweaks to counter any unpleasant side effects, its benefits would prevail. Since the mid-2000s, however, a series of shock waves has shredded the script. These include the global financial crisis of 2007–2009, the COVID pandemic, and the Russian invasion of Ukraine in 2022. These events, in addition to disruptions caused by increasingly frequent major weather events, have revealed the fragility of global supply chains, to cite just one effect. As a result, businesses and consumers have faced greater risks from geopolitical tensions and climate change. Surely these events would induce countries to work toward cooperative solutions that mitigate risks while still enjoying the rewards of global integration. That has not been the case.

As with many other issues, here the positioning of China and the United States influences the entire world's perception of and approach to globalization. The escalation of China-US trade tensions has laid bare the stark and possibly irreconcilable differences in the two countries' visions of their economic relationship. Their trade patterns could in principle be restructured such that both sides see significant benefits, but Washington's view that China has exploited the rules governing international commerce to its advantage and cannot credibly commit to honoring the spirit of the rules has created rancor and distrust. The Chinese government, for its part, sees Washington as selective regarding which rules it follows and when, holding that US actions are intended to block China's economic rise for fear of facing a rival that is its economic equal. There is no easy off-ramp from this conflict, as plans for an American manufacturing revival and the policies the country has adopted to support this objective strike at the heart of China's plans to transform its economy into one driven by innovative, high-tech, and high-value-added production.

Heightened economic tensions between the United States and China have an important implication. Even their economic relationship is now seen as a zero-sum game—where one country's expanding influence comes necessarily at the cost of the other's—rather than a mutually beneficial one. Consequently, economic forces no longer serve as a counterweight to the intrinsically competitive geopolitical relationship between the two.

This rancorous competition is in turn causing other countries to reconsider the cost-benefit trade-offs involved in globalization. Fears are mounting that countries are retreating wholesale from globalization, which could harm economic progress worldwide and even endanger the stability fostered by the commonality of interests. These fears are not entirely borne out by the data—the total volume of world trade, for instance, recovered quite well after recent crashes caused by the global financial crisis and the COVID pandemic and has continued to expand. Beneath the surface, though, changes are underway that could alter the face of globalization and its role as a force for promoting shared prosperity and stability.

It is certainly premature to mourn the end of globalization. It is, however, morphing into a new form, driven by the desire of corporations and governments to manage its negative fallout and bolster resilience in the face of risk and volatility. Trade and financial flows are now driven more by risk management than by the pursuit of maximum efficiency and returns. This has meant, for instance, that businesses are seeking to invest in and expand trade with countries more closely aligned geopolitically with their own. National governments, meanwhile, have been erecting trade barriers to protect domestic industries and their affiliated jobs, often invoking national security as a cover for economic objectives.

As countries look increasingly inward, wide-ranging implications for both economic and geopolitical stability portend trouble ahead. With even economic relationships becoming sources of discord rather than healthy competition and cooperation, a key element keeping cross-country relationships on an even keel is being eroded. Moreover, the consequences of the pullback from expansive globalization are proving to be unevenly distributed, with low- and middle-income countries again bearing the brunt. Some of these countries are just now beginning to open their economies, only to find the traditional path to development shut off as trade barriers go up around the world. This will add to economic and political instability in those countries, triggering destabilizing migrant flows toward more developed countries. In summary, the retrenchment of unfettered globalization is, paradoxically, making the world less safe and more volatile.

The Promise and the Reality

Before delving into why and how the latest era of globalization went astray, let us start by depicting its pleasanter phase, built on a foundation of elegant economic theories, which once held so much promise. We will see that as globalization's benefits were realized and, simultaneously, its problems surfaced, some surprising trends emerged that did not quite align with what economic theories had predicted.

With trade barriers as well as transportation costs falling, corporations in advanced economies found that they could take advantage of lower labor costs in developing countries. Moreover, they were able to structure lean and efficient supply chains that threaded through multiple countries, enabling cost savings by relying on specialization in intermediate products that various countries could offer. To this day, a majority of iPhones and MacBooks contain electronics and other components sourced from multiple Asian economies—Japan, Malaysia, South Korea, Taiwan, Thailand—with the final stages of production being completed in China. So even if your iPhone has "Made in China" etched on its back, much of what you would find in its innards comes from other countries.

Foreign demand for their manufactured-goods exports helped many emerging-market countries build up their manufacturing sectors, expanding their middle classes and helping them develop larger and richer economies. Trade between advanced and emerging-market countries swelled in both directions. Sales in China and other emerging-market economies account for a substantial portion of many American companies' global revenues. In 2024, Apple, Intel, and Tesla derived about one-fifth of their revenues from China, while international luxury brands like Gucci and Prada gained as much in revenues from emerging markets as they did from sales in wealthier countries.

Foreign direct investment (FDI) flows have tended to follow trade, with corporations setting up operations abroad and investing in manufacturers as well as suppliers of various kinds of inputs, including raw materials and intermediate goods. Emerging-market countries, which had long been able to secure foreign financing only in the form of debt and on unfavorable terms, were now receiving more stable flows on better terms that did not require them to assume all the risk. FDI flows to these countries surged, and investors also poured money into their equity markets. FDI and equity investment both tend to be less volatile than debt or other forms of financing, with foreign investors sharing in the risks in exchange for the prospect of better returns.

Emerging-market countries benefited from globalization in multiple ways through both the trade and investment channels. They were able to expand markets for their products beyond their national borders, enabling them to build strong manufacturing sectors that were not constrained by limited domestic demand for their products. Trade relationships with advanced economies and their more sophisticated corporations facilitated transfers of technology as well as state-of-the art production processes and managerial practices. As a result, many companies in emerging-market countries became large and modern enough that they were able to compete toe to toe with their advanced-economy counterparts, engendering greater competition, enhanced innovation, and benefits for consumers worldwide.

Foreign investment played a similar role, as multinational corporations now had reason to ensure that their suppliers in emerging-market countries were operating with the best technological and managerial practices. Foreign funds even helped create more robust financial markets with larger trading volumes and more effective regulations. India's equity markets, for instance, benefited from the participation of foreign investors, who spurred improvements in the technical infrastructure of the trading platforms as well as regulatory practices. Development of domestic financial markets, in fact, came to be seen as a key "collateral benefit" of globalization, for it enabled emerging-market countries to channel not just foreign funds but even domestic savings into more productive investments.

Like trade flows, financial flows ran both ways between advanced and emerging-market economies. Many emerging markets ran up trade surpluses (the amounts by which a country's export revenues exceed its payments for imports). These countries used their trade surpluses to accumulate foreign exchange reserves, investing them in government bonds issued by the United States and other advanced economies. In this way, if foreign investors turned their backs on an emerging-market country that had been in their favor, the country could sell those bonds to pay for imports in a widely accepted global currency while also protecting the value of its own currency.

Emerging-market policymakers, scarred by the painful crises that had enveloped some of them in the 1980s and 1990s, were determined to build up their foreign exchange reserves as insurance against such events. A symbiotic relationship developed between advanced and emerging-market countries, with both benefiting from relatively unconstrained trade and financial flows.

Much of this trading and financial activity unfolded as predicted by standard economic theories, though there were occasional oddities and some less than desirable outcomes.

Economic models predict that, while financial capital may flow in both directions, in net terms it should flow from richer countries to less developed ones. After all, wealthy countries have abundant financial resources but smaller labor forces, while developing countries have less financial capital but abundant labor.

The logic is that investing money in an additional unit of physical capital—machines or plants—in a developing country, where it can be matched with a larger pool of workers, should increase the returns on that investment. In principle, this benefits capital-poor countries, allowing them to grow faster through greater investment, unconstrained by limited domestic savings. What's more, investors from richer countries benefit by earning higher returns compared with those in their own, slower-growing economies.

The reality has proven a bit different, especially since the late 1990s. In fact, some rich countries, including Australia, the United Kingdom, Spain, and, most notably, the United States, began borrowing money from the rest of the world to finance their trade deficits (the amounts by which their imports exceeded their exports). In other words, while some investors in these wealthy countries were certainly deploying their funds across the globe, in net terms these economies were receiving more financial capital from the rest of the world than they were sending out. A large chunk of this money came from poorer countries such as China, which, in essence, were financing their richer counterparts. These "uphill" flows of financial capital from poorer to richer countries were expected to end badly—with the richer countries, whose debt obligations to the rest of the world were growing, ultimately having to tighten their belts as foreign financing dried up and the value of their currencies plunged.

Meanwhile, domestic tensions were building in some of the richer countries, particularly the United States. The flip side of China's seemingly generous financing of US trade deficits was that a lot of the money came from the earnings of Chinese companies that were exporting to the United States. Rising US imports of goods from China and other lower-wage countries were among the factors that drove many higher-wage American manufacturers out of business. At the same time, automation and other technological shifts that favored workers with higher levels of education were rapidly eroding the prospects for unskilled workers to find well-paying manufacturing jobs.

The domestic fallout in the United States eventually resulted in the election of Donald Trump as president, triggering a host of geopolitical earthquakes. Before that, the low inflation, decent growth, and overall economic well-being that characterized the period between 2000 and 2007 for both advanced and emerging-market economies came to a crashing end, although not in the way that many analysts and economists (including me) had anticipated.

The global financial crisis was set in motion by a deflating American housing-market bubble that eventually brought the US financial system to its knees. Globalization played a part in the crisis, although to this day it remains a matter of debate whether it was the proximate cause or simply added fuel to an already volatile situation. Financial flows from abroad, especially foreign central banks' purchases of US Treasury bonds, kept long-term US interest rates lower than they would otherwise have been. This encouraged various forms of financial speculation as investors sought higher returns with borrowed money. Such speculative activity was fueled by financial engineering—the creation of a slew of sophisticated-looking financial products that appeared safe but were in fact highly risky—and abetted by weak regulation. The prominence of the US financial system, in tandem with interconnected national financial markets, quickly transformed a US financial crisis into a global event.

Cross-border trade and financial flows fell in the immediate aftermath of the global financial crisis as the world economy went into a recession. Western banks were forced to rein in their global aspirations—after an extended period in which many had used borrowed money to expand worldwide—as their profits crumbled and regulators cracked down on their speculative activities.

Many large and storied banks, including Bear Stearns and Lehman Brothers, either folded or were taken over by others. The downshift in global banking accounted for a substantial portion of the overall decline in cross-country financial flows, even as other types of flows, including FDI, held up better. After all, there were still good investment opportunities around the world for entrepreneurs and for investors looking to diversify their portfolios through purchases of foreign bonds and equities.

Remarkably, the emerging-market economies not only survived the financial meltdowns in the advanced economies without themselves falling into crisis, but bounced back rapidly from what some had feared would be a prolonged worldwide recession. The major advanced countries got back on their feet more slowly, despite aggressive actions by their central banks to pump money into their economies, along with massive increases in public spending. Within a couple of years after the worst of the crisis had passed, volumes of trade in goods revived, along with FDI and cross-border investments in equity and bond markets. Economic considerations such as efficiency, cost minimization, and higher returns remained central in determining patterns of trade and financial flows. It seemed just a matter of time before globalization picked up pace again.

Meanwhile, deeper tensions were bubbling up in the background. China's meteoric rise from a small, low-income economy to the largest trading country in the world would bring these tensions to the fore.

Trade Turns into a Zero-Sum Game

Competition between two major powers inevitably becomes contentious, especially when it involves a long-established player and another that is growing into its role, with both having to adjust to their changing status relative to each other. To be sure, not all aspects of the relationship between China and the United States are necessarily and intrinsically competitive. But there is danger in the erosion of balancing forces and the expansion of areas of conflict.

For a few years after China's 2001 accession to the WTO, which was supported by the United States, both countries embraced the notion that their trade relationship could become a mutually beneficial, positive-sum endeavor. Trade between the two grew substantially, with the United States becoming China's main export market within a few years. Financial flows into China increased after 2010, when the country's government began opening its economy and markets to foreign investors. American companies eager to set up parts of their supply chains in China (to take advantage of low labor and other costs) and sell their products in its fast-growing markets ramped up their investments. US financial institutions were eager to peddle their services to a rapidly expanding middle class that demanded higher-quality services than those provided by Chinese state-owned banks.

Yet trouble was brewing. The US bilateral merchandise trade deficit with China—the amount by which US imports of goods from China exceed US exports of goods to China—was $83 billion in 2000 and marched steadily upward, hitting $418 billion in 2018. This represented an increase from 0.8 percent of US GDP to 2 percent.

There are important nuances to keep in mind when dissecting the US bilateral trade deficit with China. First, the United States runs a surplus in services trade with China. When a foreign tourist or student visits a country and spends money on hotels or tuition, that spending counts as an *export* of tourism and education services by that country. Chinese students and tourists coming to the United States, along with the money they spend, far surpass the numbers or total spending of US students and tourists in China. As a result, US exports of education and tourism services exceed US imports of similar services from China. Consequently, the overall US deficit with China—with goods and services combined—is smaller than the goods trade deficit alone.

Second, setting aside cheap baubles, only a small portion of the final value of many goods exported from China is actually created there. When a laptop or iPhone is exported from China, much of its value comes from electronic components—circuit boards, chips, screens—that are sourced from other Asian countries, as noted earlier. Yet the entire value of the iPhone is counted in trade statistics as Chinese exports to the United States.

Although these qualifications are important, they often become irrelevant subtleties in political discussions.

Imports from China came to be seen as amounting to a "China Shock," blamed for much of the hollowing out of the US manufacturing sector during the 1990s and 2000s. Many American manufacturers threw in the towel and shut down, unable to compete with the flood of cheap goods from China. Some estimates put US job losses attributable to the China Shock between 1999 and 2011 at more than two million, including about a million manufacturing jobs and others in related sectors. There were other forces, such as technological change, at play during this period, and China was hardly the only low-wage competitor to US manufacturing. Still, American politicians could not resist pinning most of the blame for the decline of US manufacturing on China.

China was becoming an American rival in other spheres beyond trade as it sought greater international influence. Coinciding with growing economic and political anxiety in the United States, fear of China gained widespread traction in US public and political circles. Doomsayers (in America) and sages (in Asia) had already begun hyping China's eclipse of the United States in economic and geopolitical power, as the Asian power's rise on all fronts was seen as unstoppable.

Moreover, China did not play by the same rules that had favored its economic rise. One prominent example was that, during the 2000s, China prevented its currency from appreciating against the dollar, even as its trade surpluses with the United States and the rest of the world widened. When a country consistently exports more than it imports, raking in more revenues than it spends, market forces would normally push up the value of that country's currency. This would make that country's exports more expensive in foreign markets and therefore less competitive, restoring the balance between exports and imports.

How did China manipulate the value of its currency to keep it from rising and thereby choking off its export machine? China's central bank counteracted market pressures on the currency through something of a Faustian bargain: It recycled a large proportion of the dollars the country received from abroad into purchases of US government bonds. That is, it offset the exchange of dollars received from its exporters' foreign sales and from foreign investors into Chinese RMB, which increased demand for RMB and would normally have driven up the currency's price. By buying up dollar assets with the dollars it received (thereby balancing higher demand for RMB with higher demand for dollars), China short-circuited this process, artificially preventing the value of the RMB from rising against the dollar. As a result, Chinese exports remained more competitive in US markets than they would otherwise have been. A useful byproduct of this strategy was that China's copious bond purchases helped the United States by financing part of the government's budget deficits and keeping US interest rates lower, which also resulted in cheaper borrowing costs for American households. In other words, China sold a large number of goods to the United States and provided financing, at low interest rates, for those purchases.

Private commercial interests have historically played a major role in shaping relationships between countries and also influencing geopolitics in important ways. The expansion of the British Empire into the Indian subcontinent in the nineteenth century was closely intertwined with the commercial interests of the East India Company and other British industry. The Opium Wars of the mid-nineteenth century and the treaties that followed between China and the major European powers, which gave those countries broad access to trade with China, remain raw in the memories of many Chinese.

These treaties are still viewed by many in China as examples of Western imperialism, in which rapacious trade relationships are used to subjugate other countries. In a 2021 speech to commemorate the centennial of the founding of the Communist Party of China, Xi Jinping remarked that, after the Opium War of 1840, "China was gradually reduced to a semi-colonial, semi-feudal society and suffered greater ravages than ever before. The country endured intense humiliation, the people were subjected to great pain, and the Chinese civilization was plunged into darkness." The period from 1839 to 1939, during which foreigners controlled large portions of China's territory, is referred to by Chinese historians as the "century of humiliation." This history continues to shape China's approach to foreign businesses and the conditions under which they are allowed to operate.

China's rapid economic growth and its government's stated policy of "opening up" the economy caused American and other Western firms to salivate at the prospect of gaining access to the fastest-growing consumer market in the world. Major US financial firms lusted after lucrative opportunities to provide wealth management, insurance, and other financial services to China's fast-expanding middle class and increasingly wealthy upper crust. American investment managers wanted to invest in Chinese bond and equity markets. Hence, the US commercial sector was keen for its government to keep the peace with China, including refraining from taking punitive actions against China for its currency manipulation during the 2000s.

For all its promises to open its consumer goods and financial markets to American and other foreign firms and to treat them fairly by granting full access to its markets, China found ways to tilt the playing field to its advantage. The Chinese government gave its manufacturing firms, both private and state owned, support and subsidies of various kinds—from cheap bank loans to subsidized land and energy. This made it easier for Chinese firms to compete with foreign manufacturers in global export markets. Additionally, China did not fully reciprocate by giving American firms free and unfettered access to its domestic markets, allowing Chinese firms to benefit from both subsidies and protection from foreign competition. Moreover, foreign firms seeking to set up operations in China usually had to do so through joint ventures with domestic companies, enabling Chinese companies to siphon technology and know-how from their foreign partners and eventually compete directly with them.

Nevertheless, American firms continued to advocate for the US government to play nice with China, encouraging officials in Washington to gently prod the Chinese government toward adhering to the rules rather than engaging in open trade conflict.

In recent years, however, this sentiment has shifted. American firms in both manufacturing and services have become increasingly disillusioned with their inability to operate freely within China. The draconian zero-COVID policy, which disrupted those manufacturing firms' supply chains from 2020 to 2022, deepened this frustration. US financial firms eager to expand in China have also struggled to navigate the increasingly hostile relationship between the two countries. American firms have had to contort themselves to avoid getting caught in the crossfire as each side tries to use them to score domestic political points. The Chinese government, for instance, has banned officials at government agencies and state-owned enterprises from buying iPhones, part of an effort to reduce reliance on foreign technology. In any event, American firms now hold a less starry-eyed view of doing business in China, recognizing that access to opportunity often comes with operational restrictions and regulations that put them at a competitive disadvantage compared with local firms.

As a result, commercial interests no longer serve as a strong stabilizing force in the US-China relationship. This helps explain why—when Trump imposed tariffs on Chinese imports in 2018 and ratcheted them up in the following years, and when the Biden administration retained those tariffs while adding further restrictions on trade and investment—the American business community did not protest as loudly as it might once have. The days when US firms eager to do business in China held significant sway over US policy are gone. Today, hostility toward China is a consistent bipartisan theme in Washington.

On a visit to Shanghai in November 2023, a friend of mine who knew the CEO of an up-and-coming electric vehicle (EV) manufacturer based there took me and a small group of economists on a field trip to the company's showroom. We were split into pairs and escorted to a row of gleaming cars, each with a driver. These were autonomous EVs, so the driver simply entered a destination into the onboard computer, and the car eased into traffic on its own. It was stunning and exciting to watch the technology in action as the car navigated smoothly around unruly delivery drivers on scooters and jaywalking pedestrians.

The real surprise came when we returned to the showroom. The CEO guided us through the car's impressive technology. Then, when we inquired about the price, we were told that a fully loaded model would set a buyer back about 180,000 yuan (around $25,000 at the exchange rate at the time), substantially cheaper than a Tesla or other EVs sold in Western markets. The CEO explained that his company was barely three years old, and once it scaled up and streamlined its production lines, prices would likely fall even further. Indeed, within a few months of my visit,

EV prices quoted by Chinese manufacturers had already dropped sharply.

As foreign economists, we could not resist asking the CEO about the role government subsidies had played in his firm's remarkably rapid rise. He assured us that his company and others like it received absolutely no subsidies. Although we were too polite to challenge our suave host, we knew this was only part of the story. Even if his company had not received direct transfers of money from the government, it had benefited from the kinds of support Chinese manufacturing firms have traditionally enjoyed, including cheap energy and land. Moreover, the government had stoked demand by offering local customers tax rebates and other incentives to buy domestically produced EVs, helping the fledgling industry compete with traditional internal combustion engine automobiles. By the time the implicit production subsidies and consumer incentives wound down, Chinese EV makers had dominated the fast-growing domestic market and made substantial inroads abroad. These tactics, which stretch the bounds of fair competition, have upset EV manufacturers in the United States and elsewhere.

It is not just EVs that have become a bone of contention between the United States and China. China's massive push into green energy, robotics, and other new technology sectors is running head-on into Washington's efforts to revive US manufacturing in those very same areas. Fears of a China Shock 2.0—a new wave of imbalance that threatens the future of American technological supremacy—have prompted an aggressive pushback from the United States. Determined to avoid repeating what many see as the ineffectual and tardy response to the first China Shock, the Biden administration imposed restrictions on US investments in and technology transfers to Chinese companies working on AI, semiconductors, microelectronics, and quantum information technologies. In addition, US companies have been barred from exporting semiconductor chips that could be used by Chinese companies in these industries. To avoid running afoul of WTO trade rules, these measures have all been framed as necessary for national security.

While we found ourselves stuck interminably in Beijing traffic on our way to dinner after a formal meeting, a Chinese official let down his reserve. We talked about our upbringing in low-middle-class families in our respective countries of birth and how much we had in common. He then expounded at length on how the United States had, in succession, seen Japan, South Korea, and now China as economic rivals after initially supporting their industrial development, and had then aggressively tried to stifle that development. He warned that, for all the positive sentiments expressed by US officials about India and their support for its economic development, the day would come that the United States would start seeing India as a rival and go after it, too. I politely dissented from his interpretation of history and noted one major difference: Among all these countries, China was the only one that the United States regarded as a geopolitical rather than just an economic rival. He responded that, setting aside geopolitics as a complicating factor, China sought only a constructive commercial relationship, but long-standing US attitudes of distrust and hostility toward any country it saw as an economic rival made this difficult.

China perceives US actions as targeted squarely against an adversary to be feared and whose development is to be squelched. The United States, by contrast, views its actions as defensive maneuvering to prevent a competitor who plays unfairly—or at least twists the rules of the game in its favor—from dominating the industries of the future, where the United States has a comparative advantage to begin with. Each side views the other's actions as hostile and as violating established rules, while viewing its own as reasonable and perfectly justifiable on national security grounds. This gulf in perceptions makes it difficult to see how the two countries can return to constructive economic cooperation, which in turn affects other aspects of their relationship.

With recriminations flying between China and the United States, once-flourishing trade and financial flows between the two countries have cooled off and are unlikely to revive anytime soon. These developments are emblematic of difficult new realities involving trade tensions, geopolitical fractures, and even disruptions caused by extreme weather events. National governments are trying to take measures to counter these vulnerabilities resulting from globalization. In the process, however, they are only making matters worse.

Government Policies Add Risks

For all its benefits, free trade has long been a political hot potato. Opening American automobile markets to imports from Japan in the 1970s brought significant benefits to American consumers in the form of more choices and lower prices. But try telling that to workers in Detroit who lost their jobs. American consumers have enjoyed cheap imports from China since 2000, but at the cost of millions of US manufacturing jobs.

There is no simple way for those who benefit from globalization to compensate those who face direct costs such as job losses. Political pressures have therefore resulted in a patchwork landscape in which trade and financial flows, rather than becoming freer over time, are increasingly subject to restrictions that give politicians cover from their upset constituents. These politically convenient solutions, whose benefits tend to be narrow, are often detrimental to economic efficiency and result in broad economic costs. It has also become a matter of political expediency to blame globalization, or specific trading partners, as the proximate cause of a country's economic problems that might in fact be the result of flawed domestic policies.

National governments must also cope with other vulnerabilities resulting from open trade. The Russian invasion of Ukraine in 2022 showed that relying heavily on a single supplier of energy products can leave an entire continent vulnerable. Before the invasion, more than 40 percent of Europe's natural gas imports came from Russia. Western sanctions on Russian natural gas exports put a severe crimp on European manufacturing, particularly in Germany, the continent's industrial powerhouse.

Government policy responses to disruptions in various forms are redirecting trade and financial flows in a manner consistent with geopolitical alignments. Such responses include trade measures (tariffs as well as import and export restrictions) but also measures designed to promote domestic technologies that effectively act as trade and investment barriers. Industrial policy—in which the government, rather than market forces, picks what it perceives as winners and losers among industries—has long been discredited, even though the practice is widespread in some form or another in most countries. Now this approach is making an open comeback.

Industrial policies in various forms are spurring the shift toward weaker global trade and financial integration. China's "dual circulation" policy, for instance, involves a state-led focus on increasing self-reliance (by boosting domestic demand and indigenous innovation) while remaining engaged with the global economy. The "Make in India" initiative targets similar objectives, including boosting Indian manufacturing by encouraging inward foreign investment, reducing administrative burdens on businesses, and, incidentally, protecting domestic manufacturers in specific sectors from foreign competition.

Such initiatives rarely invoke any aspect of protectionism, with the official narrative typically running in the opposite direction. At the 2018 World Economic Forum meeting in Davos, Indian Prime Minister Narendra Modi observed, "As opposed to globalization, the forces of protectionism are emerging. Their intent is to not only safeguard themselves from globalization, but also to alter the natural flow of globalization." He also warned that "many societies and countries are now becoming more and more self-centered. It seems that globalization is shrinking in contrast to its name. The consequences of such attitudes and wrong priorities cannot be underestimated in comparison to the threats arising out of climate change or terrorism." And yet in reality, India's average tariffs on imports have risen since 2014, when Make in India was launched.

Even advanced economies, once seen as unabashed proponents of free trade, are jumping on the bandwagon. Consider, for instance, the Biden administration's Inflation Reduction Act (IRA), which took effect in August 2022. With the professed objective of preserving US technological supremacy and promoting domestic investment in green and other new technologies, the administration put in place a number of policies that implicitly acted as barriers to free trade. The IRA aimed to boost green technologies by deploying subsidies and tax breaks to incentivize the domestic production of EVs and renewable energy components. This particular legislation riled even traditional allies in Europe, who face their own manufacturing challenges and view the United States as now contravening long-standing norms under which direct government subsidies to favored sectors have been limited. The CHIPS (Creating Helpful Incentives to Produce Semiconductors) and Science Act of 2022 provided similar incentives to semiconductor firms to set up manufacturing facilities in the United States and banned outsourcing to any "country of concern," with China atop that list. Trump undid parts of the IRA, although this was on account of his hostility to green technologies, and his other actions have more than made up for any unintended rollbacks in US protectionism.

Clearly, times have changed, and governments of all stripes feel the need to stimulate investment in new technologies. For emerging-market economies, and particularly for countries like China with unfavorable demographic trends, such investment is viewed as essential for boosting productivity growth and thereby preventing economic growth from declining precipitously. Advanced economies that face rising competition from emerging markets must contend with existential issues for their shrinking manufacturing sectors. The European Green Deal Industrial Plan, for instance, aims to make the continent a leading producer of green technologies rather than ceding these industries to the United States and China. The plan promises to lower bureaucratic impediments, coordinate policies across countries in the bloc, and offer financial incentives to companies, all in the hope of competing with US firms and reducing reliance on China for green tech supply chains.

In short, supply chain disruptions, geopolitical fragmentation, adaptation to climate change, and a host of economic and political pressures are all pushing in the same direction, causing an inward tilt to policymaking. It is not just government policies but also the actions of private corporations that are encouraging a retreat from, or at least a rethinking of, unconstrained globalization.

How Corporations Are Managing Risk

Globalization promised corporations access to markets in other countries as well as expanded sources of capital, labor, raw materials, and even production facilities. As globalization transformed every aspect of how corporations do business, though, it also led to the emergence or intensification of a variety of new risks.

One set of new risks surfaced, unexpectedly, from the pursuit of efficiency. Efficiency was once embodied in concepts such as just-in-time manufacturing and cross-national supply chains, with corporations ruthlessly cutting costs to fatten both their market shares and their profits. But the drive for efficiency has its own downsides. When a company cannot reliably deliver products it has marketed to its customers, it can suffer harm, especially in a competitive marketplace. A car manufacturer that relies on just-in-time production with minimal inventories and hires workers when needed and fires them when demand for cars is weak might reduce its costs, but it might lose the capacity to reliably make deliveries if any cog in the supply chain unravels. It might also find that hiring and training new workers when demand is strong is more expensive than keeping its workers employed through difficult times. Thus, despite its seemingly lower costs, this manufacturer might lose customers because of unreliable deliveries. Still, efficiency was the watchword for global businesses until the risks became increasingly difficult to sidestep.

A vivid illustration of how the drive for efficiency is risky came in July 2011, when Thailand experienced record levels of rainfall, resulting in devastating floods. Thailand is a small country; its annual GDP reaches barely half of 1 percent of global GDP. And yet the ripple effects of the floods ended up, by some estimates, costing about 2.5 percent of global industrial output that year. Thailand had become an important player in the supply chains of many auto manufacturers. Ford, Honda, and Toyota faced significant disruptions as a consequence of the floods. (Through happenstance, the local suppliers for General Motors and Nissan were relatively unaffected.) It was not just cars. The world's largest computer hard-disk supplier, Western Digital, which used Thailand as the production base for about 60 percent of its worldwide output, had to suspend its operations in the country. This is but one example of the fresh perils that corporations, many of which maintain complex supply chains and operations spanning multiple countries, must now navigate.

Risk is of course nothing new to companies, even if they operate in just one country. Typical sources of risk that practically every firm contends with include the availability and prices of raw materials, labor, financing, and energy, as well as factors affecting demand for their products and services, including the state of the economy. Firms can plan for such fluctuations, which affect them mostly in the short term. Shifts in technology (remember pocket cameras? The Walkman?) and consumer preferences (RIP, my beloved Blackberry) add uncertainty in a way that is difficult to plan for, unless a firm's leader is blessed with considerable foresight.

While the world has always been an uncertain and risky place, globalization, for all its benefits, has introduced a raft of major new risks for corporations. Or at the very least it has intensified existing risks, which may not be entirely new but are taking on new forms and becoming more virulent.

Climate change, as predicted by models, appears to have increased the frequency of destructive climate events and natural disasters around the world. As evidenced by the Thai floods, a breakdown in one part of a finely woven global supply chain can bring the entire chain grinding to a halt.

Geopolitical fault lines can emerge with little notice, causing massive disruption. In January 2022, despite all the warnings issued by US intelligence agencies, a Russian invasion of Ukraine seemed highly unlikely. When the invasion did happen, it quickly elicited a strong reaction against doing any type of business with Russia. The resulting disruptions intensified as countries allied with the West sought to reduce their business ties with Russia.

Government policies themselves pose an added risk. Measures enacted to address national security concerns, along with industrial policy actions designed to protect and preserve jobs in specific industries, are now being implemented through trade policy actions, as indicated in the earlier discussion of the IRA and the CHIPS and Science acts. What's more, Donald Trump's protectionist tendencies have seeped into the Republican Party, once a bastion of free trade, effectively undercutting one of its key economic pillars. Trump's reelection in 2024, and his deployment of tariffs as a bargaining tool with other countries on a broad range of issues, has injected yet more uncertainty into the future of US trade policy. For firms that operate across borders, tariffs imposed by one country, along with the cascading retaliatory actions undertaken by others, can quickly escalate into broader trade and economic hostilities, causing huge disruption.

These new sources of volatility have added to the burdens on businesses that had come to rely on supply chains built on a bedrock of free movement of goods and services. Corporations that once touted the efficiency of their supply chains have been left adrift as links in those chains become points of vulnerability. For small and medium-sized enterprises with thinner financial cushions than large multinational corporations, these disruptions can be even more difficult to manage.

In response to the escalation of various types of risks and the emergence of new ones as a byproduct of globalization, the new watchword for businesses appears to be "resilience." This involves not only reducing vulnerability to certain sources of risk but also enhancing the ability to bounce back more quickly from adversity.

How does a business build resilience? One approach is to concentrate production facilities in locations that promise relative safety from geopolitical risks. This could mean shifting production back to the home country (reshoring), distributing production across countries seen as geopolitical allies ("friend-shoring"), establishing production facilities in multiple countries to supply each of those countries' home markets, or a combination of all the above. The key point is that minimizing costs—such as labor, land, energy, and other inputs, even taxes—is no longer the main factor driving decisions about where to set up physical plants or other business operations.

Resilience can also be built through diversification, which can reduce exposure to risks associated with the concentration of production facilities, sources of raw materials, or markets for final products. For instance, even if geopolitical risks were minimized by locating a corporation's entire production base in its home country, that alone might not limit exposure to climate-related risks—unless the country had a large territory with widely dispersed geographic regions. A combination of reshoring and friend-shoring could help a company improve both aspects of resilience. Geopolitical alliances that shift unpredictably make this difficult to implement in practice—a country's allies today might become adversaries tomorrow due to shifting domestic politics or geopolitical events that drag countries into opposing camps. Canada and Mexico were among the first targets of Trump's tariff threats, with Europe following soon after, when he started his second term in office.

Still, diversification—whether through better access to raw materials and intermediate inputs, or through supply chains that avoid single points of failure—remains appealing. Similarly, targeting multiple export markets, instead of relying on just one or a few, helps mitigate risks tied to volatile demand or bilateral trade tensions. While this approach is safer, it comes with its own complications and costs, such as the difficulty of managing multiple supply chains.

A third approach entails building excess capacity and other buffers to absorb adverse shocks more easily when, as is inevitable, they occur. Buffers might include larger inventories of raw materials, intermediate goods, or even finished products—all of which would help maintain smooth production and sales.

Developing resilience through these approaches rather than focusing single-mindedly on efficiency seems logical and prudent. There is a catch, though: It is costlier. As with most situations in economics involving trade-offs of one sort or another, this is the painful and inescapable choice companies face. Bringing production back home prevents a company from taking advantage of cheaper labor or energy, in some cases making it impossible to maintain access to geographically distant, cheaper suppliers of raw materials and intermediate inputs—advantages enabled by globalization. Diversifying supply chains usually implies fewer economies of scale in production and transportation, raising costs. Maintaining inventory buffers and surplus workers—who may need to be idled during weak demand but can be deployed quickly when demand is strong—is also costly. These considerations inevitably favor larger companies. Smaller firms struggle to create such buffers or secure the credit lines that help them weather large risks.

The bottom line is that, for all its benefits, globalization has exposed manufacturers and corporations to new and more complex sources of risk. Their responses may well hinder efficiency, reduce choices, and increase costs to consumers. The more insidious result, though, is that these approaches to mitigating and managing risks might have the perverse effect of magnifying the underlying risks. For instance, retreating from markets in countries seen as geopolitical rivals to their home countries means that businesses no longer serve as bridges to help maintain good relations. In turn, this raises risks associated with geopolitical conflict.

Even countries themselves can be exposed to risks from certain facets of globalization, particularly financial integration.

Financial Flows

Cross-border flows of financial capital tend to be nimbler—or, as recipient countries see it, fickler—than trade flows. As noted earlier, foreigners can invest directly in a country's factories and financial institutions or do so indirectly through investments in equities or corporate bonds. The first type of investment, FDI, is much "stickier" than the second type, known as portfolio flows. With direct investment, a foreign investor assumes a full (or at least substantial) ownership stake by buying an existing company or creating a new one. Portfolio flows, which refer to purchases and sales of securities such as equities and bonds, constitute a far easier way to move financial capital into and out of a foreign country. For instance, selling off a factory and repatriating funds to an investor's home country is more time consuming and complicated than selling holdings in shares and bonds.

Both types of flows tend to be driven by economic considerations focused on return and risk. In addition to the set of risks that foreign investors have always faced in any country they invest in—such as macroeconomic and currency volatility, and the vagaries of domestic policymaking and politics—geopolitics now plays a role as well. As a result, these risks now include the imposition of government restrictions on cross-border financial flows.

This is a relatively new development, after a period of four decades when the trend favored reducing restrictions on cross-border capital flows. Advanced economies have largely dropped such restrictions, but many emerging-market countries, including China and India, still maintain some controls due to concerns that the associated volatility could destabilize their economies. Now even advanced economies have reintroduced restrictions on capital flows, though in narrow ways and for entirely different reasons.

In August 2023, the Biden administration issued an executive order limiting American investors, including private equity and venture capital firms, from investing in China's high-tech sectors, such as quantum computing, AI, and advanced semiconductors. The order also imposed reporting requirements on US firms making investments in other Chinese industries. The justification provided for these measures contained a stark warning that "advancement by countries of concern in sensitive technologies and products critical for the military, intelligence, surveillance, or cyber-enabled capabilities of such countries constitutes an unusual and extraordinary threat to the national security of the United States . . . certain United States investments risk exacerbating this threat. I [President Biden] hereby declare a national emergency to deal with this threat." The objective was clear: to limit the transfer of American dollars and technological expertise to China, particularly in new technology industries that the United States viewed as vital for its own manufacturing revival.

While government policies are actively limiting certain capital flows, private businesses and investors are already responding to the fracturing of the geopolitical landscape. There are signs that worldwide direct investment flows are increasingly being influenced by geopolitical considerations, even after accounting for various economic and noneconomic factors that could affect them. This is hardly surprising, as direct investment tends to follow changing patterns of trade.

Every problem presents an opportunity, and the fracturing of globalization is no exception. Countries on the right side—or at least not on the wrong side—of economic and geopolitical divides stand to benefit from the shifting crosscurrents of global trade and finance. If they are well prepared. And if they play their cards right.

China, once the factory floor of the world, remains dominant in global supply chains. Yet as its economy has grown and its workers demand higher pay, it is no longer the low-wage hub it used to be. Corporations looking to reduce costs are increasingly turning to countries like Bangladesh and Vietnam, which offer large, cheaper workforces and can compete with China in labor-intensive manufacturing. While none of these countries can match China's scale, they are gaining ground, especially with the added advantage of not being seen as geopolitical rivals to the United States and the West.

India looms large in such discussions. For a long time it was hindered by inadequate infrastructure—unreliable roads, ports, railways, and power supply—which limited its manufacturing potential. Now, with some of those deficiencies addressed and with a young and growing labor force, India is seen as a more viable location for manufacturing. Furthermore, it sits on the correct side of the geopolitical divide, with the United States and other Western powers eager to pull it into their orbit and away from China's.

Some changes already observed in the patterns of trade and financial flows are intriguing. Apple has begun to invest more robustly in India and to shift some of its phone production there to reduce its dependence on China. Meanwhile, it has become clear that US tariffs on Chinese imports will prove persistent inasmuch as trade hostility is now baked into Washington's approach, with broad bipartisan support for tariffs and other restrictions on trade with China. In response, Chinese manufacturers have increased their investments in Mexico, Vietnam, and other countries that still enjoy relatively unrestricted access to American markets. This provides an end-run around US tariffs while also diversifying their production bases, although Trump's broad-brush approach to tariffs is likely to inhibit this strategy.

In short, globalization, while not flourishing, is hardly fading away. Rather, it is shifting shape. But these changes are not entirely innocuous and might have unintended results.

Too Early to Sound the Requiem

Globalization has hardly ended, but it has taken a turn toward fragmentation along geopolitical lines, which could have important consequences for all countries. Patterns of both trade and capital flows are gradually changing in ways that mirror geopolitical alliances. While there is little evidence of a full-scale retreat from globalization, there is a clear shift toward forms of global commerce considered less risky—at least in terms of reducing vulnerability to geopolitical turbulence. Paradoxically, these shifts are likely to elevate other forms of risk.

Reduced exposure to disruptions—if reshoring and friend-shoring of production actually work as intended—could carry the important benefit of lowering the volatility of firms' output and even national GDP. But the costs are likely to be substantial. In fact, restricted trade patterns—particularly if they become more geographically localized—could ultimately increase rather than decrease vulnerability to certain types of adverse events. Weather-related disasters, such as the floods in Thailand that ruptured global supply chains for automobiles and certain electronic products, are likely to multiply in frequency because of climate change. Regional concentration could heighten the vulnerability of supply chains to such disasters. Moreover, as economic flows parallel geopolitical alignments more closely than ever, an important counterweight to geopolitical frictions is being eroded.

Thus, the fragmentation of trade and finance along geopolitical lines may not deliver the presumed benefits of greater economic stability and resilience. Rather, these forces might ultimately foment even greater volatility, both economic and geopolitical. Such developments are also leading to restrictions on the free flow of ideas and intellectual property, which hinder the global advancement of technology and other forms of knowledge. The burden of these shifts will disproportionately affect lower- and middle-income economies.

Emerging-market economies that are not politically aligned with advanced economies will find that reduced trade and financial flows result in fewer technology and knowledge transfers, hampering their development. As countries increasingly pull back from global integration, access to export markets could also become more constrained over time. This matters less for countries like China, India, and Brazil, which have grown larger, more self-sufficient, and richer than many other emerging-market economies. However, it could stifle economic progress in smaller, less-developed countries.

Low-income countries in the early stages of development need access to global markets to build up their manufacturing sectors. Their domestic markets are usually not big enough to absorb their output. Being able to sell outside their home markets enables their firms to take advantage of the economies of scale that are necessary to translate their low-labor-cost advantage into globally competitive products. An expanding manufacturing sector, with jobs that pay higher wages than agriculture and other primary production sectors, helps a country build a middle class that can support a vibrant domestic economy less heavily reliant on foreign demand. This path to development could be shut off if global trade and financial flows continue to fragment, leaving behind a large share of the world's population that will be too late to join the globalization party. For many countries in Africa, the combination of young populations and a lack of economic opportunities could prove a toxic mix. As discussed in Chapter 2, this risks fueling domestic instability and triggering migrant outflows, which could, in turn, adversely affect the political dynamics of the countries these migrants move to.

In summary, a retreat from globalization may give some countries a false sense of security, leading them to believe it renders them immune to external risks and volatility. While the costs of such a retreat may not be immediately apparent, they will ultimately be significant. Both rich and poor countries will one day come to rue their inward turn.

Why did globalization fail to deliver on its promise? For one thing, too little attention was paid to the distributional consequences. It is a reasonable proposition that free trade benefits all countries and their peoples. But in reality some countries benefit to a greater extent than others, and within any given country, the benefits are far from equally shared. Similarly, the benefits of financial globalization are often not immediately evident or widespread, while the disruptive effects of volatile capital flows are apparent and, to those already existing on the margins of economic survival, unjustifiable.

Financial globalization in particular seems to work well only when countries meet certain conditions. When a country has underdeveloped and poorly regulated financial markets, even domestic savings are not funneled toward productive projects. Foreign capital inflows only make things worse, often fueling real estate price booms, for instance, causing economic harm when those speculative booms turn into busts and capital flees the country. Along the same lines, countries beset by public-sector corruption, poor corporate governance standards, and shaky macroeconomic policies may find that foreign capital inflows exacerbate volatility in their economies rather than conferring benefits in terms of higher investment and growth.

Furthermore, it has become increasingly apparent that tighter global linkages are not always a good thing. They make pandemics, terrorism, cyberattacks, and other malignant forces harder to contain within national borders and therefore vastly more potent. Financial crimes ranging from money laundering to tax evasion through offshore tax shelters are all facilitated by the ease with which money moves across borders. As is often the case, safeguards and filters that are supposed to deter illegal activities often serve as barriers to more legitimate behavior while failing to eliminate the targeted activities.

Perhaps the benefits of globalization were subverted because the rules that should have kept trade and financial flows orderly, safe, and beneficial to all countries were flawed or inadequate, or both. Or perhaps the rules were sound but not enforced well or evenly, allowing some countries to follow rules that benefited them while flouting others. The most prominent example of this behavior is found in China, which, after gaining access to markets around the world by joining the WTO, did not entirely meet its commitments to provide similar access to its own markets. The consequence has been a backlash, with China ironically emerging as the purported supporter of those rules while the United States disregards the very rules it played a big part in designing.

For better or worse, and despite the lack of consistency in their application, rules are essential to maintaining order. But how will they be fashioned to reflect changes in economic and other forms of power? Based on what principles, and by whom, will they be written and enforced? These questions lie at the heart of international governance, a grandiose phrase for a concept that is ultimately of huge consequence to every one of us—and to which we turn next.

4

Rules of the Game

I can love a stone, Govinda, and also a tree or a piece of bark. These are things and things can be loved. Words, however, I cannot love. This is why doctrines are not for me. They have no hardness, no softness, no colors, no edges, no smell, no taste; they have nothing but words. Perhaps it is this that has hindered you in finding peace; perhaps it is all these words.

— Herman Hesse, *Siddhartha*

The European Commission (EC) takes its rulemaking seriously. This executive body of the European Union (EU) has issued a seven-page document laying down "quality standards for bananas" that touch on various characteristics used to sort bananas into three classes (the Extra class, Class I, and Class II, if you must know). "The minimum length permitted is 14 cm and the minimum grade [diameter] permitted is 27 mm"—unless the bananas are produced in the Madeira, the Azores, the Algarve (in mainland Portugal), Crete, Lakonia (in Greece), or Cyprus, in which case a length of less than 14 cm is permitted. But such bananas must be classified as Class II. A concerned consumer is only left with more questions. Is it acceptable for bananas produced in the Madeira, the Azores, the Algarve, Crete, Lakonia, or Cyprus to also possess a grade of less than 27 mm, and if so, what would the prescribed classification be? Would it matter for classification purposes if such a banana were to compensate for its slimness with greater length? Such questions could once have been referred to the EC's Management Committee for Bananas, although in 2006 this committee was disbanded and folded into the Management Committee for Fresh Fruit and Vegetables.

The EU rules on bananas were ripe for exploitation by British politicians who criticized the commission as a hidebound cross-national bureaucracy overreaching into the United Kingdom. The devious politicians went so far as to suggest that bananas with too much curvature—overly bendy bananas—would run afoul of the regulations. This was a fallacy. Whatever their shortcomings, EU bureaucrats are not unreasonable people. Bananas with slight defects in shape could still qualify as Class I bananas. Even highly bendy bananas could fit into Class II so long as the bananas retained their "essential characteristics."

It is all too easy to mock the foibles of persnickety EU bureaucrats, but any country with rules and regulations has its share of arcane, byzantine, and inconsistent ones that can be exposed to ridicule. In the United States, congressional legislation was introduced in 2024 with bipartisan support to allow childcare workers to peel bananas and oranges for children. The legislation, nicknamed the "Banana Act," was intended to override supposed restrictions on the peeling of fresh fruit on the grounds that it counted as "food preparation." In fact, there were no such restrictions in place, but the proposed legislation nevertheless garnered attention, for it resonated with people who have had to contend with other nitpicking rules.

No matter how lax your personal standards concerning bananas, your life has benefited from rules. Rules are the underpinning of smoothly functioning commercial, political, and social activities. Clearly defined rules foster healthy competition, both domestic and international, along multiple dimensions. This in turn can be good for maintaining order and discipline, especially in commercial activities such as trade and finance. Rules that are clear, transparent, and backed up by effective enforcement create predictable environments where households and businesses can thrive. Such rules foster freer flows of goods, services, financial capital, and even ideas and technology within countries and across national borders. Anarchists aside, this much is usually a matter of consensus. But that is often as far as the consensus goes.

The rub comes in agreeing on who will write the rules, enforce them, and be responsible for amending and updating them when circumstances change. The notion that rules create a level playing field that is fair to everyone almost invariably falls prey to a messy rulemaking process, which is typically controlled by the rich and politically powerful, often to the detriment of the broader public interest. This is true at practically every level of polity, ranging from subnational units such as counties or states to nations to the world at large. Still, a world without rules is far worse than one with imperfect rules, a lesson that became apparent about a century ago.

Humanity was ravaged in the first half of the twentieth century by two world wars and the Great Depression of the interwar years. As this dark period drew to an end, the nations of the world came to understand that a system anchored by widely accepted rules was essential to foster stability and enable shared prosperity. Many of the institutions that to this day define the multilateral order were created in the period between 1944 and 1948. This includes the IMF, the World Bank, the United Nations (UN), and the General Agreement on Trade and Tariffs, the precursor to the WTO.

The multilateral order is a conglomeration of rules that a vast majority of countries have agreed upon, along with the international institutions mentioned above, which have been given the responsibility to flesh out, monitor, and enforce those rules. Global power dynamics come into play at every step, and so do attempts by some countries to redefine and interpret the rules in ways that suit their own interests. This tug-of-war often takes the form of attempts to modify existing rules or create new ones that favor specific countries. These attempts can involve trying to change the rules from the inside or, in some cases, setting up new institutions to promulgate fresh rules.

When it comes to rules that govern international commerce, even the question of who sits at the rulemaking table becomes complicated and fraught. Take world trade, in which every country participates to some extent and therefore has an interest. Even pariah regimes like North Korea benefit from trade, as they sell coal and iron ore to China and a handful of other countries, and in turn purchase goods such as fertilizers and medicines.

The WTO sets the rules for the trading system in which all countries operate, but a few countries like North Korea are not members and have no say in fashioning those rules. The WTO maintains a large membership; as of June 2025, 166 countries were members, and 23 others had been granted observer status. The WTO's stated primary purpose is to "open trade for the benefit of all" by operating a global system of trade rules, acting as a forum for negotiating trade agreements, and settling trade disputes between members. It paints itself as a "member-driven, consensus-based organization."

As broad and inclusive as this sounds, and while in principle the organization indeed runs by consensus, larger economies inevitably speak more forcefully. This is particularly true in a negative sense. The United States brought the mechanism for resolving cross-national trade disputes to a grinding halt in December 2019 by blocking appointments to the WTO's appellate body, citing concerns that the dispute-settlement mechanism was unfairly harsh on the United States and too soft on countries like China. Still, the principle of equality in the WTO's voting system is important. It means that when major policy decisions lacking consensus are decided by supermajority votes, each member country, whether large or small, exercises one vote.

In international finance, by contrast, money still talks. At many of the major multilateral financial institutions, such as the

IMF and the World Bank, direct influence—as measured by voting power, claims to senior leadership positions, and other means of influencing policy—is very much tied to economic might. This has resulted in complicated power dynamics. As we saw in Chapter 2, the distribution of global economic power has shifted markedly in recent decades. But the old guard remains resistant to change, resulting in conditions that invite conflict. How this plays out will matter a great deal for governance of the multilateral order.

The United States has in recent years taken an à la carte approach to the institutions with which it engages and whose jurisdiction it accepts. Take the International Court of Justice (ICJ), which was set up in 1945 and is the principal judicial organ of the UN. The United States has been an active participant in cases against other countries at the ICJ but has refused to accept the ICJ's jurisdiction over its own actions. The rest of the world sees this as a pattern. The United States plays an instrumental role in establishing various institutions and designing their operating rules, but then proves recalcitrant when those very institutions ask that it consistently play by the rules, not just when doing so suits its interests.

The response of emerging powers, especially China, to a global order that is calcified around the power dynamics of the post–World War II era has been to set up their own institutions, where they have a greater say. This could yield positive outcomes if the rules were rewritten and enforced in a "fairer" manner. New institutions may well force older ones to raise their standards and ensure more even treatment of all members. Institutions of different vintages could thus work in concert to bolster the rules-based system.

Instead, we are witnessing a fragmentation of the system, with institutions dominated by opposing groups of countries attempting to rival each other in power and influence. Ambiguity over the rules of the game and how they will be enforced has resulted in minimal restraint on the major powers, an uncertain landscape for most other countries, and latitude for leaders with disruptive intentions, even if they come from small and otherwise weak countries.

This is not to say that institutional competition has had no positive consequences. Moves by China and other major emerging-market economies to disengage from the IMF have forced the institution to adapt in order to maintain its credibility and legitimacy with this group of rising powers. One example is the alteration in the composition of the IMF's top leadership, which used to be dominated by the advanced economies. Two of the top five management positions at the institution are now (unofficially) reserved for candidates from China and one other emerging-market economy.

Such modest changes notwithstanding, the overall picture is of a creaky system that can no longer be relied on to maintain stability in global matters, whether they involve trade or geopolitical conflicts. The weaknesses of international institutions have even grimmer consequences in circumstances where the narrow interests of individual countries conflict with the broader interests of humanity as a whole.

Global Governance Is a Matter of Life and Death

The process of making, administering, and enforcing rules is particularly complicated when the rules apply to sovereign nations. And it is particularly important because the policies of a large country often affect not just its own citizens but those of other countries as well.

Indian Prime Minister Narendra Modi once observed that in the postwar period, "global governance [has] failed in both its mandates of preventing future wars and fostering international cooperation on issues of common interest." Recent evidence certainly suggests a failure of the rules-based order to deliver much order. This failure becomes especially consequential in a world where national economic fortunes are more closely interconnected than ever. As we saw in the previous chapter, globalization is hardly behind us; it is simply morphing into new forms. Even countries striving to disengage from each other, as the United States and China seem to be, are ultimately affected by each other's policies.

This makes it all the more important for the world to adhere to a rules-based order that governs not only trade and finance but also, quite literally, matters of life and death. Global health governance has become crucial as immigration, tourism, and trade flows all act as conduits for pandemics and other public health threats. Equitable distribution of vaccines and medical resources more broadly could improve overall health outcomes. And yet, as the COVID pandemic painfully revealed, parochial interests prevailed in the moment, leaving the entire world worse off.

The World Health Organization (WHO), which is part of the UN system, provides guidance on medical issues that transcend national borders. Coordinating responses to pandemics and other worldwide health emergencies is its raison d'être. Nonetheless, as the COVID pandemic unfolded, the WHO was powerless, unable to persuade rich countries with large (in some cases excessive) vaccine stockpiles to share them with poorer countries that had great need but limited resources to acquire or distribute vaccines. Nor was the WHO successful in prevailing on China to share information early in the pandemic when countermeasures could have been more effective.

This is a vivid example of how pursuing narrow national interests can lead to worse outcomes for the entire world. In other cases, a given country may not fully internalize the costs of its policies to the rest of the world. One example of such "negative externalities," as discussed in Chapter 1, is greenhouse gas emissions. The unwillingness of China, India, and the United States to take drastic actions to curb them not only affects those countries but also has global consequences. When addressing cross-national problems, which inevitably involve spillovers and externalities, a lack of global coordination represents a significant hurdle.

Similar examples abound in the realm of international finance. Wild speculative swings can destabilize national financial markets and, depending on the forces at play and the size of the country experiencing instability, have spillover effects on the rest of the world. Because of the dominance of the US dollar, disruptions in US financial markets or even moves by the Fed to raise or cut US interest rates have sizable effects on the rest of the world. And there are many examples of meltdowns in one emerging-market economy setting off "contagion effects"—international investors pulling their money from the entire group of emerging markets, including those in sound economic condition, simply because events in one economy cause them to reassess the riskiness of investments in any of those countries.

Clearly, the world needs rules that work. Global institutions have been set up precisely to design rules and promote common goals that might be harder to achieve if countries prioritized their own narrow, short-term interests. This tension is much harder to reconcile in practice than in the high-minded rhetoric often heard when national leaders gather. For instance, multilateral institutions like the IMF could mitigate unpleasant developments in international finance, such as monetary policy spillovers and contagion effects, by pushing the major economies to adopt better economic policies and by providing a financial lifeline to countries exposed to contagion. As we will see in this chapter, the enforcement of global rules becomes a challenge in practice when the rules collide with national priorities.

Before evaluating the current structure of the rules-based system, it is worth considering what an ideal structure would look like—one that serves all countries well. This will help us measure how far the present system falls short of that ideal before examining the forces driving change, for better or worse.

Rules About Rulemaking

A long-standing view, articulated centuries ago by philosophers such as Thomas Hobbes and Jean-Jacques Rousseau, holds that "there is no freedom without the law." This sentiment encapsulates the important truth that constraints on the behavior of individuals, households, and other social units, not to mention countries, can in fact be liberating. But bridging the gap between individual prerogatives and the interests of a broader community takes work. It requires codifying permissible actions and behavior. Some of the principles that govern the formation of international rules are similar to those adopted at the societal or national level.

By design, rules help build a common understanding of how one should act in particular circumstances. Stopping at red lights and proceeding on green makes everyone better off because it allows for smooth traffic flows. In the United States, when traffic lights fail, flashing red and flashing yellow lights carry specific connotations. Even if everyone obeys those rules, traffic moves much less smoothly than when the lights are functioning properly. In general, as in this example, imperfect rules are in most circumstances better than no rules.

Rules are needed even in the context of war. This seems odd. A war arises precisely because a ruler or a country decides to violate the territorial integrity of another country (or perhaps reclaim territory that was usurped by force). All countries have decided that, even in those circumstances, certain humanitarian rules are necessary to ensure that civilians do not become the direct targets of warfare. Unfortunately, those rules are rarely enforced, though they might serve as a deterrent, as a head of government could eventually be hauled before a war crimes court for ordering or allowing the rules to be breached. Even more regrettably, in most cases when the rules are violated, only the losing side is held to account—and even then, only when it is not a major power.

Human beings also care a great deal about fairness. The pain of standing in a slow-moving queue is magnified tenfold if anyone unfairly jumps ahead in the line. Of course, if there is a clear rule for skipping a queue, then the resentment is dampened. At some Hindu temples in India, you can pay a modest fee to be admitted into a special line that speeds your path to the inner sanctum, with far less time spent among the plebeians, perhaps even buying you a little more time before the deity to make your case for receiving the deity's blessings. And nobody seems to complain when I board flights ahead of most others—between customers with disabilities and families with children under two—without even standing in line, thanks to my hard-won elite status earned through extensive international travel.

Fairness, in both perception and reality, is a key desideratum of any set of rules. Other elements of well-functioning rules that help them gain wide acceptance include being clear, easy to interpret, and consistent.

Even if rules make everyone better off, there is usually a tussle in determining the exact rules, as they can be tilted, either explicitly or implicitly, to favor certain individuals or groups while maintaining a patina of fairness and equality. So the question regarding who gets to write the rules becomes a contentious matter, requiring rules of its own. This process invariably reflects power dynamics. Parents set rules to be followed by their children (although in certain families, such as my own, the father's sphere of authority is limited to the family dog, who occasionally deigns to respect his wishes). The gray zone of rules when children are turning into adults is a tricky one for any family. Such complications are not limited to families.

The IMF (along with the World Bank) was founded at the Bretton Woods Conference, held in July 1944 in the eponymous town in the American state of New Hampshire and attended by forty-four Allied nations. The institution began operating in 1947, with forty members, including China and India. The structure of the institution and its charter were determined largely by the United Kingdom and the United States, the two major economic powers. The renowned British economist John Maynard Keynes, and a longtime US Treasury official, Harry Dexter White, played key roles in this process. The USSR attended the conference but did not become a member. The Axis powers—Italy, Germany, and Japan—became IMF members by 1952. These countries then set about repairing their reputations and, with the help of the Marshall Plan, their economies.

Voting power at the IMF is apportioned among countries on the basis of economic variables such as shares of global GDP and trade. To this day, the G7 countries (Canada, France, Germany, Italy, Japan, the United Kingdom, and the United States) dominate the IMF with 41 percent of the voting share, roughly in line with their collective weight in world GDP. This voting share is boosted to a majority by other advanced economies that typically follow the G7's lead.

Thanks to their rapid growth in recent decades, China and India now account for 20 percent of global GDP, but their combined voting share is just 9 percent. Thus, when it comes to major policy changes, the traditional powers continue to control the rulemaking process at the most important international financial institution (IFI). The IMF is but one example of this phenomenon. Clashes between the rapidly growing new powers' quest for influence and the unwillingness of the old powers to cede theirs are rocking the multilateral rules-based system and undermining its legitimacy.

In addition to the question of whether every country merits one vote or whether votes are weighted by criteria such as GDP, there is the matter of how decisions are made. Voting systems invariably involve a trade-off between efficiency and equality. Broadly, they fall into three categories—unanimous, majoritarian, and supermajoritarian—each occupying a distinct point along the efficiency-equality spectrum.

Unanimous systems, which require consensus on every policy decision, protect the interests of all countries but can paralyze the functioning of international institutions inasmuch as one recalcitrant member can hold up decision-making. Hungary by itself repeatedly blocked EU aid to Ukraine in its war against Russia, supposedly to avoid prolonging the war and promote peace. Beyond fulminating openly and loudly, there was little the other twenty-six countries could do to sway Viktor Orbán, Hungary's democratically elected but authoritarian leader, who had become a pariah within the group.

Majoritarian systems, which grant one vote per country and require only a simple majority for policy decisions, can generate more balanced outcomes by making coalition-building important. Both these systems can cause larger members of an institution to disengage, though, if they believe that a group of small countries can thwart them at every turn. Such disengagement undercuts an institution's effectiveness.

Supermajoritarian systems, which require a large majority for policy decisions, offer greater balance by preventing one or a few countries from blocking the majority while also ensuring that major decisions have broad support. When voting rights are tied to economic size rather than distributed equally among countries, supermajoritarian systems provide additional safeguards—at least from the larger countries' perspective. But in some cases this setup gives a single large country veto power over major decisions. At the IMF, for instance, major actions require an 85 percent supermajority, and the US voting share is 16 percent. As a result, other countries often feel that their interests can be overridden at the whim of the United States.

In short, there is no ideal voting system that can fully bridge differences between an individual country's interests and the collective interests of an entire group. Maintaining legitimacy among all countries inevitably collides with effective decision-making and enforcement. Political scientists and, of course, economists have tried to develop voting rules that force each member to consider how its choices affect other members. In 2008, when the United States was the sole country blocking an increase in the IMF's financial resources, I proposed that a small portion of voting rights be auctioned off to the highest bidders (with a limit on how much voting power any single country could gain through this process). The logic was simple: Countries willing to contribute more than others to the IMF's pool of resources ought to play a larger role in determining how the institution is run and in its policy decisions. Such a mechanism could be supplemented with safeguards to ensure that small countries with limited resources were not crowded out from decision-making.

For all their logical appeal, this and other clever schemes have gotten little traction. As economic power shifts and old institutions remain static, their effectiveness and legitimacy has been sapped away.

Another problem with rules is that an individual, or country, can in many cases benefit from violating them if everyone else follows them. If one person (with a cheap ticket and no special boarding privileges) waltzes to the head of an otherwise orderly queue to board an airplane, they enjoy easier access to overhead bin space. Such behavior makes it less likely that rules will be followed, even though everyone is better off if they are. The cheater—and everyone else—would be at a disadvantage if the boarding process were a disorganized scrum.

Rules have little value without a clear mechanism for enforcing them. Effective and consistent enforcement of rules is therefore essential, which brings up two issues. First, who will carry out the enforcement? Second, what is the penalty for breaking a rule? Some airlines ensure that their gate agents shoo away anyone trying to board a plane before their boarding group has been called, with the ensuing embarrassment likely serving as a deterrent to others contemplating breaking the rules. The reality, though, is that rules tend to apply with disproportionate force to the poor, weak, and vulnerable—whether individuals or countries—while the rich and powerful are able to skirt them, and in some cases ensure that they do not apply to themselves at all.

Recognizing that undisciplined fiscal policies adopted by any of its members could threaten the credibility and durability of the entire group, the EU in 1997 put in place rules limiting national budget deficits and public debt levels as part of the Stability and Growth Pact. These rules were even more relevant and important for EU members that adopted the euro as their common currency two years later. Reckless spending and high debt levels in any eurozone country were rightly seen as posing risks to the monetary union.

Germany, with France's support, insisted on strict rules. A member country's government budget deficits could not exceed 3 percent of its annual GDP, and public debt levels could not exceed 60 percent of GDP. Any deviations would require the offending government to pay a penalty. Proud of its fiscal probity, Germany wanted to ensure that its spendthrift Mediterranean counterparts, such as Greece and Italy, did not derail the common currency by using it as a cover to run up larger budget deficits.

In an outcome rich with irony, Germany and France were among the first governments to violate the deficit rule! The two biggest countries in the eurozone increased government spending in 2003 to combat economic slowdowns. Needless to say, the rules were bent for them—after all, they were breaking the rule in an entirely justified and sensible manner (or so they claimed), and doing so for the collective well-being of the eurozone—and neither had to pay a penalty.

By the time the eurozone debt crisis erupted in 2009, the Teutonic affection for fiscal prudence had revived. Countries like Greece and Italy were lectured to, in no uncertain terms, with the message that they needed to fix their public finances and economies. The unmistakable subtext was that it was their undisciplined policies that had put not just their own economies but the entire eurozone project in peril.

This brings to mind an adage that an official in the Indian Administrative Service brought up during a chat about rules in India, when I noted inconsistencies in how a particular set of rules had been applied across similar cases. As this person wisely put it, "The rules depend on who you are and whom you know." When rules are applied unevenly, they only foment cross-country tensions and instability rather than promoting orderly outcomes.

Breaking a rule must have consequences if the rule is to have any meaning. Sometimes, those consequences can make everyone worse off. Take, for instance, a child who commits to finishing her homework before joining the rest of the family for a picnic at a nearby park. If she does not finish her homework in time, it would make the day less pleasurable for everyone to leave the child behind—a worse outcome for the entire family. So the child ends up joining the picnic in any event, whether or not the homework gets done. If everyone knows this, the commitment has no value in the first place.

Such was the case with France and Germany in the example regarding limits on budget deficits. If the eurozone's two largest economies entered a recession, the entire region would suffer. But as with parents and children, inconsistency in applying rules makes them harder to enforce in normal times.

Which brings up another popular adage concerning rules— that it is better to ask for forgiveness for breaking them than for permission. This principle might matter little when individuals are navigating bureaucracies within a country, but at the international level such a cavalier approach by national governments is harder to disguise and can chip away at the very foundations of a rules-bound system.

If they make everyone better off, why aren't rules universal and pervasive? Their very existence suggests giving up some element of autonomy. In a society, this means sublimating individual desires and prerogatives in favor of a set of codes that should benefit everyone. In an international context, it might mean sacrificing a degree of national sovereignty to promote global welfare. This raises the difficult issue of managing the actual or perceived loss of national sovereignty when agreeing to a system of global governance with commonly accepted standards and rules.

It asks a lot of a purportedly strong leader to explain to constituents the benefits of sound international governance, which can seem abstract, distant, and disconnected from their day-to-day lives. It is even harder for a leader to resist the easy temptation of linking popular grievances to malign foreign factors, including international institutions and their rules, as an excuse for festering domestic problems.

The tension between global standards and national interests—sometimes a real tension and sometimes a political cudgel—often infects domestic politics, resulting in outcomes that inflict broad damage. The Brexit vote in 2016 that took the United Kingdom out of the EU illustrates how this apparent friction can be parlayed into domestic political divisions. By any measure, the United Kingdom benefited a great deal from being in the Union, with goods and services flowing freely across its borders to and from countries on the Continent. Still, the trope of an unaccountable, unelected transnational bureaucracy over which the British people had no control, that paid little attention to their needs and could not be influenced (much less sacked), but that nonetheless affected their lives in small and large ways (see rules regarding acceptable banana dimensions), was played to the hilt by devious politicians. In short, when a system of rules is seen as lacking legitimacy and accountability, perverse and damaging consequences often follow.

While rules that work satisfactorily can be written for normal circumstances, it is exceptions that test the very framework of accepted rules. For a well-functioning society or international system, this means rules alone are insufficient; they must be backed up by norms that are often difficult to codify. Moreover, rules are not written in stone (with the possible exception of those handed down to Moses) and need to evolve to remain relevant and useful.

Black swan events, which are highly improbable but not impossible, are well documented. Economists (and physicists) use the concept of a "five-sigma" event to describe extreme outcomes. The Greek letter sigma denotes the standard deviation of a variable—say, the price of oil—in historical data. The standard deviation, in case memory of your high school statistics class is scratchy, measures how much a variable tends to fluctuate around its long-term average. Based on historical patterns, the probability that the price of oil will vary five standard deviations or more from its average is tiny but, importantly, not zero.

In finance, a number of five-sigma events—such as the global financial crisis—have occurred in recent years. Large banks that once seemed rock solid collapsed and almost took down the entire US financial system. Then there are events that, until they happen, are considered impossible or at least inconceivable. Let's return to the example of crude oil prices. Suppose we assume that prices can range only from zero to $1,000 a barrel. Over the past five decades, oil prices have mostly remained between $5 and $140, so that broader range should surely cover all possible outcomes. And yet in April 2020, at the beginning of the COVID pandemic, the price of a barrel of Brent Crude briefly dropped to *minus* $30! Sadly, this did not mean you could fill up your car's gas tank and get paid for doing so. Rather, with oil demand in free fall and storage facilities full, oil that had already been pumped had to be loaded onto stationary tankers, incurring costs while waiting for prices to rebound.

This episode shows how the unthinkable can on rare occasions turn into reality, rendering it difficult to write rules that account for outcomes that are entirely out of the ordinary and that apply in any possible scenario. As a result, norms that provide guidance for acceptable behavior in all circumstances are as important as rules that apply to particular situations. Norms arise from a shared understanding of basic values and are fortified by tradition, which makes their origins opaque within a given society and even more so in the international sphere.

The US Constitution is a hallowed document that is invoked by the principled and unprincipled alike to justify their actions. The notion that the Founding Fathers—a group of wise but imperfect humans fashioning a document full of compromises at a difficult time in US history—understood, down to the level of specific details, what would be best for the country for all time is ludicrous. And yet that vision colors the thinking of many American citizens, abetted by some unscrupulous people who surely know better but nevertheless maintain this fiction because it suits their narrow purposes.

Principles like those that undergird the US Constitution may be immutable, but their translation into rules must leave room for evolution in response to changing circumstances. Financial regulations written in an era of paper currency and bearer instruments must adapt to a world where payments and other financial transactions are largely digital. Governance structures, too, must evolve alongside the rules.

But change is hard. Once people, businesses, or even countries adapt to a set of rules, they instinctively resist altering them. Even flawed rules work well for certain segments of society, which then resist reforms for the greater good if those changes threaten their narrow interests.

The interplay between money and influence, and its adverse effect on the structure and operation of the rules-based order, is vividly exemplified by the evolution and management of the international financial system.

Governing the International Financial System

In global finance, the IMF and the World Bank are the principal international institutions, counting nearly all countries in the world as members. The IMF appraises the macroeconomic policies of all its member countries and offers short-term loans when a country runs low on funds to prevent the collapse of its banking system or currency. The World Bank provides development financing. So a country turns to the IMF if its currency is under attack and falling in value relative to others, while it turns to the World Bank for building infrastructure like a dam or bridge, or for advice on improving its health care system. These two institutions collectively bear the weighty responsibilities of maintaining global financial stability, navigating the world economy through crises when they do occur, and protecting vulnerable countries. This requires that they maintain legitimacy and credibility across all groups of countries, which in turn requires them to encourage large countries to implement policies that serve both their own long-term interests and the world's, while also preserving the financial resources necessary to limit the spread of crises.

Both the IMF and the World Bank have suffered from the perception that they are unwilling to stand up to traditional powers such as the United States and the United Kingdom, even as those countries undertake reckless policies that have adverse effects on the world economy. Emerging-market countries believe that the rich countries enjoy favorable treatment from the IMF in particular. On the flip side, the United States has long believed that the IMF has mollycoddled China, failing to take it to task for currency manipulation and other antimarket practices. The Trump administration has taken things one step further, with open hostility toward the IMF and World Bank driven by the notion that these institutions' recommendations and policies are not always perfectly aligned with US interests (defined narrowly).

Meanwhile, the IMF's lending practices have been criticized by its internal watchdog for the uneven treatment of countries it provides financial assistance to. The IMF requires borrowing countries to adopt reforms such as reining in budget deficits, restraining money supply, and modifying regulations to improve the business climate. Funding is in principle cut off for countries that do not stick to these commitments.

Large countries like Argentina and rich countries like Greece, however, have been treated more leniently, continuing to receive funds despite violating their commitments. A survey of national policymakers conducted by the IMF itself showed that, when it was providing financial support to eurozone countries hit hard by the debt crisis, many member countries felt excluded from the decision-making process and "thought European countries were treated more favorably." Countries that are poor or small or both, meanwhile, often believe they are treated too harshly by both institutions, which typically impose tougher conditions on their loans and brook no deviations from their reform commitments.

These are not the only reasons for the erosion of the prestige and legitimacy of these IFIs, especially among developing and emerging-market economies. Their governance structure has ossified. The IMF is governed by a large executive board of twenty-five directors, representing key countries (as well as groups of smaller countries), which oversees its operations and makes major policy decisions. The World Bank has a similar board, separate from the IMF's.

Every major publicly listed company has a board, which typically meets once or twice a quarter to hold management to account and provide guidance on strategic matters. The boards of the IMF and World Bank each meet roughly two to three times a *week*. Given this frequency, board members—along with their large support teams—set up home in Washington. The members make decisions at the behest of their national authorities, so they do not vote based on the objective merits of each matter, but they are involved in practically every policy decision. As you can imagine, this is a huge drain on money and time. Proposals to make the executive board a nonresident body that meets less frequently and mainly provides high-level strategic guidance have gone nowhere. After all, it is the same board that would have to vote itself out of residence.

A more egregious issue, illustrated by earlier examples, involves voting rights at the IMF, which are in principle distributed based on various measures of a country's size and importance in global trade and finance. As already noted, the United States has veto power over the IMF's major policy decisions, which requires a supermajority. For other policy decisions that require only majority approval, the United States and other advanced economies hold sway with their combined voting share. This distribution of voting rights is at odds with the economic reality that emerging-market economies now rival the advanced economies in overall size and also in GDP rankings. Japan, with an economy that is one-fourth the size of China's, has a slightly larger voting share than China does. India's economy is larger than either France's or the United Kingdom's, but it has a smaller voting share than either.

This situation should change, but again, the executive board must approve any changes. The Europeans are loath to give up their power, and all the advanced countries are reluctant to grant China more power, especially veto power. They fear that China could pressure other emerging-market and developing countries to form a bloc that would secure majority voting power.

The IMF does have a rule that voting shares are adjusted every five years based on a formula that accounts for a country's share of global GDP, trade, and other economic factors. However, the executive board must approve any such modifications. In other words, the advanced economies—who currently control a majority voting share on the board—would have to approve the loss of their own majority. As a result, the formula has essentially been ignored since 2010. Ironically, even as it is disregarded in practice, this formula remains a subject of power struggles within the institution, for even minor tweaks can affect country rankings in voting power. This no doubt reflects the awareness that, eventually, the IMF will have to acknowledge the shifting economic power dynamics, and the formula will matter when that day comes.

The enormous symbolism embodied in IMF voting shares—and the zero-sum nature of reallocating them, since all shares must sum to 100—means that any changes will inevitably involve pitched battles between countries seeking to preserve or improve their positions in the pecking order. Moreover, a mechanical application of the current formula using recent data will benefit China to the greatest extent while only modestly helping India, Indonesia, and a few others. Additionally, the formula would shrink the voting shares of many other emerging-market and developing economies, particularly those in Africa and Latin America. With their weak economic performance in recent decades, the GDPs of those countries have put them further behind the rest of the world. Thus, for low- and middle-income countries that are not eager to have China speak on their behalf, such revisions will hardly improve the IMF's perceived legitimacy.

The advanced economies have held leadership of the two institutions firmly in their grip. The United States has traditionally ceded to Europe the privilege of choosing the IMF's managing director, the head of the institution. In return, the Europeans support whomever the United States nominates to head the

World Bank and also the second-in-command at the IMF, its first deputy managing director. There are consolation prizes for other members—at the turn of the millennium, two more deputy managing director positions were added at the IMF, with one of them reserved for Japan and the other rotated among emerging-market countries in Africa and Latin America, two regions that lacked representation at the top levels.

China grew increasingly frustrated with its disproportionately limited clout at the institution, an annoyance that intensified when its economy overtook Japan's in 2010 to become the second largest in the world, yet nothing changed. To appease China, in 2011 a new deputy managing director position was created, with the understanding that it would be reserved for China. This is how two of the IMF's top five management slots came to be allocated to nationals from emerging-market countries. (It should be noted that in 2019 the Europeans picked Kristalina Georgieva, a Bulgarian national, to head the IMF, a position she still held as of 2025; Bulgaria is regarded by some as an emerging-market country.)

In addition to the IMF and World Bank, there is another selective institution that matters greatly in the world of finance: the Bank for International Settlements (BIS). The BIS, which describes itself as a "bank for central banks," is owned by sixty-three of the major central banks and serves as a forum enabling those banks to cooperate on issues of mutual interest. For instance, the BIS hosts the Basel Committee on Banking Supervision, which develops global standards that serve as a template for national regulatory authorities. Deviating from those standards would make it harder for a country's commercial banks to gain an international presence, as regulators elsewhere would be wary of allowing them to operate in their jurisdictions.

The heads of the major central banks meet roughly every two months at BIS headquarters in Basel, Switzerland. In principle the heads of all central banks enjoy similar status at these deliberations, and policy decisions are made mostly by consensus. However, as a regular participant told me with a sardonic grin, "There are a few firsts among us equals, and they tend to get their way on major policy issues."

In short, even as economic and financial power become more widely distributed across advanced and emerging-market countries, changes in the relative influence of various country groups at major IFIs have been glacial at best and nonexistent at worst. Understandably, this has not pleased the rising powers. Faced with this frozen landscape of global governance, China decided to take matters into its own hands.

China Makes Its Move

As China's economic power grew, so did its leaders' desire for greater influence in international economic affairs. They recognized, however, that the country's clout at multilateral institutions such as the IMF and World Bank would be constrained because the traditional powers would not readily cede their grasp. The Chinese are quick learners, with a pragmatic approach to international relations and adept at adjusting their strategy as circumstances evolve. By the 2010s, when even the global financial crisis failed to shake loose the grip of the advanced economies on these institutions, China launched a revamped strategy to promote its economic and geopolitical ambitions more effectively.

China now employs a multipronged approach to expand its role in setting the global agenda. First, it is gradually increasing its influence within international institutions and establishing at least a toehold in regional organizations, even those outside its immediate sphere of interest, a strategy that allows it to push for change from the inside. Second, it is creating new multilateral institutions where it gets to call the shots, allowing it to control the rules of the game while also nudging existing institutions toward reform. Third, it is forging cooperative arrangements with like-minded countries to build trust and deepen economic ties with prospective partners, an effort that could even draw would-be competitors into its orbit. Let's take a look at each of these approaches.

The first element of China's strategy involves increasing its influence in existing multilateral institutions. China seems to have accepted that its voting shares—though well below what it could reasonably claim (based on the institutions' own formulas) relative to its shares of world GDP and trade—will be slow to change. Instead, through aggressive behind-the-scenes campaigns, it has ensured greater representation at the institutions' senior leadership levels. As noted, one of the four deputy managing director positions at the IMF is now allocated to China.

China has also begun marking its presence in regional financial institutions, focusing on those where it has the opportunity to play a major role, even if through indirect influence over other members. China has established beachheads at the African Development Bank, the Caribbean Development Bank, and the Inter-American Development Bank. Africa engages in trade more extensively with the EU as a whole, but China is the single country that accounts for the largest share of Africa's trade. For many Latin American countries, China has become the largest export market. So China's presence in these organizations allows it to begin playing a role—modest at first, but easily scalable—in the regions' economic governance.

China has shown an initial willingness to engage with the existing multilateral institutions on their own terms rather than seeking change as the price of entry. This playbook harks back to China's accession to the WTO in 2001. After a long and difficult series of negotiations, China agreed to most of the standard conditions for WTO membership, which gave it expanded access to foreign export markets but also came with a commitment to open its own markets to foreign companies and investors. Now that China is a large and powerful member of the WTO, it can play a greater role in influencing how the organization defines and applies rules for international trading.

In 2016 the European Bank for Reconstruction and Development (EBRD) welcomed China as a member, recognizing that Chinese funds could serve as a useful complement to its own financing of various projects. Astonishingly, China was willing to sign on to the institution's mandate, which limits its operations to countries that are "committed to and applying the principles of multiparty democracy [and] pluralism." The very first article in the institution's charter states that its members are "committed to the fundamental principles of multiparty democracy, the rule of law, respect for human rights and market economics." It is remarkable that China was willing to join the EBRD despite the inconsistency of the mandate with the tenets of the Communist Party of China. Perhaps because China stages elections, some in China contend (and some on the outside accept) that the country practices a version of democracy that simply differs from what the West thinks of as free and open. Another plausible interpretation is that China projects openness to compromise when it seeks membership in existing institutions. Over time, it then strives to subtly influence those institutions from the inside rather than through brute economic or political force exerted from the outside.

The second prong of China's approach to global agenda-setting has been to more actively assert its ascendance in international finance by bankrolling new institutions. China's leaders recognized that it could put its money to good use by funding large-scale projects in Asia—a crying need for countries in the region that have lacked funds. Thus was born the idea for the Asian Infrastructure Investment Bank (AIIB). The bank's stated goal was to finance infrastructure projects such as roads, railways, and airports in the Asia-Pacific Region.

The United States was caught flat-footed by the rush of countries—including some of its close economic and political allies—that lined up to join the China-led AIIB when it was launched in 2016. Somewhat petulantly, and unwilling to confer any legitimacy on the institution, the United States and Japan have stayed out of the AIIB, but that has not slowed the parade of countries eager to become members. By 2024, the AIIB boasted 110 members and a capital base of nearly $100 billion. China has contributed $30 billion, the largest amount by far of all the members, and has a voting share of 27 percent. The AIIB's headquarters is located in Beijing.

China has argued that many of the procedures followed by existing multilateral institutions are unnecessarily bureaucratic and complicated, noting that the AIIB will put greater emphasis on running a lean bureaucracy and making decisions swiftly. China has asserted that the AIIB not only demonstrates governance as effective as that of existing institutions, but will do even better. In the AIIB's governance structure, one sees many positive elements: a simple and transparent formula for setting countries' voting shares, the absence of any single country's veto power over major decisions, and a nonresident executive board that supervises but does not unduly interfere with the management of the institution. These are exactly the sorts of changes that have long been sought at the IMF but have proved difficult to implement because of the entrenched interests blocking them. Moreover, developing and emerging-market economies, which dominate the AIIB, play more prominent roles there than at other IFIs, even if they do so in China's shadow.

The AIIB is a conspicuous example of China's impatience with marginal changes in global governance. It has grabbed the reins and is seeking to rewrite the rules in a way that ostensibly improves on the existing order, which China and other emerging markets see as having been defined by and mainly serving the interests of the major advanced economies.

The AIIB helps Beijing legitimize its efforts to extend its economic and political influence while subtly influencing the rules of the game. By setting up an institution that aspires to establish best practices in governance and transparency, China seeks to show that it can provide constructive global leadership that enhances rather than detracts from the extant international economic order. The AIIB's management aimed not only to meet but to exceed existing standards. Yet it has struggled to shift the perception, perhaps warranted, that the AIIB is primarily controlled by the Chinese government, with other countries' participation serving mainly to lend legitimacy and soften any blowback.

The AIIB is a textbook example of China's increasingly savvy and disciplined approach to international economic relations, one that emphasizes constructive engagement over brute financial force. Beijing is using the AIIB as a tool of international economic diplomacy that supplants its earlier roughshod bilateral approach, which sparked resentment even among some countries that were recipients of Chinese financing. Whether the change is one of substance or form is less clear. Any country receiving AIIB funding knows full well that although the project has to be approved by the AIIB board, the funding is ultimately contingent on support from China.

As the third prong of its approach to global institutions, China has strategically aligned itself more closely with other major emerging-market economies to present a united front. It has taken on a leadership role in the BRICS, the group created in 2009 including Brazil, Russia, India, China, and South Africa. These economies collectively account for one-quarter of global GDP and a population of three billion, roughly two-fifths of the world's total.

Together, these countries are demanding a greater say in the running of major institutions and in the design of changes in the rules and procedures governing international finance. However, they have a history of sharp differences and even armed conflicts between themselves. China shares borders with both India and Russia and has engaged in military skirmishes with each of them. Still, the leaders of this group declared at their 2012 summit that their discussions were "inspired by a shared desire to further strengthen our partnership for common development and take our cooperation forward on the basis of openness, solidarity, mutual understanding and trust." Such statements were met with skepticism about whether the BRICS had sufficiently aligned interests to achieve anything of substance.

China, the largest economy in the group with a vast stock of foreign exchange reserves, saw its opportunity to lead and seized it. Spurred by the offer of a large contribution from China, the BRICS set up an arrangement in 2014 to pool a portion of their foreign exchange reserves. The BRICS Contingent Reserve Arrangement has amassed a pool of $100 billion, with China committing $41 billion. The five countries have not actually put this money into a pool; instead, they have simply committed to providing the agreed-on amounts if any one of them needs funds to respond to a currency crisis.

The following year, the BRICS set up the New Development Bank (NDB) with the aim of supporting "infrastructure and sustainable development projects" in their economies. The initial $50 billion of subscribed capital was derived from equal contributions from the five members, who also enjoy equal voting rights, with none of them holding veto power over decisions made by a majority of the members. The NDB, with the support of all its founding members, has sought to broaden its reach and influence by bringing more countries into its fold. Four members—Bangladesh, Egypt, the United Arab Emirates, and Uruguay—were added during 2021–2023, with much smaller contributions and voting shares. The founding members' voting shares have been slightly reduced to about 19 percent each, but, importantly, parity has been maintained among them.

Behind the scenes, things were not so chummy. An intense dispute arose between Beijing and New Delhi over the location of the NDB's headquarters. As usual, China got its way, with Shanghai chosen as the location. As a consolation prize, the first president of the institution was an Indian. To maintain the semblance of parity, the two immediately succeeding presidents have been Brazilians, although this has done little to counter the widespread view that China is the dominant power in the institution.

In any event, the BRICS have shown that they can put money on the table in a coordinated way and overcome concerns about how their sometimes divergent—and often conflicting—economic and geopolitical interests could hamper their cooperation on the world stage. K. V. Kamath, the first president of the NDB, put it this way: "Our objective is not to challenge the existing system as it is but to improve and complement the system in our own way." By fostering stronger financial ties between key emerging-market economies and creating alternatives to the existing global financial architecture, this growing bloc of countries is chipping away at the dominance of advanced Western economies. With its vast financial resources, China has become the first among equals in this group.

Refashioning the Rules-Based System

As I've argued throughout this book, competition is usually healthy, resulting in better outcomes. This ought to be true even in the case of competition *between* global institutions, although the calculations in that case can be rather subtle because such institutions are intended, by their very nature, to promote cooperation among all nations. Still, when it comes to issues like development aid, prospective borrowers might be drawn to lenders offering cheaper loans more expeditiously and with fewer onerous requirements. Such competition could benefit the poorest and least powerful countries, which usually find themselves at the mercy of IFIs and their internal power dynamics.

The first phase of competition between long-standing and new IFIs appears healthy—raising standards and pushing every institution to do better. There is a major, if so far latent, risk that this competition will precipitate a race to the bottom as the institutions try to appeal to a broader membership and garner more business. For instance, in the business of making development loans, one can well imagine institutions competing to finance new projects by offering not only better terms but also looser qualifying standards. While this might seem to favor recipients of aid and development finance, it could ultimately lead these countries further into debt. Money that comes with few strings attached—lacking any measures to raise labor and environmental standards or to control corruption—will only enrich elites while doing little to help the country's broader citizenry, who will nevertheless get stuck with the bills owed to outside financiers.

The governance structures of new institutions like the AIIB and NDB are designed to aspire to higher standards than those of existing ones. This is certainly the case on paper, although it is equally clear that Beijing controls both membership and decision-making at these institutions. As China becomes ever more authoritarian and state-dominated, and as its domestic political system grows increasingly centralized and opaque, it is hard to imagine that these characteristics will not influence its governance of these institutions.

Changes to the international order usually arise from extreme circumstances or shifts in economic power that make the existing order untenable. Examples of this pattern abound. The Group of 20 (G20)—a roughly equal mix of major advanced and emerging-market economies, including the G7 as well as countries like Brazil, China, and India—was created before the global financial crisis but sprang into relevance in the crucible of that crisis. The dollar's displacement of the British pound sterling as the dominant global currency reflected the waning might of the UK economy and the simultaneous waxing of the US economy. Today, it is the rise of China, India, and other emerging-market economies that is shaking up the world economic and financial order. Each of these shifts has tested the adaptability and resilience, if not the very survival, of a rules-based global order.

This order is coming under threat from other corners as well. The United States is blocking the work of and disengaging from institutions like the IMF, World Bank, and WTO that it played a key role in creating and that are essential for setting and enforcing the rules of global governance. The Trump administration's distaste for multilateral institutions runs even deeper. On his first day back in office in January 2025, Trump set in motion America's withdrawal from the WHO, citing the institution's mishandling of the COVID pandemic and its vulnerability to inappropriate political influence from some member states (read: China) despite their modest financial contributions relative to that of the United States.

The withdrawal, either de jure or de facto, of the world's leading power undercuts the financial stability and effectiveness of these institutions. Other Western-aligned nations such as Japan, the United Kingdom, and the collection of European countries are wracked by their own problems and are in no position to provide enlightened, effective leadership to these institutions. This situation leaves other countries adrift, without a clear set of rules to guide their behavior—or, crucially, rules they can be confident other countries will follow.

In the other corner, China is gaining ascendancy in the world economic and financial order—not, as the United States and other Western economies would prefer, by participating in existing institutions under the current rules of the game, but on its own terms and by co-opting other countries into the system of rules it seeks to dictate. China is setting up its own institutions and corralling other emerging-market and developing countries into their ambit. Given the nature of China's internal governance, it is difficult to imagine these institutions pressuring their members or aid recipients to foster democratic institutions, increase government transparency, or adopt better labor and environmental standards.

Meanwhile, smaller countries, often those with the most at stake in matters of global importance and those most vulnerable to the policies of large nations, are led to view existing institutions as mostly focused on perpetuating the power and governing philosophies of the large countries. The proliferation of new institutions might also primarily serve the interests of their major shareholders, rather than helping marginalized countries gain influence to advocate for their interests in a reset of the existing multilateral system.

Even the rules governing regional blocs like the EU are fraying due to uneven enforcement. The unfairness of rules that hold smaller and newer members to account while failing to constrain the behavior of larger countries is proving untenable. The political forces that have enabled figures in the mold of Donald Trump to claim power are also undermining long-standing security alliances like NATO that are meant to foster geopolitical stability through the deterrent effects of collective defense. Trump has made no secret of his reluctance to unconditionally fulfill this core NATO obligation, leaving the periphery of the alliance exposed to territorial aggression.

One particularly disheartening example of the breakdown in international norms and governance is the lack of any accountability for or restraint on Israel's devastation of the entire population of Gaza in response to the atrocities perpetrated on Israeli civilians by Hamas terrorists in October 2023. Domestic politics in Israel, with a leader seemingly viewing extreme military aggression as essential to preserving his tenuous hold on power, and the United States, with criticism of even the most egregious of Israeli policies and actions all too easily twisted as being antisemitic, have allowed the persistent violation of basic humanitarian principles.

All told, the post–World War II rules-based system of global governance is at risk of crumbling, buffeted by a shifting world order rather than shaping it to humanity's greatest benefit. Both old and new institutions are coping with challenges to their legitimacy and, by extension, their credibility. This hinders their effectiveness in tackling problems of international scope and in fostering cooperation where it could lead to superior outcomes at both the national and international levels. Rather than serving as a source of stability, the struggle to define the contours of the global governance system and control its levers is generating greater friction and instability.

With the world teetering as it adjusts to two strong powers at opposite ends of the scale, middle powers such as India could provide much-needed stability. These countries, especially smaller, low-income countries that are less resilient and lack self-sufficiency, have a strong incentive to prevent disruptions in global trade and finance or a breakdown of the rules-based system. A refashioning of cross-country alliances could also help shore up the gaps in global governance. The reality, however, is proving less comforting.

5

Middle Powers and Alliances

When a shepherd goes to kill a wolf, and takes his dog to see the sport, he should take care to avoid mistakes. The dog has certain relationships to the wolf the shepherd may have forgotten.

— Robert M. Pirsig, *Zen and the Art of Motorcycle Maintenance*

India's foreign minister, S. Jaishankar, a suave and eloquent former diplomat, became a cult hero for his clear articulation of the country's interests during the Ukraine war and for forcefully asserting his government's willingness to stand up to the United States and other Western powers rather than simply dutifully falling in line with their demands to isolate Russia economically. At a session of the Indian parliament in December 2022, he defended the government's decision to continue receiving oil imports from Russia. By sidestepping the sanctions intended to restrict Russian oil exports while also benefiting from the price caps imposed by Western countries on those exports, India could buy large quantities of Russian oil and natural gas more cheaply. An opposition politician criticized the government's stance, declaring that, since attaining independence in 1947, India had not embraced neutrality in conflicts between an oppressor and the oppressed, between an elephant and an ant.

Jaishankar responded that India had consistently urged dialogue and diplomacy rather than supporting Russia in its aggression against Ukraine, arguing that the government's priority was to mitigate the economic effects of the war, including higher food and energy prices, on the Indian people. He stated, "If it is your contention that our position has been in putting the interests of the Indian public first, I plead guilty to it. Yes, I put the interests of the Indian public first." This unleashed a flood of fawning articles in local newspapers, with many approvingly citing this sentiment in their headlines, further burnishing Jaishankar's image.

India has become the master of issue-based alliances, aligning with countries or groups depending on the matter at hand and adopting the approach that best serves the country's interests. Access to cheap Russian oil was the determining factor in India's decision to sidestep sanctions on Russia. At the same time, India has been eager to cultivate a close relationship with the United States, which helps it avoid allying too closely with China. A disputed border and fears of being outmuscled by its neighbor's much larger economy have kept India wary of China, even though the two countries often find themselves on the same side of issues where the interests of emerging markets diverge from those of the United States and other rich countries.

Still, notwithstanding its adroitness in managing this balancing act that has kept it more or less on the right side of both great powers, one wonders whether India could find itself bereft of true partners who would stand by it through good times and bad if it is perceived as fickle in its associations.

At a conference in New Delhi in October 2023, I posed this question to Minister Jaishankar after he had delivered a keynote speech and opened the floor to questions. I first noted that India had pursued targeted alliances based on specific issues. While acknowledging that this approach might help India maintain its strategic autonomy, I asked whether it also carried the risk of relatively shallow, potentially unreliable alliances that might not serve India well in times of trouble. The session moderator wanted to wrap up as time was running short, but the minister insisted on answering the interesting question that had been posed. He agreed with my characterization, noted that India had little choice, and asserted that, while the approach carried undeniable risks, it had served the country well. He concluded that "being in the middle is not the answer, but being on the extremes is not the answer either."

The implication was that the solution—for India, at least—was to avoid occupying a fixed spot on the spectrum between the two great powers, while retaining enough flexibility to shift with changing issues and circumstances. The risk to a country of engaging in issue-specific alliances, however, is that it affords little protection during periods of serious geopolitical stress, as neither superpower feels particularly compelled to defend the country's interests—unless they happen to align perfectly with the interests of that superpower at that moment. This is the conundrum that much of the world faces as the globe's two superpowers jockey for power and influence. But in this challenge lies an opening for countries in the middle to exert their influence, which could collectively be quite substantial, in positive ways.

For a country like India, rising tensions between the West and China offer certain economic opportunities, as we saw in the discussion of globalization in Chapter 3. Yet such opportunities could be overwhelmed by the breakdown of the rules-based international order if those tensions were to boil over. Although India would benefit from acting as a peace broker of sorts and doing what it can to bridge the growing divide, it has resisted that role and instead chosen to forge its own path. The calculus made by the Indian government is leading it to take actions that may serve its short-term interests but also risk contributing to global instability. Other middle powers, especially those in Asia such as Indonesia and Vietnam, have adopted similar stances.

Some small countries, meanwhile, have already thrown in their lot with one side or another, recognizing that, unlike a large country like India, which has room to maneuver, they could end up as collateral damage if they attempt to stay neutral. A few of these countries, perhaps ostracized by either great power, have little choice in the matter; shunned by the United States, the likes of Iran, Pakistan, and North Korea have tied their economic and geopolitical fortunes to China.

The remaining countries in the middle form a sizable, heterogeneous group that runs the gamut from rich to poor, large to small, and democratic to de facto authoritarian. Some are rich in legacy wealth but less productive in current output. Others are rich in human and natural resources but bereft of economic conditions and institutions that allow them to prosper. Many have been plundered by corrupt elites or torn apart by factional rivalries. All these disparities make it difficult for these countries to work together toward common objectives—to the extent those even exist—leaving them mostly to chart their own courses.

Ongoing changes in the world order represent a treacherous time for some of these countries and a time of opportunity for others. Some are better positioned to thrive in a new configuration while others will struggle. Policies and strategy will count, but so will luck and personalities. Geopolitical realignments offer an opening for even marginalized countries to ally with groups that are trying to expand their collective footprint. At the same time, such realignments raise the prospect that some countries will become even more marginalized in the competition between existing groups or the creation of new ones.

A broad set of partly overlapping and partly nonintersecting alliances is operating in the shadow of competition between China and the United States. Alliances that promote a cooperative approach to economic and security issues can make up for the limited power that individual countries possess and enhance the group's collective power, but alliances themselves are not immune to shifting political winds and other changes. As democracy finds itself on the ropes, institutions fray, free markets succumb to government intrusion, and countries retreat from global integration, many alliances are being reshaped.

Will countries be forced to choose sides as great-power competition intensifies, or will fence-sitting become the norm, with many countries attempting to hedge their bets by diversifying their relationships? An even more consequential question is whether the formation and expansion of alliances, along with the positioning of individual countries within this landscape, will serve as a balancing force or foment greater turbulence. The answers to these questions, and their implications for the stability of the world order, are not reassuring.

Challenging Choices

In *The History of the Peloponnesian War*, the ancient Greek historian Thucydides writes of the decades-long war in the fifth century BC between Athens, which had been the dominant power in Greece, and Sparta, the upstart that ultimately displaced Athens as the hegemon. The Peloponnesian War is often considered a parable for the inevitability of military conflict when a rising power challenges the dominance of a large, established power. China's rise and its challenge to US dominance seems to fit this paradigm exactly, foreshadowing open warfare between the two.

We must learn from history, which has essential lessons for us. But context is important as well. Unlike previous instances of hegemon-versus-upstart conflicts, this one is less about direct control of each other's territories. China and the United States are trying to maintain or expand their spheres of influence and can do so without directly engaging in armed conflict that touches each other's national soils, although there is an ominous, overhanging threat of direct military engagement in other parts of the world. The contentious relationship between two superpowers, more evenly matched economically and militarily than in other recent rivalries, creates difficult choices and challenges for the rest of the world.

The two major powers and their allies share an interest in bringing other countries into alliance and keeping them there. This offers an unsavory choice: to face either China's rapacity in coveting both territory and influence or the vicissitudes of the United States in its current political alignment, making it precarious for any country to throw in its lot with either major power.

China has come to be viewed by many countries as a friend and economic savior—one that provides funds with few overt strings attached to those that desperately need the money for development and other programs, but that have no recourse to private capital. Yet, as discussed in Chapter 1, there are other types of strings attached, and some countries that have fallen into China's grip have ended up regretting their dependence on its funds. Moreover, China has expected countries receiving its funding to line up behind it on a range of issues, including cutting diplomatic ties with Taiwan and supporting the Chinese position in contentious votes at the United Nations.

The United States, for its part, has come to be regarded as a powerful yet fickle ally—once admired in much of the world, but never fully trusted, with its politics often turning insular and successive administrations adopting very different approaches to global engagement. Under Trump, the United States has become aggressive in its dealings with other countries and vindictive toward those that do not align with its policies.

During his first presidency, Trump threatened at one point to pull the United States out of NATO, the compact that has long anchored the close political and military alliance between Europe and North America. To make things worse, in January 2025, on the eve of taking office for his second term, he refused to rule out the use of military force to take over the Panama Canal and even Greenland, part of the sovereign territory of Denmark, a

NATO member. His secretary of state, Marco Rubio, reaffirmed that it was not a joke and confirmed America's interest in buying Greenland or, if need be, taking the territory by force. Whatever the seriousness of such threats, the very fact that the US political system could return to office a president willing to trifle with the country's long-standing treaty obligations surely makes all countries in or contemplating treaties with the United States wonder whether they are on shaky ground.

One way to frame the two extremes of the unsavory tradeoff faced by countries around the world is as a binary choice between picking a side or adopting a neutral posture.

The first approach has the advantage of creating a close relationship with a major power, which can come in handy during times of economic or geopolitical stress. For instance, in the immediate aftermath of the global financial crisis, practically every country in the world wanted access to US dollars to protect its own financial system. To meet this demand and prevent a broader collapse of global financial markets, as we saw in Chapter 2, the Federal Reserve set up bilateral currency swap lines that allowed other central banks to borrow dollars using their own currencies as collateral. Aside from the central banks of the major advanced economies, only a small handful of other economies were able to secure currency swap lines from the Fed. Australia, Brazil, Mexico, and South Korea were among the select few, all countries whose economic and geopolitical interests are closely aligned with those of the United States. India was among the countries that sought but did not receive a swap line, for it was not seen as having a close enough relationship with the United States.

The downside of this approach is that close proximity to a single power exposes a country to its whims, including unpredictable internal political dynamics. Even while fostering a closer trade relationship with China in recent years, South Korea has long been an ally of the United States on most matters in international forums. And yet this did not protect it from being hit by

Trump-era tariffs during his first presidency, when he targeted all trading partners with which the United States had trade deficits.

The second option in this binary classification is to choose diversification, which involves forsaking a close relationship with either major power to mitigate the risks of alienating the other. The vast economic power and self-centered policies of the two major powers have led a number of countries to view this as the only viable choice, even if imperfect.

In Robert Pirsig's cult classic *Zen and the Art of Motorcycle Maintenance*, the author's alter ego, Phaedrus, explores various alternatives to being impaled on either of the two horns of a dilemma. The equivalent of the diversification strategy is to attempt to go *between* the bull's horns, which could work in evading both but might end even more disastrously in a double impalement. When neither of the two major powers has a stake in a country's fortunes, that country is vulnerable to volatility from global events and, in some cases, even from heightened internal strife and atrocities. The peoples of Haiti and Sudan, for example, must feel that their suffering garners scant attention compared with events in other parts of the world where China or the United States have clear economic or geopolitical interests, such as Zambia and Ukraine.

These are not the only choices, however, as Phaedrus well knows given his training in logic. One can employ additional creative strategies, such as trying to sing the bull to sleep or throwing sand in its eyes—both of which require a high level of skill in the bullring and carry even greater risks of failure. In any case, they are not readily available in the international arena, where countries interact with each other repeatedly over time.

Yet another alternative is to refuse to enter the arena altogether, even if this means having to pay a penalty. This alternative is the equivalent of becoming self-sufficient, thereby limiting a country's exposure to the vagaries of geopolitical shifts. This approach sometimes extends even to international trade and financial flows. The concept is appealing but comes at the enormous cost of denying a country the benefits of trade. When India threw off the yoke of British occupation in 1947, it applied the concept of *swadeshi*, self-reliance, to eliminate the scars of colonialism. Unfortunately, though, this isolationism and the socialist bent of its initial postindependence governments held back India's economic progress for decades. This contrasts starkly with China, which began to free a significant portion of its economy from state control in the 1980s and subsequently embraced integration into the global trading system. Self-sufficiency, if it means limiting participation in the world economy, exacts a significant cost for the ostensible benefit of greater economic safety and security. Even though it has now become a large economy, India no longer regards this as a viable strategy.

Several countries have found it profitable to be more explicitly neutral without disengaging from global trade and finance. For many decades Switzerland benefited from a secretive banking system, using neutrality as a shield to deflect the prying eyes of other countries' banking regulators, which made it an alluring magnet for investors with large sums of money whose provenance they preferred not to reveal. However, even Switzerland found it difficult to remain on the fence in the face of Russia's naked aggression against Ukraine. Russian oligarchs suddenly and unexpectedly found that they and their money were no longer welcome. Some of their financial assets were even frozen by the Swiss government. It remains to be seen if these actions will erode Switzerland's position as an international financial center. In any case, neutrality is not an option for other countries that lack Switzerland's wealth.

Another approach—one that is not an option for a lone bullfighter in a ring—involves entering alliances, which helps a country strengthen relationships with a select group of counterparts. This approach can offer some protection for a smaller, weaker country and can be combined with other strategies. Even alliances with like-minded countries, however, often come with trade-offs.

The Economic Community of West African States, formed in 1975, was designed to promote the economic integration of fifteen countries in West Africa and enable the group to speak with a unified voice on matters of global importance. Instead, the political instability and economic woes of its two largest members, Nigeria and Ghana, along with the smaller members' concerns about their economic interests and influence being sidelined, have only highlighted rifts within the group.

This array of choices is hardly soothing to countries in the middle that face increasing pressure to get off the fence and choose sides. Some countries have unreservedly thrown in their lot with China or the United States, while others have tried to hedge their bets at the risk of falling into disfavor with one or both. The middle path, sidling up to both powers while simultaneously avoiding the full embrace of either, certainly has many advantages. Diversification is after all a time-tested strategy for reducing risk without compromising returns, but this approach faces its own challenges.

The choices and strategies adopted by the middle powers play an important role in determining the overall balance of power in the world. A complex and constantly shifting set of considerations, including domestic political dynamics, influences how these countries position themselves. The preferred strategy of diversifying economic and geopolitical relationships is difficult to execute successfully and carries its own risks. One country in particular has the size and economic clout to deploy this strategy to maximum effect; its experience reveals the complications involved and the potential downsides.

India Hedges Its Bets

India is playing the diversification game as well as it can be played. As a democracy with an independent judiciary and a free-market orientation—although these attributions perhaps deserve some qualification—it should find a natural alliance with Western countries. At the same time, as a low-middle-income country with economic priorities that distinguish it from richer countries, it has more in common with other emerging-market countries. Now, as a rising economic power in its own right, it is trying to carve out a distinct sphere of influence for itself.

To protect its own interests and avoid taking sides, India has tried to stay relatively neutral as geopolitical tensions flare up in various regions. This harkens back to India's tradition as a leader of the Non-Aligned Movement, which, at the height of US-Soviet tensions in the 1970s and 1980s, represented the effort by a number of countries to avoid becoming too closely aligned with either power. At the time, when it was not entirely obvious which side would prevail in dominating the global order, it was a prudent strategy.

Now, as the world's fifth-largest economy, and with the prospect of becoming the third-largest economy within a few years as it rapidly catches up to Germany and Japan, India has been courted by the two superpowers. Yet India's leaders have been circumspect about aligning too closely with either one for fear of having to compromise its short-term interests. Instead, India has tended toward one pole or the other depending on the specific economic or geopolitical issue at hand, while trying to maintain an overall gloss of neutrality.

India has been especially wary of China, which it views as both an economic competitor and a hostile neighbor due to border skirmishes over disputed territory in India's northeast region. Concerns that cheap Chinese goods could overwhelm India's manufacturing sector have led to tariffs and other restrictions on imports from China. Additionally, both economic and security concerns have prompted bans on Chinese phone manufacturers and their technologies.

In a 2024 interview, India's commerce and industry minister, Piyush Goyal, was asked about the prospect of India's joining a regional trade agreement that included China and Japan. Goyal was direct and unambiguous in his response, stating that participation in such an agreement, which would no doubt be dominated by China, would amount to giving China free access to Indian markets. He then drew a sharp distinction between China and India, referring to China as a "non-transparent economy, very opaque in its economic practices, where both trading systems, political systems, the economy—the way it is managed—is completely different from what the democratic world wants."

While touting its credentials as the world's largest democracy, India has been equally wary of allying itself too closely with the United States. Since the British partitioned India and created Pakistan when ceding independence in 1947, the United States has consistently provided significant military and development assistance to Pakistan. This money was intended to serve US geopolitical interests, as India's nonalignment was seen as pulling it closer into the orbit of the Soviet Union. Indian political leaders thus viewed the United States as siding with Pakistan in border tensions, which occasionally escalate into conflicts and even wars.

Indian Prime Minister Modi and Trump hit it off early on in Trump's first term, with Modi astutely sparing no effort to pander to Trump's ego. This began raising hopes in Delhi that, with China and India increasingly at loggerheads on territorial and economic issues, Washington would serve as a reliable counterweight against Beijing. To Modi's surprise and dismay, his honeymoon with Trump was short-lived. Trump took note of the US trade deficit with India, placing it in the same category as China, and imposed tariffs on imports from India. Trump's hardline stance on immigration, which affected Indian workers in the United States, further soured the relationship, even though Modi and Trump continued to profess their admiration for each other.

The Biden administration, in a concerted effort to sway India from its relatively neutral stance on geopolitical matters, worked to convince the Modi administration that, given their shared visions, a stronger economic and political alliance with the United States was in India's best interests. High-level US cabinet officials traveled to Delhi to argue that a closer alignment with the United States would benefit India and to fortify the bilateral relationship. Yet Indian governments now and in the future are likely to remain wary of such overtures. Under both Trump administrations, the United States has proven an unreliable partner, and even under other administrations it has been seen as a fair-weather ally primarily interested in pushing its own agenda.

Operating in China's shadow has made it challenging for India to take the lead among the middle powers, leaving it to chart its own course. However, its growing economic clout has given it leeway to pursue a more assertive foreign policy.

India's presidency of the G20 in 2023 presented the government with a well-timed opening to highlight the global validation of the country's economic and geopolitical strategies. India's economy was performing much better post-COVID than that of others in the group, and its neutral geopolitical stance had not resulted in significant costs to its international standing. Indeed, the Biden administration was quick to forgive India for refusing to participate in the sanctions imposed on Russia following its invasion of Ukraine.

India made a mighty effort to emphasize its position as a neutral and honest broker, using its presidency to unite the G20 membership and advance progress in areas of common interest, such as better coordination of banking regulation, while downplaying areas of conflict. Maintaining this fine balance took some astute framing of the G20 agenda and extensive behind-the-scenes diplomacy to keep tensions from blocking progress in areas where there was broad agreement on the need for change—such as reforming the IMF and other multilateral institutions—even if the specifics of those changes were difficult to agree on.

In a remarkable tour de force, India accomplished what had seemed inconceivable after the start of the Ukraine war: persuading all G20 members—including China, Russia, and the United States—to sign off on a joint communiqué. One could argue that the communiqué was milquetoast, but in fact it included fairly pointed language about the war and several other issues that, over the previous eighteen months, had left the G20 splintered and unable to reach such an agreement in any of their meetings since the war began. But the celebration was tempered. At the last minute, Chinese President Xi Jinping was a no-show at the national leaders' summit, which was the pinnacle of India's presidency of the group. Xi's absence highlighted the tensions between China and India, with China far from eager to contribute in any way to enhancing India's prestige on the global stage. The absence of Xi and Putin also underscored the fractured status of the G20, with the advanced economies on one side, China and Russia on the other, and a few like India in the middle.

India has the capacity to play a stabilizing role in the global order, but this will be difficult to do if it continues to pursue its strategy of issue-based alliances. Yet Indian government officials argue that this strategy is essential to India's capacity to play a constructive role, as neither of the two major powers has entirely noble intentions, and each needs an incentive to actively seek India's cooperation rather than taking it for granted in every circumstance. If the G20 outcome, however modest it might seem, is any indication, these officials may have a point. But India's unwillingness to take a stand when international norms are violated, such as its position of neutrality on the Ukraine war for the sake of short-term economic benefits like cheaper oil, leaves it without a clear set of principles guiding its policies and actions.

For India, the calculations are subtle even in matters of broader global governance. Anything that increases the influence of emerging-market countries as a group often results in China's gaining the most and, in relative terms, widening its power gap with India. For instance, India has always been ambivalent about IMF reforms that would increase the voting shares of emerging-market economies in line with relative economic size. For this would mean that India's gain of a slightly larger voting share would pale in comparison to China's substantially larger gain.

An emphasis on protecting its own short-term interests, whatever that might imply for the rest of the world, leaves India poorly positioned to take a leadership role in global affairs. A more assertive external policy based largely on its self-interest is certainly defensible as typical behavior for major powers, despite their high-minded statements about promoting the global good. However, this approach makes it harder for India to serve as a credible and widely trusted stabilizing force as the world around it faces ever greater instability.

The Rest of the Middle

The economic and political fortunes (and plights) of many countries are tied to how they fit into a rapidly shifting world order. In Asia, home to some of the most dynamic economies in the world, the fraught choices come into sharpest relief.

China, India, and Japan have staked out their positions on the geopolitical spectrum. Other Asian countries are caught in a difficult situation. Many of them, including larger economies such as Indonesia, Malaysia, Thailand, and Vietnam, have strong trade and financial linkages with China. With Japan's economy receding in importance and being overshadowed by China's despite remaining a wealthy one, these countries face a strong economic imperative to maintain cordial relationships with China. But they are wary of China's interventionist impulses, with countries like the Philippines, which experiences direct territorial conflicts with China and suffers the consequences of its wrath, being left in particularly vulnerable positions.

The United States remains influential in the region, although the first Trump administration's withdrawal from the Trans-Pacific Partnership (TPP) and its lack of positive engagement with medium-sized Asian countries stirred doubts about the attitudes of future US administrations toward the region. Smaller countries, which tend to be buffeted by global crosscurrents more than larger ones, face particularly complicated balancing acts as the two superpowers seek their allegiance. This group includes Singapore, which has close economic ties to China but is more akin to the United States in most ways, especially in its free-market orientation.

This tightrope walk is hardly new to Singapore, having been part of its reality ever since it became an independent and sovereign state in 1965. Singapore's former prime minister Lee Kuan Yew, in a 1966 speech, referred to a Chinese proverb: "Big fish eat small fish; small fish eat shrimps." He then noted that some types of shrimp have developed an effective defense mechanism: They are poisonous and can harm the fish that eat them. In reality, though, survival is a challenge for any shrimp when the big fish are thrashing about and roiling the waters.

Singapore's phenomenal economic progress has raised its per capita income to a level slightly above that of the United States. Its prosperity has elevated its stature—after all, economic success is hard to argue with—and given it greater room to maneuver. Still, Singapore has little choice but to remain in China's good graces. For all its wealth, its annual GDP of roughly $550 billion renders it a pygmy relative to China, whose economy is nearly thirty-five times larger. Singapore has formed extensive trade and financial links with China, but it fancies itself a free market and an open democracy with a strong sense of the rule of law, values that naturally align it more closely with Western countries than with China. Singaporean leaders have taken great pains to nurture their relationships with both countries, paying frequent visits to both Beijing and Washington.

Bilahari Kausikan, an influential Singaporean diplomat, acknowledged the difficulty in keeping the Chinese and Americans simultaneously happy, noting that both were sometimes displeased with Singapore for pursuing its own interests. He declared, "Singapore does not exist to give joy to American or Chinese hearts. So long as neither side is so unhappy that it dismisses us as unredeemable, we can live with their unhappiness and manage it." Managing the unhappiness of China and the United States has gotten harder as the two superpowers have grown less happy with each other.

China is Vietnam's largest trading partner, one of its biggest investors, and its second-largest export market, after the United States. Caught between its economic dependence on China and a fear of close entanglement with either superpower, Vietnam has tried to formulate a policy of independence and at least military self-reliance. This policy is encapsulated in its defense doctrine of "four nos": no taking sides between China and the United States, no military alliances, no foreign military bases within its borders, and no use or threats of force against any other country. Articulating such a doctrine publicly offers a degree of protection from superpower pressure. It remains to be seen whether Vietnam's neutrality can be sustained when the chips are down.

Despite their close economic ties, China and the Philippines have had a rocky relationship, with territorial disputes over the Spratly Islands, an archipelago in the South China Sea, often flaring into maritime confrontations. Chinese military vessels have clashed with Philippine fishing and military vessels near disputed shoals in the region. The US-Philippines Mutual Defense Treaty, signed in 1951, in principle gives the Philippines some protection against Chinese military aggression; yet the Philippines cannot afford to antagonize China for fear of facing significant economic consequences, such as loss of access to Chinese markets for its exports and reduced Chinese investment. Furthermore, with Trump in the White House, the Philippines can scarcely count on the United States to honor its treaty obligations and offer military support when needed.

Much of Asia will thus remain caught in the crosscurrents, striving to avoid being smashed on the rocks rather than serving as agents of harmony.

With respect to legacy wealth, both economic and cultural, Europe remains a heavyweight. Many of the great historical empires were based on the continent, with some extending their dominions to far-flung parts of the world. The Industrial Revolution was born in Europe and helped establish many of the global centers of power. And although the world wars set off a gradual decline in Europe's prominence, the creation of the EU in 1993 and the grand project of European monetary unification, culminating in the introduction of the euro in 1999, were intended to restore Europe to its former glory. That did not happen. In fact, the continent has faced mounting pressure from the premature creation of a monetary union that was not backed up by a more comprehensive economic and banking union.

This circumstance continues to define the state of the European unification project, which remains riven by crosscurrents and a failure to coalesce fully around a grand vision. Becoming mired midway on the path to full integration has actually created even greater risk. Centrifugal political forces have been pulling the region apart, and despite European leaders consistently reaffirming their commitment to greater unification, the realities on the ground have been less inspiring. Brexit severed the close links between the United Kingdom and continental Europe, while the eurozone faces ongoing economic and political tensions.

In a speech delivered at the Sorbonne in April 2024, French President Emmanuel Macron was blunt in his assessment of Europe's future: "We must be clear about the fact that today, our Europe is mortal. It can die. It can die, and it all depends on our choices. These choices have to be made now." He argued that

Europe was at risk of becoming a "vassal" of the United States (clearly a recurring source of dread for French leaders, as we saw in Chapter 2) unless it pursued partnerships with all global regions. Macron contended that this approach was essential if Europe aimed to serve as a stabilizing force and as a "power of balance that speaks to the rest of the world, rejecting the bipolar confrontation that too many continents are settling into. Having an Arctic strategy, an Indo-Pacific strategy, a Latin America strategy and a strategy with the African continent means showing that Europe is not just a piece of the West, but a continent-world that thinks about its universality and the planet's great balances, that rejects confrontation between regions and wishes to build balanced partnerships."

The reality has diverged from those lofty aspirations. With Europe at battle with its inner demons, the continent has hardly been an economic or geopolitical powerhouse. Europe's ability to play an equilibrating role in the world has also been constrained by the surge of nationalism within its own ranks, as many countries on the continent struggle to contain populist movements. Macron himself dissolved the French Parliament in June 2024 in response to his party's loss to the far-right National Rally party in the EU's parliamentary elections. His gamble of calling early elections ended in a temporarily deadlocked national government. Yet again it was India's Jaishankar who best summed up the situation Europe finds itself in: "Europe has to grow out of the mindset that Europe's problems are the world's problems but the world's problems are not Europe's problems."

Africa, the second-most populous continent after Asia, is home to several countries with enormous yet unrealized potential. Rich in natural and human resources, Africa boasts a favorable demographic structure, with higher fertility rates and a smaller share of the population beyond working age compared to most other regions. This trend is likely to continue in many countries, including Ethiopia, Nigeria, and Tanzania, in sharp contrast to the declining working-age populations seen elsewhere in the world, as noted in Chapter 1. The challenge for Africa has always been how to transform its vast resources into output that improves the well-being of its peoples.

Many African countries have been wracked by brutal sectarian conflicts, political instability, and rampant corruption. Consequently, the continent as a whole has proven incapable of punching at its weight because its leaders have so far been unable to speak with one voice or tackle deep-rooted institutional problems.

These problems are familiar to African leaders, and some countries in the region do attempt to play significant roles on the world stage. South Africa is part of the emerging-market group known as BRICS, but its inclusion initially stemmed from the convenience of completing the initialism for an investment bank's marketing campaign. Arguably Nigeria, the continent's largest economy in 2008, had a stronger claim to BRICS membership when the group held its first summit in June 2009. Then again, "BRINC" was not an ideal moniker for a group around which to build a marketing campaign or that aspired to greatness on the global stage. Luckily, with Nigeria's economy faltering and its currency (the naira) plunging in value in recent years, South Africa's status as the continent's representative in BRICS has become justifiable, as its economy overtook Nigeria's by 2024.

The African Continental Free Trade Area, which came into force in 2019 and covers all fifty-five countries on the continent, could prove an important step toward unifying Africa, enabling it to speak with one voice and increase its clout in global affairs. At their summit in New Delhi in September 2023, G20 leaders agreed to include the African Union as a member, giving it a more prominent platform. Still, the harsh reality is that the major powers see much of the continent as of little economic or strategic importance. Even South Africa, with a population of sixty-four million, has an annual GDP lower than that of Denmark, with a population of six million. A few other African countries draw attention only because they are endowed with mineral deposits, but this advantage, as noted earlier, has mostly just fomented internal instability. Many of the large African countries—including Algeria, Egypt, Ghana, Kenya, and Morocco—are beset by economic woes, in some cases made worse by external debt burdens, and political instability. Thus, even if Africa expands its presence on the international stage, economic and political insecurities make it hard to view the continent as a stabilizing force.

This is unfortunate, because any instability in geopolitics and global finance causes the greatest relative harm to Africa's already vulnerable populations. For example, with the major global powers unable to agree on measures to forcefully tackle greenhouse gas emissions, many African countries whose economies depend heavily on agriculture are already suffering from the environmental volatility associated with human-induced climate change. This undermines food security and worsens the threat of conflict over dwindling resources, in turn fueling displacement and outward migration.

Latin America also harbors numerous countries with great but unfulfilled economic promise. Like Africa, it has been wracked by corruption and political instability. Many Latin American countries have in recent years strengthened their ties with China, whose industrial machine has shown a voracious appetite for commodities and other imports from countries like Brazil and Chile.

The region's relationship with the United States has always been complicated, with US interference in its politics often stoking resentment. Even though the dollar is the de facto national currency in many Latin American countries and American financing has been important for the region, frustration with US policies and with the dollar boils over periodically. Brazilian President Luiz Inácio Lula da Silva, whose annoyance with the dollar was noted in Chapter 2, has floated various ideas to bypass the dollar, including the creation of a BRICS currency and a regional currency called the "sur." In 2023, he tried to revive the Union of South American Nations, which was formed in 2011 but faded into obscurity as right-wing leaders such as Brazil's Jair Bolsonaro (president from 2019 to 2023) wanted to have nothing to do with left-wing leaders in the region. Lula also called out the American economic embargo on Cuba, characterizing it as illegal.

By contrast, Argentine President Javier Milei has been unabashed in his admiration for the United States. In a speech in April 2024 emphasizing the dangers of communist ideas, he invoked commonalities in the histories of the two nations: "We both belong to the Western tradition with a culture, a political history and a way of living in society that is largely shared. A tradition that has at its base the ideas of freedom, the defence of life and private property, which were the banner of the founding fathers of both nations when they drew up their first constitutions.... The best way to defend our sovereignty is to strengthen our strategic alliance with the United States and with all countries that embrace the causes of freedom."

This rhetoric marked a pronounced shift in Argentina's official posture. Before Milei's election victory in November 2023, China had not only provided substantial loans and other types of funding but also set up a financial lifeline for Argentina in the form of a currency swap arrangement between the two countries' central banks, to the tune of about $18 billion. This arrangement gave the Argentine central bank access to RMB funds at short notice. With the economy foundering and the Argentinian peso collapsing in the run-up to the 2023 elections, then-President Alberto Fernández received permission from Beijing to use about a third of its swap line, partly to pay off a loan from the IMF. The Chinese government welcomed the arrangement, pleased that it would draw Argentina closer to China while also raising the RMB's profile through a major international transaction.

Milei, however, had other plans. He had no desire to rely on China's assistance and made this clear to the country's special envoy, who attended his inauguration as a representative of Chinese President Xi Jinping. The envoy apparently communicated that China expected Argentina's support on diplomatic matters in exchange for the release of any funds. Milei instead secured funding from the Development Bank of Latin America and the Caribbean to cover the loan payment to the IMF. This affront, coupled with Milei's talk of replacing the Argentinian peso with the dollar, was too much for Beijing to bear. In a fit of petulance, China temporarily froze the currency swap arrangement.

Brazil's and Argentina's differing attitudes toward the United States and China, along with their (and other Latin American countries') shifting approaches over time—shaped by domestic political shifts—are emblematic of the region's inability to play a collective stabilizing role. Moreover, faced with their own domestic economic and political instability, Latin American countries' relationships with the rest of the world are likely to remain transactional and reactive rather than driven by a consistent region-wide strategy.

All these modes of survival in a byzantine geopolitical environment are playing out against the background of new and shifting alliances. Forming alliances offers the potential to amplify the limited impact that individual middle powers have in promoting stability. In some cases, these alliances help countries build closer ties with major powers, without exposing them to pressures they might find difficult to resist on their own. Ideally, coalitions of countries foster collective purpose and harmony, maintaining a balanced competition between groups. However, the internal dynamics within these alliances are often as intricate as the relationships between them, sometimes sowing discord rather than unity.

Atrophying Alliances

Global alliances have proliferated since World War II, as even great powers recognize the advantages of collaborating with like-minded countries to pursue common goals—or at least thwart the ambitions of other powers. Some of these alliances have begun to fray at the edges, while others struggle to manage a range of objectives that lack coherence.

Certain alliances have clearly defined memberships and structures that enable cooperation. Others, including assemblages like the Global South, are less well defined and, perhaps due to intellectual languor, reflect the use of cardinal directions to distinguish between rich and poor countries. The North-South divide lacks both clear boundaries and organizational structure—a fact that has hardly restrained the widespread use of these terms.

The G7 was once a dominant force made up of the world's major economic powers. It stood in counterpoint to the Soviet bloc, which was economically far less powerful but had military might to match. Despite the substantial decline in the G7's collective economic prowess in this millennium, its cohesion, and therefore its influence, has persisted thanks to its members' shared economic and political values. Populist governments with more openly nationalistic orientations have infected even these countries, with Italy under Giorgia Meloni, the United Kingdom under Boris Johnson, and the United States under Donald Trump standing out as the most egregious examples. Nevertheless, the group remains bound together by its members' shared core values, which remain distinct from China's, as well as their historical associations.

As the G7 grew less representative of global economic power, it became untenable to exclude emerging-market countries from a body meant to provide global leadership, despite those countries' less advanced development and divergent political structures. This led to the creation of the G20 in 1999, as noted earlier, bringing together major advanced and emerging-market economies. The global financial crisis of 2007–2009 breathed life into the G20, as it became clear that any hope of saving a crumbling world economy would rest on the joint efforts of both advanced and emerging economies. The G20 passed this difficult test but began to fray under the even harsher test of noncrisis periods, when parochial interests resurfaced.

It is difficult to envision the G20 uniting to make progress on any major issue facing the world today. Even where there is ostensibly some agreement, such as the need to address climate change, broad and vague statements are touted as progress in the absence of serious commitments, let alone true action. Countries like Saudi Arabia that are firmly opposed in practice to a broadly shared climate agenda, despite paying elaborate lip service to it, have been effective at blocking consensus. Moreover, countries committed to tackling the problem have different ideas about how to do so and varying degrees of resolve. In recent G20 meetings, even issuing a joint communiqué—typically a set of exalted aspirations rather than concrete commitments—has proven too much. Although India managed to persuade the group to agree on a joint statement pertaining to Russia's invasion of Ukraine, the sheen of unity faded quickly. And now, with Trump back in power, chances of the G20 presenting a united front on any issue have receded further.

Even the G7, a more homogeneous group than the G20, is not quite the unbreakable alliance it once seemed. Rifts broke out at the June 2018 G7 summit held in Canada. Trump, then in his first term, had already upset the other six countries with various trade restrictions. In the lead-up to the summit, Trump affected a hostile attitude toward other members, chiding them for disinviting Russia from the group's deliberations (a move made in 2014 following Russia's annexation of Crimea) and arguing that Russia needed to be at the table for the deliberations to be meaningful. French Finance Minister Bruno Le Maire was blunt in his view of the United States' isolation on this and other issues, stating, "What this G7 is going to show is that the United States are alone against everyone and especially alone against their allies." He added pointedly, "We will be divided—it will not be a G7, it will be a G6 plus one."

The summit went as well as could be expected in light of these tensions, but the leaders were still converging on a joint communiqué to be issued at the end of the summit. Trump left early as the discussions turned to topics he cared little about—climate change, oceans, and clean energy—and headed to Asia for a meeting with North Korean leader Kim Jong Un. While on the plane, he was informed that, at a press conference, Canadian Prime Minister Justin Trudeau had referred to US tariffs on Canada, imposed on national security grounds, as "insulting." Trudeau said Canada was considering retaliatory tariffs on the United States, adding, "Canadians are polite and reasonable but we will also not be pushed around." Upon hearing this, Trump blew up. He instructed his aides to withdraw US endorsement of the communiqué and proceeded to excoriate Trudeau as "very dishonest and weak." Trump's trade advisor Peter Navarro was even less diplomatic, declaring, "There's a special place in hell for any foreign leader that engages in bad-faith diplomacy with President Donald J. Trump and then tries to stab him in the back on the way out the door. And that's what bad-faith Justin Trudeau did with that stunt press conference."

The Biden administration put the G7 back together, though it is hard to imagine that the other members have the same confidence in the group's durability that they once had, especially with Trump now back in office. Meanwhile, the G20 has persevered, with each country that assumes the presidency (which rotates annually) doing its best to unite all members around common interests and cooperation on matters of global importance. While it is possible the G20 will rise to the occasion when the next global economic or financial crisis strikes, it is just as likely that the group could slide into irrelevance or, even worse, an acrimonious splintering. This would be a distressing outcome, because the G20 remains the one body large enough to encompass all the major advanced and emerging-market economies, yet small enough to allow for reasonably rapid coordination of policies, even if full cooperation remains difficult.

The benefits of free and open trade have been the motivating force behind pacts that eventually underpin deeper alliances. Regional trade agreements, which permit cross-border trade with few restrictions among participants, are pervasive around the globe. Among the newest, the African Continental Free Trade Area, mentioned earlier, is also the largest when measured by the number of member countries. Regional agreements tend to be easier to set up, as countries situated in close geographical proximity and with similar attributes naturally have more incentives to enter into trade pacts. Still, establishing trade agreements has proved challenging in regions where countries have dissimilar political systems and varying stages of development.

Trade accords are sometimes seen as the leading edge of broader integration across various dimensions, from economic to social. The African Union articulated the goals of the Continental Free Trade Area as "creating a single African market for goods and services facilitated by free movement [of] persons, capital, [and] investment to deepen economic integration, [and to] promote and attain sustainable and inclusive socio-economic development, gender equality, industrialization, agricultural development, food security, and structural transformation." The EU states that its member countries "believe that by working together they are stronger and better able to tackle today's big challenges, such as climate change and the digital transformation of our society, major health and security threats like the COVID-19 pandemic, and Russia's war of aggression against Ukraine." These objectives, while noble, are so broad that they can strain trade agreements, particularly when they collide with domestic political dynamics.

As discussed in Chapter 3, trade agreements have increasingly been viewed as a means to promote additional aims, such as encouraging other countries to adopt the environmental, labor, and other standards established by one or more countries in the group. Such agreements can also acquire a geopolitical dimension. When the Obama administration announced the formation of the TPP in 2009, China was not invited—and there was no mistaking the symbolism of the inclusion of a number of China's Asian neighbors. The TPP was seen as a tool that Japan and the United States could use to create at least a modest counterweight to rising Chinese influence throughout Asia. Furthermore, the United States insisted on including in the treaty a range of labor and environmental standards, as well as policies to limit government intervention in foreign exchange markets. The smaller countries in the group acquiesced in the interest of gaining better access to US markets for their exports. By including some of China's key trading partners in the agreement, the United States aimed to subtly influence the standards to which China would be held by those partners.

The TPP was signed by all twelve countries' governments in February 2016, but the agreement still needed to be ratified by their national legislatures. Eleven countries did so well before the two-year deadline, avoiding the risk of the agreement being annulled for lack of full ratification. The exception was the United States—the TPP's main architect. The Obama administration, which had artfully negotiated the deal, was unable to secure its ratification by the US Congress and left the decision to the next administration. Both candidates in the November 2016 US presidential election—Hillary Clinton and Donald Trump—expressed reservations about the TPP, which was facing a great deal of domestic pushback.

In January 2017, within days of taking office, Trump pulled the United States out of the TPP. In one stroke, he had ceded economic and geopolitical influence to China, whose government probably could not believe its luck. The move also destroyed the other TPP members' trust in the United States, as leaders in those countries had expended political capital to overcome opposition to ratification in their own countries.

Trump did not stop there. He simultaneously unleashed a wave of vitriol against the North American Free Trade Agreement (NAFTA) with Canada and Mexico, calling it "one of the worst deals anybody in history has ever entered into," and threatened to pull the United States out of NATO if other members did not increase military spending. He had, in effect, put the world on notice that all of America's traditional economic and security alliances were open to reassessment, renegotiation, and possibly even reversal. As with the context of US isolation within the G7, this is likely to influence the attitudes of even long-standing US allies, who may now reconsider the sturdiness of their relationships with the United States.

For all his bluster, the businessman in Trump recognized the necessity of maintaining smooth trade in the highly integrated North American economy. In October 2018, the United States-Mexico-Canada Agreement (USMCA) replaced NAFTA, accomplishing Trump's goal of putting America first, even if only in name rather than in the country's long-term interests. USMCA is not an initialism that rolls off the tongue, but it does carry one virtue: It will be harder for a future American president to refer to it derisively and mockingly as Trump did with NAFTA, perhaps rendering it more durable!

Although Trump's administration celebrated the revamping of NAFTA as a victory, his actions further eroded trust among US allies, who could see that even two of America's closest trading partners were not immune to the unpredictability of American domestic political dynamics. This concern was only reinforced by Trump's threats, early in his second term, to impose sizable tariffs on imports from Canada and Mexico on the pretext that the two countries were not doing enough to control the flows of illicit drugs and illegal immigrants to the United States.

China, meanwhile, took full advantage of the void left by the United States' disengagement from Asia under the first Trump administration. In November 2020, the ten members of the Association of Southeast Asian Countries joined China and four other countries to set up the Regional Comprehensive Economic Partnership (RCEP). The United States and India opted out, which in effect meant that, despite Japan's presence, the group would be dominated by China.

The RCEP is a clear marker of rising Chinese influence and the corresponding decline of US influence in the Asia-Pacific region. The trade pact more closely ties the economic fortunes of the signatory countries to China's and will over time draw them deeper into China's economic and geopolitical orbit. Additionally, Trump's pullout from the TPP gives the United States less leverage to pressure China into modifying its trading and economic practices in line with US labor and environmental standards, intellectual property rights protections, and other issues related to free trade. Abrogating the TPP, which was at its heart an American project, and standing aside while the RCEP filled the void is one of the most significant "own goals" by the United States under Trump, with ramifications that reverberate beyond trade.

To counter China's rising influence in Asia through the RCEP, the Biden administration attempted to re-create an agreement from the ashes of the TPP. In 2022, the United States launched the Indo-Pacific Economic Framework (IPEF), even adding countries like India and South Korea that had not been part of the TPP. The framework had four pillars, the most prominent of which was trade. Unlike the TPP, the IPEF did not need congressional approval as it was not meant to be a trade agreement that would lower tariff barriers among its members but merely a commitment to abide by consistent trade practices and standards. By the end of 2023, under strong pressure from Democratic Party politicians fretting about possible job losses in their states due to any expansion in imports resulting from the IPEF, the United States had in effect toppled the trade pillar. Yet again, the United States led its partners to the mountaintop and then stranded them there.

How alliances come into being, as well as their approach to membership, has implications for their durability. Membership in any alliance is usually seen as a privilege that confers benefits while also entailing responsibilities. Sometimes the symbolism of who is in or out of a particular alliance is as important as the substance of the benefits it offers or the objectives it seeks to advance. The stability of an alliance, and the touchier question of whose interests it actually represents, has implications for its ability to effectively advocate for common interests and contribute to broader stability.

Some alliances are meant to be exclusive, with participation restricted to those invited by existing members, while others aim to be inclusionary and open to all those who wish to enter. China has implicitly shifted toward an inclusive approach, recognizing that it confers advantages over the US approach, which limits the reach of its alliances and makes membership in organizations under its control highly selective. China has embraced countries across the regions encompassed by its Belt and Road Initiative, has opened membership in the Asian Infrastructure Investment Bank to all interested countries, and has been eager to add members to both the BRICS group and the BRICS-led New Development Bank. The key consideration in all these cases, of course, is that China holds the levers of power, regardless of the ostensible governance structure or how widely voting power is in principle distributed. While China has indicated its aim to lead by consensus rather than by diktat, it is hard to envision any member of these initiatives and institutions effectively challenging China.

Western-led alliances, in contrast, have typically adopted an exclusionary approach, with membership seen as a privilege to be earned through good behavior or at least good intentions. This has generated resentment over the implicit judgments passed by existing members on the economic and political structures of prospective members.

Even within some of these groups, the sands are shifting. China has not shied away from using the lure of membership in the BRICS as a tool to strengthen its claim to being the leader of the so-called Global South. This ambition is cloaked in the guise of strengthening the group's voice in global affairs. But the subtext is clear: China benefits in two ways. Bringing more countries, especially US rivals, into the fold strengthens the group's standing as an alternative to the US- and Europe-dominated West. By choosing which countries are let in and reaping their loyalty in return, China strengthens its de facto leadership and weakens the other original members, including India.

In August 2023, the BRICS held a summit in Johannesburg. Russian President Vladimir Putin did not attend the event in person, as there was an International Criminal Court (ICC) warrant out for his arrest on charges of war crimes related to Russia's invasion of Ukraine. As a signatory to the Rome Statute that established the ICC, the South African government was in principle obliged to arrest Putin when he touched down on the country's soil. South African President Cyril Ramaphosa had made it clear that there would be no such arrest on his watch. Still, to prevent any awkwardness, or perhaps reflecting concern that the South African government might, in an untimely manner, decide to take its international obligations seriously, Putin stayed away, participating through a video link and sending his foreign minister to stand in for him at the obligatory photo ops. The leaders of all the other nations in the group were present.

There had been rumblings prior to the summit that China would ram a set of new members down the throats of the existing BRICS countries. India and South Africa had indicated their displeasure with this idea, especially as the proposed list reportedly included countries like Iran and Venezuela. For India, the notion of being part of a group that included such international pariahs was unappealing. Rather than rushing the expansion, the Indian government pushed hard for the BRICS to establish criteria for membership and to announce those criteria at the end of the summit, leaving any actual invitations for a later date.

China would have none of this. It insisted on extending formal invitations to several new members at the conclusion of the summit. Under extreme Chinese pressure, the other members folded, though they did eliminate some of the more unsavory prospects from the list. The leaders announced the expansion of their group, effective in 2024, to include Argentina, Egypt, Ethiopia, Iran, Saudi Arabia, and the United Arab Emirates (UAE). Other than the two major oil-producing nations, the final set of invitees was a motley group, united perhaps only in their distaste for the United States. (The summit took place before Milei became president of Argentina.) One senior South African official, in a private conversation, later described it to me as "an unprincipled expansion," explaining that no logical principle could justify this particular set of candidates for the first round of BRICS expansion. Then again, maybe the choices hinted at a higher purpose: laying the groundwork for one day changing the group's name to BRICS IESUS, a nod to the Latin transliteration of the Greek name for "Jesus," thus bringing it closer to the Lord.

For India, the inclusion of Saudi Arabia and the UAE, two countries it regards as friends, made the bitter pill easier to swallow. Prime Minister Modi tried to put a positive spin on a diplomatic defeat, arguing that India had been equally keen on the expansion, and that he was "happy that our teams have together agreed on guiding principles, standards, criteria, procedures for expansion of BRICS." He added that such an expansion, bringing in new member states as "partners," would enable the group to better reflect changing times and the evolving world order. In reality, though, this was a clear win for China. The episode illustrates how alliances that ostensibly represent the interests of a broad group of emerging-market countries can be dominated by one country and serve its interests. It also demonstrates how even larger middle powers often find themselves and their priorities sidelined when they get caught up in great-power competition.

Alliances can make mistakes, sometimes adding countries to their rosters whose values do not quite align with those of existing members. Such actions are usually driven by the belief that the new members will come to see the benefits of membership and will bring their economic, political, and social systems in line with those of current members. However, expanding a group's membership, even with the noblest of intentions, can sometimes backfire, especially if it is difficult to reverse.

In 1952, Türkiye was invited to join NATO, an important step for a country seen as democratic and opening up to liberal values. That was indeed the case for many decades, although progress was uneven. The election of Recep Teyyip Erdogan as president in 2014, which resulted in Türkiye's turn toward an increasingly authoritarian, illiberal, and theocratic state, dispelled that illusion. By then it was too late. Erdogan single-handedly blocked the accession of Finland and Sweden to NATO and made it clear that he would extract a hefty price for allowing either country to enter the alliance. Moreover, he blatantly flouted sanctions imposed on Russia for its 2022 invasion of Ukraine.

The NATO charter lacks a provision for suspending, let alone ejecting, member states, leaving much of the bargaining power in Erdogan's hands. He finally relented on Finland's and Sweden's NATO accession only after the two countries had committed to combating Kurdish groups that Türkiye had designated as terrorist organizations and agreed to extradite a few Turkish citizens whose return Erdogan had sought. The deal had to be sweetened by a US sale of F-16 fighter jets to Türkiye.

In 2004, the EU brought two former Soviet-bloc countries, Hungary and Poland, into its fold. The application and vetting process was arduous and protracted. With both countries seen as throwing off the shackles of their communist pasts and moving rapidly toward becoming market-oriented liberal democracies, the hope was that EU membership would accelerate their development and support the institutionalization of liberal values. But then the political winds shifted dramatically in both countries. In 2006, the twin Kaczynski brothers took the reins of power in Poland; in 2010 Viktor Orbán did the same in Hungary. Both governments adopted socially conservative policies and did their utmost to quash the independence of their judiciaries and organs of free speech. EU bureaucrats were hardly inclined to acknowledge that including these countries might have been a mistake, or at least a hasty and premature move. In any case, the Union was stuck with these recalcitrant members, as it could not credibly threaten to throw either of them out, a process even more cumbersome than incorporating new members. The EU, which strives to work by consensus, was forced to find a workaround when Orbán, who had expressed solidarity with Putin on certain matters, refused to approve additional financial aid to Ukraine in late 2023.

Perhaps the lesson of such machinations is that although broadening an alliance is an attractive proposition, it is not without danger. In the worst circumstances, expansion could destroy an alliance rather than strengthen it. The above examples illustrate that countries lacking power and influence are either swept along as part of an alliance or, when they do wield influence, it is often in ways that undermine collective interests and fuel disharmony.

Another issue—one that has implications for both their own stability and that of the world—is how such global alliances perceive and are likely to react to flashpoints in world affairs. One ticking time bomb is the existential threat faced by a middle power that finds itself unable to join any alliance.

Taiwan's Travails

It is easy to paint doomsday scenarios for human civilization. After all, there are now nine known nuclear powers in the world, with others, like Iran, waiting in the wings and some, like North Korea and Pakistan, internally unstable and unlikely to gain the world's attention for any reason other than occasional nuclear warhead rattling. Even if nuclear annihilation is not how the world ends, numerous other scenarios could reshape the global order. One in particular illustrates how the great powers might collide with each other and how a middle power caught between them could have little control over its own destiny. Any attempt to change the fragile status quo over Taiwan could easily put the world's two major powers in direct conflict. Such an outcome would likely be driven by domestic politics in China and the United States, with Taiwan having little agency in the matter.

Mao Zedong is revered as the father of the People's Republic of China, even though his legacy was blighted by the Great Leap Forward, which proved disastrous for the economy and resulted in widespread famine, with a death toll estimated in the tens of millions. Deng Xiaoping is celebrated as the architect of modern China for introducing a series of far-reaching free-market-oriented reforms that set the country on the path to becoming a major economic power. Xi Jinping, who in 2022 amended the country's constitution to extend his tenure beyond the previous two-term limit, is seen as an even more powerful leader of modern China than any of his predecessors, including Mao and Deng.

Having consolidated his power, Xi's objective is to leave behind a major legacy that will enshrine him in the history books, at least those written in China. Reunification of the Mainland with Taiwan would surely accomplish this. But how? And when? These questions have been the subject of much intrigue in Beijing and beyond, particularly as there appear to be factions within the Chinese military with competing views on the advisability of taking military action to achieve this outcome and on accelerating the timetable for such an action. Another element that enters into the calculation is whether the ensuing damage to China's economy, the likely result of an outright conflict with Taiwan, would overshadow another aspect of Xi's legacy: elevating China to the status of an upper-middle-income economy.

Economic considerations could also play a role in evaluating the likely timing of an attempted reunification by force. Competing theories abound about whether economic weakness in China is likely to make an invasion more or less likely. The "cornered tiger" theory posits that a weak economy could increase domestic pressure on the Chinese government, which might seek to alleviate it by rallying the population around the flag and initiating an invasion. The more aggressive elements of the military could be emboldened by economic missteps, weakening the dovish factions in the government and precipitating this outcome. An alternative view is that the government would prefer to attack from a position of strength, which would help it manage the disruptions that would inevitably follow an overt attack. In this view, a stronger economy would buffer China from the pain of any financial sanctions that could be imposed by the United States and other Western countries.

There is, of course, more than one way to skin a cat. China could achieve a de facto takeover of Taiwan in far simpler ways. Beijing has already initiated small steps, including incursions into airspace that breach Taiwan's territory, each of which, on its own, would not be substantial enough to warrant retaliation but could over time establish new realities on the ground and in the air. These actions would gradually tighten China's military and economic grip over the island, complemented by efforts to foment domestic dissent in Taiwan regarding the advisability of keeping China at arm's length.

In the calculus over any action China might take in its approach to Taiwan, the passage of time cuts both ways. China could gamble that its economic heft increases with every passing day and its vulnerability to US financial sanctions wanes. Moreover, the costs to the United States of losing access to Taiwan's manufacturing base will decrease over time as it becomes less reliant on Taiwanese suppliers of chips and electronic equipment, which might in turn limit the aggressiveness of the American response to military action taken by China.

The cost to China of waiting is that, with US military help and more time, Taiwan would be better prepared to repel at least the initial waves of an outright attack. There is little doubt that

China's military superiority will allow it to eventually overwhelm Taiwan. Still, the prospect of significant military losses, especially casualties involving people whom leaders in Beijing consider every bit as Chinese as residents of the Mainland, would be unpalatable.

Taiwan arguably has some cards of its own to play. It is a major producer of advanced semiconductor chips, which are essential for smartphones, defense and AI systems, and a vast range of other high-end electronics and computing systems. This makes Taiwan a more attractive takeover target for China but also creates a "silicon shield" that should trigger US protection if it were to face any hostilities. The United States clearly has a direct stake in preserving access to Taiwanese chips to maintain its technological supremacy and prevent its high-tech industries from being kneecapped if that access were cut off by China. But Trump's desire to bring manufacturing back to the United States led him to pressure Taiwanese chip manufacturers to set up production facilities stateside. Thus, although Taiwan is in principle tightening its economic ties to the United States, it finds itself eroding its own protective shield and exposing itself to US political currents.

Even so, under most scenarios a Chinese initiation of direct conflict with Taiwan is likely to draw in the United States as well, a major factor as Beijing weighs its options. American political dynamics are a wild card, of course. Had Vladimir Putin planned his invasion of Ukraine to coincide with Trump's time in the White House, the US reaction would have been very different, given Trump's puzzling on-again, off-again admiration for Putin.

Trump is by no means a staunch proponent of the long-standing one-China policy that the United States has maintained, which supports Taiwan's self-governance while not recognizing it as an independent nation. During the 2024 election campaign, Trump asserted that Taiwan "stole our chip business" and should pay the United States for defending it. He has reportedly questioned the need for a US military presence on the Korean peninsula, adding, "Even more than that, what do we get from protecting Taiwan, say?"

Few things unite Democrats and Republicans as much as hawkish posturing over China, so the likely US reaction cannot easily be inferred from the political affiliation of the White House's occupant alone. If recent experience is anything to go by, even one-party rule, which is the situation in 2026 with the White House and both houses of Congress under Republican control, does not guarantee certainty about the US response. After all, American measures to help counter the Hamas attack on Israel, a close US ally, or the Russian incursion into Ukraine, a country on the doorstep of NATO, fell prey to the isolationist and anarchic wing of the Republican party. If the US political configuration shifts to a divided government, with one party controlling even a single house of Congress and the other in the White House, the response would almost surely be slower and less effective. Without a strong economic imperative, it is far from clear whether a Chinese attack on Taiwan would necessarily lead to direct confrontation with the United States.

For all its wealth and dynamism, Taiwan's destiny is hostage to forces beyond its control. Taiwan has little capacity, through its own policy choices, to promote stability while preserving its autonomy.

The Muddled Middle

Whereas the war between Athens and Sparta had only regional consequences, the power struggle between the United States and China is felt worldwide. Countries are now in the difficult position of deciding whether to pick sides between the two or find alternative approaches to hedge their bets. This is instigating various geopolitical realignments as countries scurry to optimize their economic and security interests while trying to avoid becoming collateral damage as the two superpowers and various regional powers jockey for influence. Some traditional allies are falling out, while odd combinations of bedfellows are coming together.

The hope that countries in the middle, which have a strong interest in stability and de-escalation of tensions between the two major superpowers, will serve as a stabilizing force seems increasingly forlorn. As we have seen in this chapter, larger middle powers like India and Indonesia, as well as economically developed and relatively wealthy ones like Singapore and Taiwan, often find themselves buffeted by forces beyond their control and unable to advance their priorities. Moreover, there is little evidence that they are using their limited influence or shaping their alliances in ways that contribute to stability.

In many middle powers, economic and domestic political factors have converged in a way that has turned these countries into agents of instability rather than promoters of regional or geopolitical stability. Broad coalitions that should be tamping down this instability have been weakened by forces undermining their cohesiveness and unity of purpose. Long-standing alliances like NATO and the EU are fraying as populist pressures intensify the doom loop. New alliances, often opportunistic and lacking common values or shared long-term interests, are likely to prove fragile as well.

Against this turbulent backdrop, we must consider one other factor that has played a transformative role throughout human history: technology. From the invention of paper and the printing press to the creation of railroads and airplanes, technological innovations have radically reshaped global power. Now a wave of new technologies, built on digital platforms, is shifting the playing field in important and unpredictable ways. These advancements provide smaller and less powerful countries with potent tools to expand their capabilities, while also giving powerful countries more ways to propagate their interests. Will these changes foster greater balance and stability? Or will the darker side of technology prevail?

6

New Technologies: Panacea or Peril?

Consider the auk;
Becoming extinct because he forgot how to fly, and could only walk.
Consider man, who may well become extinct
Because he forgot how to walk and learned how to fly before he
thinked.

—Ogden Nash, "A Caution to Everybody"

After a three-and-a-half-year hiatus waiting out the COVID pandemic, I returned to China in July 2023 with much excitement at the prospect of catching up with old friends and getting the pulse of the economy. My first stop was at the "Summer Davos" in Tianjin, a major event put on by the World Economic Forum (WEF). Little did I anticipate that my appearance there would precipitate threats of physical violence and bodily harm.

The WEF's signature annual event, held in the Swiss ski village of Davos, is a magnet for the world's financial and political luminaries, who fly in, many on private jets, to bemoan the state of the world and offer brilliant ideas to set things right. As a rising superpower, China felt it needed its own WEF event, where it could highlight its accomplishments and dictate the tenor of discussions. Klaus Schwab, the founder of the WEF, could hardly turn down the prospect of securing a platform in China and strengthening the organization's credentials as a worldwide convening power.

The Summer Davos conferences, some of which I had participated in during pre-COVID times, had grown into high-profile events, with many top Chinese and foreign officials and businessmen in attendance, and with the Chinese premier usually making a speech. The 2023 conference, the first held in person after a three-year break, was different. The new Chinese premier did give the headline speech, and many senior Chinese government officials did indeed attend. However, with US-Chinese tensions running high, especially in view of China's support for Russia in its war against Ukraine, hardly any officials or businessmen from the United States and Western Europe were in evidence. Russians and Africans were there aplenty.

In addition to speaking at a session devoted to the Chinese economy, I gave a talk about my book *The Future of Money* to a small but packed room. To my satisfaction, the event was also livestreamed, and the video would be made available on the WEF website after the conference. During the question and answer period following my remarks, an audience member asked for my views on central bank digital currencies (CBDCs), digital versions of central bank money. I spoke about how CBDCs offered many advantages over cash, especially in their convenience. I added that it was important to have safeguards in place to prevent CBDCs from being used as instruments of social policy. Otherwise, for instance, a government could program its CBDC to make it difficult to use to purchase illicit drugs, pornography, or perhaps even alcohol, ammunition, contraception, or other reproductive services. The point was that the advent of digital money opened up exciting possibilities but could also facilitate darker outcomes, where a government might use its control over CBDCs to interfere directly in the lives and choices of its citizens.

Some two weeks after returning to the United States, I woke up one morning to a deluge of emails spouting all manner of vitriol and suggesting I go back to India; some even hinted at violence against me and my family. My university phone voicemail filled up with similar messages. I soon got a call from an Associated Press reporter asking about the context of my comments, whether I was paid by or working for the WEF, and whether I had advocated for replacing physical currency with digital dollars and for restricting them from being used to purchase guns and ammunition.

I went online right away, as one naturally does in such circumstances, and soon found edited clips of the video from my session circulating on various right-wing (based on a quick check of their contents) social media accounts. Whoever picked up the video, edited it, and built a narrative around it was clever enough to hit the right buttons (but without adding any outright commentary): Behold this privileged brown man from an elite East Coast university, working for a "globalist" cabal with socialist backing that is plotting to take over the world and, most of all, snatch guns out of the hands of honest, law-abiding citizens who only want to be left alone to pursue their cherished Second Amendment rights to the fullest.

Thus did I experience the power of certain elements of modern technology that I regularly use and champion—social media and digital finance—when they were turned against me. This personal saga, while of no consequence and little interest to anyone other than me and my family, stands as a metaphor for larger issues. Tangential though it might seem to the issues discussed in this book, technology in its various manifestations has the potential to tilt the geopolitical power balance. Whether that is for better or worse remains to be seen.

Technology may be the answer to many of humanity's problems. It may also spell doom for civilization. These propositions are equally tenable and not mutually exclusive. While technology reflects human resourcefulness, it will take considerable resolve on the part of citizens and governments to harness it for humanity's benefit rather than ruin.

Many seemingly intractable problems—food scarcity, endemic poverty, pandemics and other health scourges, to name just a few—are becoming solvable through innovation. The expansion of material resources enabled by new technologies should reduce conflict and foster greater harmony among nations. At the same time, technology that has brought us closer together has also fueled the reemergence of tribalism in its most virulent forms. X (the rebranded version of Twitter, which might have been driven into the ground by the time this book is published) and Facebook are prime examples, making it easier to spew hate and stoke acrimony with a speed and at a scale that amplify their damage to the social fabric. The benefits and perils of these technologies extend beyond national borders, adding another layer to their effects.

Technological forces are influencing global economic and geopolitical realignments in important ways. In principle, these forces could rebalance power by making it easier for low-income countries to compete with richer ones by leveling the playing field in many areas. For instance, the proliferation of digital payment systems and currencies could erode some of the advantages held by established currencies, such as their global availability and recognition. However, trusting technology by itself to deliver these outcomes is backfiring. Instead, technology is leading societies toward darker outcomes, shifting conflicts between countries into other arenas and adding new sources of instability to the world order.

Three sets of technologies—financial technologies (fintech), artificial intelligence (AI), and information technologies (IT)—are transforming the world for better *and* for worse. Fintech gives everyone, rich or poor, easier access to a wide range of financial products and services, helping to democratize finance. Yet the digitalization of money could be perverted, granting governments and corporate conglomerates greater control over both our economic and social lives. Similarly, while AI can strengthen a country's institutional framework by providing a more robust informational foundation, it can equally be weaponized to undermine that foundation. IT, including social media, helps bind communities together even as it drives wedges between them, often stoking nationalistic tendencies.

The negative aspects of these technologies feed off each other in damaging ways. AI and social media form a toxic mix that can spread distorted information that erodes trust in both the information itself and the once-reliable sources that curated it. Cryptocurrency lubricates the financing of illicit activities, further fraying the social fabric. Meanwhile, technology provides autocratic governments with new tools to control their citizens and stir chaos and confusion in other countries. Instead of acting as a neutral force, technology is becoming an instrument of power, shaping and driving geopolitical realignments.

It is striking that the development and adoption of some new technologies are occurring at exponential rather than linear rates, amplifying their influence. However, this also means that technologies like AI can race ahead of regulations and the creation of guardrails, leaving them vulnerable to negative consequences and potential misuse as instruments of malevolence.

The Digital Revolution in Finance

Finance is the lifeblood of modern economies, enabling households and businesses to manage savings, credit, and risk. In many parts of the world, access to basic financial products has been limited by underdeveloped financial markets, pervasive poverty, or both. In some countries, the banking system is just not up to the task of serving the entire population, and stock and bond markets are still in their nascent stages. Even when capable of doing so, banks and other financial institutions are typically loath to serve low-income clients, as the cost of providing services on a small scale typically outweighs potential profits. Informal finance—from moneylenders to family support to community-level pooling of resources—can help but is no substitute for an effective, well-functioning financial system.

The lack of financial inclusion—broad and easy access to financial products and services—has major consequences that go beyond financial outcomes. It leaves households that exist on the margins of society highly vulnerable and often reluctant to support beneficial economic reforms. These households, which often make up much of the population in low-income economies, feel disconnected from any potential gains and are more affected by the inevitable short-term dislocations such reforms cause. For those living hand to mouth and unable to access credit in hard times, the distant promise of better prospects is often no match for the immediate but fleeting benefits offered by populists, such as cash handouts.

Technology has been a boon to efforts to broaden financial inclusion at a rapid pace. Simple mobile phones have become portals for conducting banking transactions, not just enabling digital payments but also connecting households of all income levels to the financial system. In middle-income countries like China, Brazil, and India, as well as poorer ones like Somalia and Tanzania, digital payments are becoming the norm, displacing physical currency. This shift is a godsend to consumers and businesses, including small mom-and-pop shops and street vendors, allowing them to avoid the risks associated with handling cash, including damage, loss, and theft. The ramifications go beyond the convenience and efficiency of payments.

Take India, which, though it started later than China, has now made impressive progress in digitalizing its economy. The government set up and now manages a national payments infrastructure, the Unified Payments Interface, which processes payments and transfers money between people, businesses, and government agencies. Actual payment services are still provided by banks and other service providers, but the common infrastructure makes the process cheap, swift, and seamless. The government complemented this initiative with a massive project that gives every citizen access to a digital identity system and bank accounts linked to those identities. This combination, referred to as the India Stack (with identity, payment, and data-management layers), has been transformative.

Digital payments have become widespread, and even low-income households have access to bank accounts for managing savings and credit. The government is switching to electronic cash transfers to indigent households instead of providing food and energy subsidies that were complicated to administer and caused untold hassles for recipients. This marks quite a change from what I experienced during my childhood in a middle-class family in India. I remember, with little fondness, the ration cards that secured my family a monthly allotment of rice and sugar at subsidized prices. Procuring and updating the ration cards inevitably involved bribing the relevant public officials. Shopkeepers at government-authorized outlets dispensing the rations would invariably try to tilt the scales (literally) to stiff consumers by giving them smaller portions. The digitalization of the economy has alleviated such petty corruption, smoothed many frictions that made doing business difficult, and given India's citizens a sense of being vested in the country's economic success.

Digitalization will not by itself root out corruption or satisfy economic aspirations, but it gives people of all economic classes a potent tool and a fighting chance to improve their lives. And in one important way—by providing cheap, widespread, and efficient access to digital payments—it has enabled emerging-market countries to leapfrog more advanced ones. We in the United States still extensively use cash, checks, and credit cards, making payments a much slower and (for businesses) more expensive proposition than in China or India.

Digital payments are not particularly complicated technologically, yet they have been transformative in scope. It would take a different kind of technological leap to bear the promise of more fundamental change in the way financial transactions are conducted and in how the relationship between the state and its citizens is structured.

The advent of the first cryptocurrency, Bitcoin, in 2008 was a huge step forward for the libertarian dream of escaping the clutches of governments, central banks, and the big bad private banks, credit card companies, and other institutions of centralized finance. The promise of the blockchain technology bequeathed to the world by the (still anonymous) creator of Bitcoin was that cryptocurrency would enable payments to be made without relying on traditional third-party intermediaries, which had come to be seen as increasingly untrustworthy. Instead, trust would be based on computer algorithms that harness the power of transparency and the community to ensure the system's security.

Blockchains are electronic ledgers that contain transparent, secure, and immutable records of all transactions conducted through digital wallets whose balances are maintained on those ledgers. Transactions recorded on a blockchain are validated through a process of consensus among the computer nodes that are active participants on a particular chain. This is all done without having to rely on paper currency, bank deposits, credit cards, or payment companies such as PayPal or Venmo. And yet cryptocurrency transactions are secure, can be executed without setting up an account at a financial institution, and can be conducted while preserving anonymity (which, unfortunately, leads to their use for illicit activities). Sounds like magic, and having written a book about digital currencies (*The Future of Money*, mentioned earlier), I can tell you that the technology is mind-bogglingly creative and innovative.

Blockchains could conceivably be used not just for commercial transactions but also to improve the accessibility and security of official records and to reduce public corruption. In India, for instance, land records were once maintained in dusty physical ledgers, rendering it difficult to track them down, and exposing them to fraud and manipulation. Maintaining such records on a blockchain has helped create a secure and transparent record of land ownership that is easy to access and verify. Similarly, storing government procurement data on blockchains not only streamlines contracting and payment processes but also, through increased transparency surrounding contract details—amounts, contractors, performance metrics—can reduce avenues for corruption.

Blockchain architecture has even spawned decentralized autonomous organizations (DAOs), where the rules are created and enforced by an online community through open-source computer code, with no appointed leaders or managers. This is a highly democratic and nonhierarchical organizational structure, with no central governing body and with members acting in the best interest of the entity. People power at its finest.

DAOs are proliferating in blockchain-based decentralized finance, with some cryptocurrency exchanges such as Uniswap now structured as DAOs. DAOs are not limited to finance. The Constitution DAO was set up in 2021 as a crowdfunding project to purchase an original copy of the US constitution that was to be auctioned off by Sotheby's. The plan, agreed upon by the members of the DAO through a vote, was to give the copy to the Smithsonian Institution and have it available for public display. The DAO raised over $40 million but was outbid by Ken Griffin, a hedge fund billionaire, perhaps showing that traditional finance still has some fight left in it—or perhaps that money still beats people power.

Even if it doesn't replace traditional institutions, blockchain technology has opened up the prospect of the democratization of finance, for both the providers of financial services and those who use the services. The barriers to entry in providing financial services, especially beyond digital payments to products designed for managing savings and credit, are enormous. The cost of setting up brick-and-mortar operations and putting in place teams of accountants and lawyers to satisfy the needs of regulators can be prohibitive. This confers huge advantages of incumbency on existing institutions, particularly large ones, and reduces competition. Meanwhile, as already noted, banks have no incentive to sign up low-income or low-net-worth customers, who find it difficult to gain access to even minimal financial services.

Decentralized finance can help obviate these constraints by making it easier for innovative firms to offer even bespoke financial products to a broad clientele at low cost. Once a digital operation is set up, the cost of servicing an additional customer is trivial, making it far easier to scale up such operations. Other key attributes of decentralized finance built on blockchains include full transparency of transaction records, permission-free access, and censorship-resistant content. In other words, inasmuch as no institution manages the system and it operates beyond the reach of governments and regulators, anyone can participate, without needing permission or facing any official restrictions. This makes it particularly attractive for eluding the tentacles of authoritarian regimes, which seek to control access to finance in addition to other aspects of their citizens' lives.

In principle, decentralization helps level parts of the playing field between the rich and the poor within any society, in addition to providing a tool to undermine authoritarian regimes. After all, regimes that restrict their citizens' freedoms are the most vulnerable to technological disruptions that bypass their control.

After a long period in which fiat currencies issued by national central banks faced little competition, the digitalization of finance has enabled privately issued currencies to nibble at this dominance. Cryptocurrencies such as Bitcoin, though, are proving too volatile in value to serve as a reliable means of payment. It's hard to depend on a currency when one day it buys you a large cappuccino and a flaky croissant but the next only a small cup of coffee. To fill this gap, other cryptocurrencies have sprung up that use the new technology but maintain stable value. Ironically, these "stablecoins" derive their stability from being backed one-to-one by reserves of fiat currencies, which is entirely at odds with the libertarian ideal of forgoing central bank money altogether.

Stablecoins are competing with official currencies, even if only as mediums of exchange rather than independent stores of value. Still, any competition is good; in principle, it forces the issuers of a currency, whether private or official, to be disciplined with their policies for fear of undermining the currency's utility or value.

This competition is spurring central banks to issue their own digital currencies—CBDCs. With cash on its way out, central banks are eager to ensure that their money remains relevant for retail transactions. CBDCs are seen as useful in making digital payments widely accessible and promoting financial inclusion, filling in gaps left by the private sector.

China is racing to issue its own CBDC, the eCNY (or digital Chinese yuan). Brazil, India, Japan, and a host of other countries, big and small, are experimenting with CBDCs and could soon begin rolling them out. These developments are giving hope to the forlorn detractors of US dollar supremacy; perhaps the digitalization of other currencies, while the Fed dawdles, will give them a leg up in international finance.

As of early 2023, the Fed had in fact completed some technical groundwork on a digital dollar. But the concept quickly took on a political tone in the United States, with a mere mention setting conspiracy theorists in a tizzy, as we saw at the beginning of this chapter. Mainstream politicians like Florida Governor Ron DeSantis have weighed in, claiming that a digital dollar would be a tool through which "Davos elites . . . [attempt] to backdoor woke ideology like Environmental, Social, and Governance (ESG) into the United States financial system, threatening individual privacy and economic freedom." Fortunately, thanks to legislation put forward by DeSantis to ban the use of CBDCs in his state, at least the good residents of Florida have been inoculated against the ravages of a digital dollar, should it ever come to pass.

In 2023, the Fed launched FedNow, a suite of improvements to retail and wholesale payments that aims to accomplish much of what a digital dollar would. FedNow is hardly setting the pace for the rest of the world. It would simply bring the United States up to speed, enabling instant bank transfers, around-the-clock settlement of electronic payments (rather than just during business hours on weekdays), and other features that have long been standard in many other countries. This is odd for a country that leads the world in so many other areas of technology and suggests that the United States risks falling behind in fintech and in international currency power.

However, the rapid introduction of CBDCs by China and other countries will by itself hardly undermine US financial power or erode the dollar's dominance. While digitalization of a currency offers convenience and efficiency, those benefits cannot make up for a lack of trust in the issuing country's institutional framework. Therefore, a fundamental reordering of the global currency landscape is unlikely to occur solely due to changes in the technology of money.

Shouldn't the digitalization of currencies at least diminish the advantages of size, making a small country's currency as available and usable as that of any large country? In this case, too, changes are coming—but in yet another paradox, they may favor bigger, economically powerful countries, or even megacorporations.

In principle, certain financial technologies level the playing field, enabling poorer and smaller countries to compete more effectively with larger, richer ones. In practice, the worldwide proliferation of digital currencies could inflict the greatest harm on countries that are small and less developed. National currencies issued by their central banks could lose ground to CBDCs issued by the major economies and possibly even to private stablecoins if they were to become widely available. If well-known and deep-pocketed companies like Amazon and Google were to someday issue their own stablecoins, citizens of small, poorly governed countries might prefer those to the currencies issued by their own central banks. Even for larger countries whose central banks lack credibility and whose currencies therefore suffer from volatility and loss of value to inflation, digital technologies threaten to displace their domestic money with foreign alternatives.

The shift toward regulated, centralized cryptocurrencies (stablecoins) as well as official digital currencies could actually increase government oversight of households and businesses. Digital "smart money" that replaces cash could become an instrument of government control, with authoritarian regimes using it for surveillance and even ostensibly benevolent governments conceivably employing it to promote their social objectives, as I warned at my Summer Davos appearance.

Thailand has brought the perils of digital money into sharp focus. To fulfill a promise made during an election campaign and with the hope of giving the country's stagnant economy a boost, in August 2024 the government initiated a program designed to distribute money to low-income households. Fifty million Thais who fell below certain income and savings thresholds saw about $280 each, roughly half the monthly per capita income in Thailand, deposited into their digital wallets. Thailand had not yet rolled out its CBDC nationwide, but the digital wallets operated much like a digital version of the baht, the Thai currency.

Many worthy attributes distinguished the Thai transfer program. It was well targeted, directing funds to poorer individuals who would especially benefit and were likely to spend rather than save the money. The funds went directly to recipients, reducing the corruption often associated with money channeled through public agencies. The funds had to be spent within six months, an excellent way to stimulate consumption while limiting leakage into savings, which would not immediately boost economic activity. Funds could only be spent at authorized small shops within recipients' local areas. Criminals and others with a history of fraud were not eligible, and merchants with spotty tax payment records could not participate. The funds could not be used to purchase alcohol, cigarettes, or marijuana, or for online shopping.

These limitations seem entirely defensible. But they are also deeply disturbing, for they show how easily digital money can be subverted for social-engineering purposes. The Thai government in effect decided that only "worthy" individuals and merchants could benefit from the program, that funds must be spent in specific areas, and that certain products deemed undesirable could not be purchased. It is not hard to envision a future where wider CBDC usage is similarly restricted to "good" citizens and "acceptable" expenditures, as defined by the government.

As digital currencies, both private and official, go mainstream, they threaten to give big corporations and government a better view into our financial lives and greater control over how we spend our money. Thus, in an ultimate irony, the revolution that Bitcoin instigated might end up destroying whatever vestiges of privacy are left in modern financial markets.

What's worse, the cryptocurrency revolution invoked the notion of decentralized trust but has instead undermined institutionalized trust without providing a durable alternative. Blockchain was supposed to lead us to a world of decentralized and democratized finance, but it has so far led to speculative activity and fraud. Much of blockchain-based finance has evolved into financial engineering that enables various forms of speculation, with the democratization of finance remaining a distant promise. It must be acknowledged that, while falling short of its grand ambitions, the cryptocurrency revolution has nevertheless catalyzed important developments in both domestic and international finance, particularly dramatic reductions in costs and processing times for cross-border payments. Whether these developments serve as forces for equalization of economic power and stability remains to be determined.

In short, for all their benefits, the proliferation of digital currencies, both official and private, is hardly an avenue for stability through constructive competition. Rather, these new technologies might further concentrate financial power in the hands of a few countries, exacerbate financial fragmentation, and become tools through which countries try to promote their geopolitical objectives.

Fintech has the most direct impact on the world economic and financial order, but other technologies hold even more radical potential for change, with far-reaching implications for finance and beyond.

Artificial Intelligence

AI is a transformative technology that uses "big data"—immense collections of electronic data (such as numbers, words, images, or other content)—and machine-learning algorithms, supported by massive computing power, to replicate certain mechanistic aspects of human intelligence. AI already pervades our daily lives, from facial recognition to text prediction to autocorrect functions in word processing and email software (not that AI is perfect by any means—to my consternation, my first name is often autocorrected to "Sewer"). Whether AI can mimic the creative aspects of human intelligence—the serendipitous connections and flashes of deep insight that are the hallmarks of nonmechanistic thinking—is an open question. Still, AI can clearly accomplish certain tasks that would ordinarily require human intellect and perform many operations much more quickly than humans.

AI is deemed a general-purpose technology since it can be deployed in a number of areas, from financial analysis to health care to areas once thought secure from algorithmic intervention, such as graphic arts and music composition. It has the potential to make the transfer of knowledge easy and cheap across countries, which could, in principle, allow even poor countries to benefit from advancements in a wide range of fields. However, as with any emerging technology, the practical outcomes remain unclear. The broad commercial implications of AI are intensifying competition between countries, often through restrictions on trade and technology transfers, rather than cooperation in developing and harnessing the technology to humanity's benefit.

As we consider what standards to employ in evaluating AI and its potential impact across domains, we must first examine the specific nature of the technology. Machine-learning algorithms have long been used to identify, characterize, and reproduce patterns in data, a process that underpins a specific type of AI referred to as predictive AI. If predictive AI is viewed as the efficient use of data to answer specific questions, the standards for evaluation are clear: accuracy, speed, and reproducibility of results. In customer service, for instance, the relevance, precision, and latency (response time) of AI-generated answers are important quantifiable benchmarks of performance and dependability. Whether you like it or not, such applications are already mainstream, and you've probably interacted with AI-powered chatbots when seeking help with consumer products, customer service, or banking issues.

Generative AI is the true game changer. Large language models (LLMs) like GPT use machine-learning algorithms trained on vast amounts of data to create new content. ChatGPT (the AI chatbot powered by GPT) does a perfectly adequate job of composing emails, blocks of text, even speeches. I have used it myself to write and refine computer code, which allows me and my research assistants to work more efficiently and avoid errors. These tasks just scratch the surface of generative AI's capabilities as it rapidly approaches the ability to mimic human intelligence— not only generating text and computer code but also creating new products and services, even poetry and digital art.

AI has the potential to improve efficiency and welfare for consumers, businesses, and perhaps governments as well. Examples abound, even in such areas as health care. Finding a new cure or combining chemicals to create a compound with curative or other desirable properties yields well-defined benefits. AI can search for such possibilities more efficiently than humans. In these areas, too, one can envision quantitative standards for evaluating the performance of different AI models.

The standards for evaluating AI output are much murkier in fields long dominated by human creativity. Consider an AI that generates a new piece of art or music, both already in the realm of possibility. These are amazing creations in their own right, yet it is far from clear whether the standards of creativity we apply as a matter of course to humans should also apply to autonomous AI output. For re-creating a particular image, reproducibility is a clear criterion. But when the goal is to create something completely new, that metric is no longer relevant, and the standards become increasingly ambiguous. While we humans ponder these standards and contemplate guardrails to mitigate potential adverse effects, AI is quickly becoming pervasive.

AI has already permeated my classroom and those of my colleagues at Cornell University. It is hard to imagine that some students in my undergraduate finance class are not using it to meet my strict deadlines for written assignments. These are usually due at ten a.m. on Mondays, and I suspect that, for those starting at nine a.m. on the day of the deadline, relying on AI is pretty much the only option. I teach a small class of around twenty-five to thirty students and require each of them to come up with an independent research idea and develop it into a paper through multiple stages. This allows me to monitor and limit their use of AI to some extent. I encourage them to use it to assist with their research and clean up their writing, but not to generate a topic or write the entire paper (though I may be giving myself too much credit for being able to distinguish original work from AI-generated ideas and text). This is a time-intensive process for me and an infeasible one for my colleagues who teach larger classes.

AI's value in generating ideas or approaching issues from a critical perspective is far from obvious. In fact, as a teacher I worry that using it robs my students of the clarity of thought that comes from shaping inchoate ideas into words and organizing those words into a coherent narrative. The grueling (and therefore thoroughly enjoyable!) process of writing this book—the material was reorganized many times, and each chapter was rewritten multiple times, with no help from AI—was essential to sharpening the ideas. The content and structure of the book in its final form look very different from where I started. (You might still not care for the end product, but it could have been a lot worse.) Using AI indiscriminately could affect the very genesis of ideas and intellectual creativity. More fundamentally, it could also erode our ability to exercise critical judgment amid the information overload that has become the reality in our daily lives.

There is ample evidence to suggest that AI will augment productivity; indeed, even by 2024 there were already perceptible signs of a productivity boomlet in the United States, attributable in significant part to AI. Both economists and technologists are divided, though, on whether AI will wipe away entire categories of jobs or boost job creation. The latter positive effect could result from two forces. First, AI could make it easier for workers with limited education and skills to compete for jobs. Basic mastery of internet use is sufficient to deploy some AI tools, which could liberate low-skill workers from the drudgery of repetitive tasks and, in effect, upskill them by freeing up their time for other tasks. The advent of automated teller machines, for instance, did not eliminate bank tellers but freed them up to offer more personalized services (although the popularity of online banking is now causing the number of bank branches and tellers to decline). Second, AI could turbocharge many industries and create entirely new categories of jobs, particularly in high-tech manufacturing. The opposite argument is that AI will displace low-skill workers and those who lack the technical chops to fully harness its potential. Rather than being frustrated by incompetent and unhelpful call-center employees and customer service agents, one is more likely these days to encounter incompetent and unhelpful AI chatbots.

I see both these aspects in my own work life, but the positive ones are more pleasant to talk about (I've had my fill of customer service chatbots). AI allows me, practically instantaneously, to accomplish tasks that I once assigned to my research assistants, both undergraduate and graduate students. It is now easy to create charts from a dataset or check computer code, tasks that would have taken my RAs hours to execute well. And if those RAs were in the middle of exams, it would take days. I haven't reduced the number of RAs on my team, however. Instead of attending to more mundane tasks, they can now perform highly sophisticated analysis of data patterns and advanced econometric modeling exercises.

Similarly, outcomes at the national level cut both ways. The effects of AI on low-wage, basic manufacturing are likely to be limited. It is in the services sector that AI could have larger impacts. AI helps Indian back-office processing firms provide accounting, payroll, logistics, and other business services much more efficiently and cheaply to American and other overseas clients. At the same time, American firms can now deploy AI to undertake many tasks previously assigned to Indian workers. Those workers are hard-working and inexpensive, but an AI is even harder-working, more reliable, and cheaper. It is not just call-center and technical support jobs that could be affected. Even the business of reading and interpreting X-rays, a task currently handled by doctors, can be carried out by AI with remarkable accuracy and reliability.

Although a machine-learning algorithm itself is neutral and free of racial, gender, or other sorts of biases, the historical data used to train AI models are not always free of biases. If white households have found it easier than black households to get mortgages simply due to their race, even after controlling for income levels and other factors that should affect lending decisions, then training an AI on a historical dataset of mortgage originations could cause these long-standing racial biases to seep into the AI's outcomes. Ferreting out and mitigating the effects of such biases in the data is far from straightforward.

A much harder question is whether generative AI can align with human values. Many technologies are inherently free of values like altruism, compassion, equity, and justice. This is perhaps as it should be, for it is up to humans to use technology in ways that promote values we hold dear. Those values are typically not codified in any form that an algorithm can learn from observed data. The technologies we release into the world are capable of transforming and even creating new products, services, and works of literature and art. It ought to be concerning, while we are being dazzled by the possibilities, that there is little control over the values or value systems implicitly embedded in those new creations.

Perchance there are offsetting benefits. AI is not just value-free but also, at least in principle, free of the sort of pettiness—the prejudices, the tribalism—that characterize us as human beings, especially when we approach issues at a cross-national level. On a more positive note, as we think about global governance problems that appear intractable, maybe what we really need is the hand of AI to devise creative solutions that guide us toward a better state of the world. That would be a profound contribution from a technology devised by humans, one that might allow us to rise above the differences that hold us back.

AI, like other technologies, is not entirely benign. In its malign aspects, it bears some similarities to cryptocurrencies. While AI empowers end users in principle, it might also provide new avenues for fraud and speculation. Rather than building or reinforcing trust, AI can undermine it in various ways, particularly by making it harder to differentiate between actual and malicious information. Deepfakes—audio, photos, and videos that, thanks to increasingly sophisticated AI tools, are becoming harder to distinguish from genuine materials—are rapidly spreading into all areas of social and political discourse. This is further eroding trust in traditional institutions and information providers, creating a fertile ground for malcontents of various sorts, including hostile foreign governments.

Even the promise of widely accessible and open-access technologies that should intensify competition, and thereby benefit consumers and society, might prove to be a mirage. Rather than fostering competition, both AI and fintech could lead to greater concentration, especially if large, established firms co-opt them and use it to strengthen their market power. In other words, technologies meant to deliver broad benefits might instead further concentrate economic power at both the corporate and cross-national levels.

China and the United States are now in a race to dominate the development of AI, turning yet another transformative technology into a forum for competition rather than a platform for collaboration that could benefit humanity as a whole. With easy access to capital, control of computer chips essential to this technology, and an environment that fosters radical innovation, the United States had a head start, one that seemed insurmountable. But the emergence in January 2025 of DeepSeek, an LLM developed by a Chinese AI company, marked a breakthrough of a different sort. Despite operating at a fraction of the cost and with far less computing power than its American counterparts, DeepSeek matched the performance of existing LLMs like ChatGPT. Thus, China seems to have accomplished with AI what it has done with trains, electric vehicles, solar panels, and many other manufactured products: improved enormously on an innovation that was not necessarily homegrown by reducing costs and increasing efficiency, thereby enhancing its commercial potential. This has set the stage for a pitched battle between the two countries over the strategic leverage to be gained by exploiting AI.

The global consequences of AI are not obvious at this early stage. AI enables countries with limited human capital to compete more effectively in global markets for goods and services. Equally, though, we must be aware of the risk that smaller and less developed countries will be overrun by the new technologies, with their workers and manufacturers lacking the skills and financing to adopt and implement them. It is reasonable to hope that the risks are mainly transitional and that outcomes will eventually tilt back toward the benefits. But all evidence from the evolutionary path of many technologies suggests that the malign effects usually tend to skew, rather than level, the playing field—both within and between countries.

Information Technology

Information is now more accessible than ever, thanks to rapid advances in information and communication technologies. Social media in its various manifestations has become a source not only for updates from family and friends but also for recipes, sports scores, and news. Thanks to Instagram and TikTok, my high school–aged younger daughter is far more aware of political news and international affairs than I and others in my generation ever were at her age. This certainly makes for lively discussions at dinner (and also shows me how far behind I am on new social trends, memes, and what passes for music these days).

Social media offers benefits beyond just enabling social connections. Its value in promoting the flow of information blocked by official channels has in some cases helped evade the tight control imposed by authoritarian regimes. The Chinese government's abrupt reversal of its zero-COVID policy in December 2022 was precipitated by protests that were often coordinated via social media and whose messages were disseminated widely through the same channels. In Russia, antiwar and antigovernment messages proliferated on social media following Putin's invasion of Ukraine. In both countries, governments responded by shutting down access to traditional social media platforms, allowing only state-approved narratives to circulate through controlled channels. More secure apps, such as Telegram, have remained harder for these governments to rein in.

Although social media can help expose and disseminate information that governments would rather keep secret, easier access to vast spigots of information does not necessarily result in a better-informed populace. The barrage of content now at our fingertips has not been matched by filters that can sort accurate and authentic information from disinformation and misinformation. This lack of filters undermines trust in all sources, with the credibility of information increasingly judged by its capacity to confirm existing priors and prejudices, rather than its ability to offer alternative perspectives on issues that provoke strong emotions.

As with many of the phenomena discussed in this book, the proliferation of digital news media and other information sources has not yielded better outcomes through competition but instead has produced fragmentation, deepening societal fissures. Social media aggravates this fragmentation by reinforcing echo chambers that bind like-minded people together while alienating others, contributing to political polarization in democracies.

I see another irony in how new IT tilts the balance in favor of less open societies. Open societies, which have long thrived on the free flow of information, now struggle to contain the spread of disinformation—whether internally or from outside agents. Opportunities for multiplying and amplifying disinformation are increasingly available, allowing countries of any size to expand their influence by shaping both access to and the very nature of publicly available information. These same tools can be used by authoritarian regimes to undermine liberal democracies.

There is one area where the malign intentions of both large and small countries have acquired added potency: the use of social media platforms to interfere in democratic elections. Not only China and Russia but even small countries like North Korea now have easy access to tools that can exploit social media networks to distort information, spread misinformation, and create or intensify rivalries between economic and social groups in other countries, especially at election times when emotions run high.

Such outcomes point to an inherent asymmetry in IT. In principle, the ease with which high-quality and reliable information can be disseminated should make it possible to squeeze out inaccurate or intentionally misleading information. In practice, however, the structure of media and information platforms has led to the opposite outcome. Large platforms have little incentive to filter out bad information. They have attracted broad, diverse audiences by limiting the filters placed on the quality of content while reinforcing loyalty to the platform through algorithms that selectively feed users information that conforms to and corroborates their existing beliefs. Thus, while technology has fostered the concentration of power in the hands of large platforms, it has also led to the fragmentation of information sources and the quality of content available on those platforms.

These developments have undercut the role of trusted purveyors of information, with each now perceived as serving an agenda behind the content they choose to create and disseminate. The weakening of institutions like the free press, including by political leaders who resist accountability, has put us on a path that will be difficult to reverse.

Guardrails

Free markets work well to allocate an economy's resources efficiently. The price mechanism, which reflects demand and supply conditions, helps achieve this efficiency, while competition maintains balance. But we have learned many times over that markets rarely operate in this idealized form. Early entrants into a marketplace often grow quickly in size and use their advantages to outmuscle or squash competitors, thereby increasing their dominance. Network effects, seen in the widespread use of a product or service that encourages others to adopt it, make it difficult for competitors to take on established rivals, especially when those rivals succeed—and sometimes even when they stumble.

Google's dominance in internet searches largely results from its better performance compared to the alternatives (ever tried Bing before its AI enhancements?). Then there is Twitter, which created a social media platform of enormous influence. Elon Musk's takeover of Twitter, which he renamed X, drove away advertisers and users. Despite strong demand for a platform like X, no serious direct competitor has emerged, though alternatives like BlueSky and Threads have certainly gained some traction. Other platforms, including Facebook, Instagram, and TikTok, dominate their own niches, accreting enormous power and influence. This type of concentration has become the norm with many new technologies. Their digital nature enables expanded reach, reinforcing network effects.

Without regulatory guardrails in place, many of the new technologies built on digital platforms are leading to greater concentration of wealth and influence, exacerbating economic inequities and undermining social trust. Regulation is a complex matter, though, as it is not always feasible to simply extend or slightly modify existing rules to cover new technologies.

Take decentralized finance, which by definition is managed not by traditional institutions but by freelance developers who create and modify open-source computer code, leaving no specific party responsible for it. If bugs appear in the code, there is no organization to take responsibility; the expectation is that once the bug is documented, the community of developers will quickly fix it. Regulation struggles to mitigate the risks posed by such bugs because there is no centralized entity that can be held to account. Whereas AI developers are typically companies like OpenAI and Google, which can be regulated, the ways in which their code and the resulting capabilities are used are much harder to regulate.

The challenges of regulating social media and information platforms run up against the tenets of free speech. Open and democratic societies are rightly wary of regulating speech that might be considered inaccurate, offensive, or even dangerous because those characteristics are not generally easy to define. Freedoms of association, speech, and expression are essential to holding those in power accountable for their actions and policies. Striking the right balance between safeguarding these freedoms and preventing the misuse of social media to spread disinformation and misinformation—both of which can undercut trust in government and other institutions—is no easy task.

New technologies inherently come with risks. The ubiquity of cell phones and social media has taken a toll on children's attentiveness and mental health, even as it has allowed them to remain engaged with each other and become better informed about the world. Similarly, the risky nature of cryptocurrencies could affect not just individual investors but also broader financial markets.

Open-minded regulators rightly view these technologies as potentially useful to society and want to establish guardrails that mitigate their risks. The challenge lies in doing so without stifling innovation, while limiting the systemic consequences of risky outcomes—particularly if those risks fall disproportionately on those least able to absorb them.

The emergence of cryptocurrencies, many of which, like Bitcoin, have become purely speculative financial assets with no intrinsic value, has placed this tension starkly on the table. Investor protection is important for shielding naïve, unsophisticated retail investors from taking on risks they may not understand and whose consequences they may be ill equipped to manage. If such risks were confined to sophisticated investors, such as venture capitalists, the concern would be less acute, barring any large-scale systemic consequences. So the challenge involves balancing regulations—not to eliminate risk altogether but to create sufficient protection for vulnerable investors and to prevent broader breakdowns in the financial system.

Medical doctors tell me that their friends, family, and random acquaintances can rarely resist describing their latest health-related symptoms in great detail, expecting an on-the-spot diagnosis. I face a less consequential version of this phenomenon. Once people learn about my previous book (which I sneak into every conversation, given the slightest chance), they inevitably ask about my views on Bitcoin and whether they should invest in it. My answer is straightforward: If you are endowed with high risk tolerance, can afford to gamble with part of your savings, and have an otherwise well-diversified portfolio, then go right ahead. Investing 5 to 10 percent of your wealth into Bitcoin might yield fantastically high returns—if the dreams of Bitcoin maximalists pan out and its value goes to the moon. Equally likely (and in my view more so) is that the value of Bitcoin eventually crashes. If you are the betting type and can stomach losing a small portion of your portfolio, there's no harm in gambling.

At cryptocurrency conferences where I have been invited to speak, I have encountered another reason to worry. I have met many individuals, including some elderly folks, who have gone all in on Bitcoin. The slightly more sophisticated among them have invested in a broad range of cryptocurrencies. These investors have just enough knowledge to endanger their portfolios—they understand the need for diversification but believe that distributing their savings across multiple cryptocurrencies meaningfully reduces risk. What they often fail to recognize is that most cryptos tend to rise or fall together. A young investor placing all his chips on Bitcoin and losing his shirt worries me less than older investors who may have larger nest eggs and much less time to make up for any losses through new savings from their labor income.

These investors view cryptocurrencies and related financial products as assets subject to government oversight—and therefore as reasonable investments. This impression often stems from the fact that US investors are required to report cryptocurrency holdings and any capital gains on them to US tax authorities, so surely they are legitimate assets. Moreover, in January 2024 the US Securities and Exchange Commission began approving cryptocurrency exchange-traded funds, which allow investors to easily trade Bitcoin and other cryptocurrencies without having to buy and hold them directly. Casual investors tend to interpret SEC approval as a signal that these are well-regulated, mainstream financial products. In its statement approving exchange-traded products linked to Bitcoin, the SEC cautioned that Bitcoin "is primarily a speculative, volatile asset," that the SEC has not approved or endorsed it, and that investors in such products face myriad risks. That part of the message typically receives less attention from investors lured by the prospects of high returns, who regard SEC approval as an implicit endorsement. These examples point to the dangers of weak regulation—rules that provide minimal investor protection (limited to fraud, not naïveté) while still conferring legitimacy on an entire class of financial products.

Cryptocurrency proponents celebrated Trump's second presidential victory, seeing in him a kindred spirit. Trump was once a Bitcoin skeptic—calling it a scam—but changed his tune as the industry proved to be a cash cow during his 2024 election campaign. With a new presidential administration stocked with crypto proponents, the crypto industry is getting exactly what it wants: legitimacy provided by government oversight and light-touch regulation that is not terribly intrusive. This combination amounts to a toxic mix for both the financial system and investors. Financial regulators will ease up on regulating cryptocurrencies and crypto-related financial products. Crypto creators, promoters, and exchanges will be able to operate freely, while banks and investment managers will face fewer constraints when dealing in crypto assets. These changes will boost the broad adoption of crypto by both retail and institutional investors.

Trump and his acolytes even floated a proposal to create a "Strategic Bitcoin Reserve," a government-owned digital stockpile, which would give Bitcoin an official imprimatur. Then, amid various actions taken to enhance Bitcoin's legitimacy, Trump simultaneously undercut that legitimacy by highlighting the purely speculative nature of cryptocurrencies as an asset class. He did this by issuing his own meme coin—the Trump coin, or $Trump—just before he took office in January 2025. The creation of this coin, which was intended as a purely speculative asset with no intrinsic value, highlights the Trump administration's embrace of cryptocurrencies along with his dismissive attitude toward government regulation. It is remarkable for a government leader, let alone the leader of the free world, to create and promote a vehicle for rampant speculation and to profit from it directly. The Trump coin, however, did not encounter totally smooth sailing. It soon faced strong competition in monetizing the family name—Melania Trump issued her own meme coin, $Melania, two days after the launch of $Trump.

Cryptocurrencies have taken strong hold in many emerging-market economies, where people have less faith in local financial products. In India, middle-class and rich households have long relied on gold as a vehicle for their savings. Now a large number of Indians—by one estimate over a hundred million (7 percent of the population)—have embraced cryptocurrencies as well, as either an adjunct or an alternative to gold. This despite the government's attempts to limit the trading and ownership of cryptos through various sorts of regulations, including high capital gains and transactions taxes. At one point, it restricted banks from enabling cryptocurrency transactions (the ban was overturned by the courts).

Such public attitudes highlight the conundrum that governments and regulators face. The proliferation of cryptocurrencies reveals declining trust in government and in traditional finance. A government's measures to limit this proliferation are therefore seen as attempts to prevent erosion of its own power. And regulation that is too tight would certainly choke off any benefits, including beneficial changes in traditional finance, that could be catalyzed by the new technologies. But if and when the world of crypto crumbles, especially if it has become a widely held financial asset, governments and official regulators will no doubt be criticized for having been asleep at the wheel, failing to protect retail investors from the ravages of crypto. It is a no-win situation for officials, especially those inclined to promote financial innovation.

Another complication is that some new technologies are not easily constrained by national borders, requiring governance to be considered at the global level. Blockchain-based finance, for instance, is conducted on the internet rather than through any particular country's financial plumbing. Tight regulations simply push some of the activity offshore without constraining the availability of these products. Such was the case with Sam Bankman-Fried's cryptocurrency exchange, FTX, which was technically headquartered in The Bahamas but provided services to American customers, despite being prohibited from doing so. US regulatory agencies had no direct oversight of FTX, which became one of the largest cryptocurrency exchanges in the world. The Bahamian authorities apparently took a more relaxed approach to regulating FTX than the United States likely would have. FTX finally collapsed in November 2022, and one year later Bankman-Fried received a twenty-five-year prison sentence in the United States for perpetrating extensive fraud.

The new, more favorable US attitude toward cryptocurrencies is likely to encourage other countries to let down their guard in regulating them. A country with a well-developed financial system such as the United States can cope with the risks emanating from broad adoption of cryptocurrencies, but such risks could spell doom for others, especially poorer developing countries.

AI poses similar challenges. The European Union jumped ahead with aggressive regulation, while US regulators are giving the technology more room to run. The result is that Europe is falling behind in AI innovation but might still suffer from the negative aspects of this rapidly proliferating technology. The challenge for regulators worldwide is to develop a cohesive regulatory structure rather than a fragmented one. Fragmentation would not only fail to corral new technologies but could also squelch some of their more positive aspects. The commercial possibilities of AI are undercutting such efforts, with China and the United States, in particular, prioritizing dominance over careful management.

A global regulatory framework applied consistently across countries will be necessary to improve the cost-benefit trade-offs associated with these new technologies. This is easier said than done, however, as many developing countries lack the regulatory expertise and resources needed to police these technologies. In addition, there are the usual challenges in determining the right framework: Who writes the rules, who is at the table when the rules are written, and who enforces them?

As we have seen, these issues are complicated in every aspect of global governance. Digital currencies and AI are no exceptions, especially given their emergence at a time when geopolitical tensions are running high, making this an acutely contentious process. In the absence of global frameworks, smaller and less developed countries—those with limited regulatory capacity and few mechanisms to resist the onslaught of new technologies—may find themselves at a disadvantage rather than benefiting from a level playing field.

Dashed Dreams of Plenty

It is a tantalizing prospect that technology could foster abundance by meeting the essential necessities of all human beings—food, clothing, shelter—while freeing people from the drudgery of both physical and mental labor. Technology might not as easily address the craving for human dignity or a sense of purpose, but maybe those abstractions are less important or, at least, can be postponed until the basic needs of all humanity are met. One could even dream that such abundance would reduce conflicts within and between countries, as there would be no compulsion to fight over scarce resources. However, humans' tribalism, their emphasis on relative rather than absolute standards of living, and the importance of cultural and religious identity make it hard to foresee an end to conflict, even in a world of abundance. Still, at least it would be a world without hunger, homelessness, and other forms of economic deprivation.

India's Green Revolution, initiated in the mid-1960s, is a prime example of how technology can improve agricultural yields and increase crops' resilience to weather and pestilence. In many parts of the world, hunger and food scarcity persist, but these are usually consequences of dysfunctional governments, policies that limit cross-border agricultural trade, and poor macroeconomic management. Some countries still face scarcity, but the global supply of food is generally sufficient to sustain the population. Food may be an easier problem to solve than water shortages, as water is an even scarcer resource in many regions. Here, too, technologies that improve desalination and wastewater recycling can help expand the availability of these vital resources.

Even when it comes to core sustenance, though, a gulf exists between the well-off and the vulnerable populations, especially those in fragile nation-states, who face severe resource constraints but are the least likely to benefit from new technologies. During periods of global economic and geopolitical stress, food security itself becomes the subject of nationalistic policies.

Russia's invasion of Ukraine, a country that previously accounted for about 10 percent of global wheat exports, disrupted exports from that country, pushing up wheat prices in 2022. Then, as food prices surged worldwide with the post-COVID global economic recovery, India banned exports of white rice in July 2023 to hold down domestic prices. India is by far the world's largest rice exporter, accounting for about 40 percent of the global rice trade in 2022—more than the next four exporters combined. India's export ban sharply drove up prices quoted by other exporters such as Thailand and Vietnam. Even in richer countries, where households spend relatively modest shares of their incomes on food, these price increases took a toll on household budgets. For countries in sub-Saharan Africa that rely on grain imports and were already strapped for resources, this was a much tougher blow.

In short, even where technological solutions exist to help populations meet basic necessities, few safeguards are in place for the truly vulnerable—countries and people—who remain exposed to volatility and strife fomented by narrow-minded national leaders and geopolitical ructions. The fruits of technology alone will not rescue us from the doom loop.

A Better World or a Darker One?

The brief tour of technology provided in this chapter has not even touched on phenomenal developments in fields such as bioengineering, green energy, medicine, and much more. Mankind has faced down many disasters and potential catastrophes, with innovation and new technologies increasing the profusion of resources in ways that not only address these problems but even improve material standards of living. Humanity is certainly poised for a better future, at least if advancing technology is taken as a sign of progress.

Technology has given us the capacity to create resources in greater abundance than ever before. If cross-border conflicts are mainly driven by competition for resources, then such abundance should no doubt serve as a deterrent. Certain resources, like land, cannot readily be expanded through technology, though even this constraint might relax if fanciful visions of life in space or on currently uninhabitable regions of the earth become reality. Still, it is not just absolute wealth but relative wealth that seems to matter to people and nations. And power, by definition, is a relative concept. Thus, technology may simply change the nature of conflict rather than help us avoid it.

AI and blockchain are remarkable, highly innovative technologies with enormous potential to generate beneficial outcomes. While their use requires technical expertise, they are largely nonexclusive and not subject to the same cost barriers as proprietary technologies. Open to anyone who has an internet connection, they are easily accessible and resistant to censorship (unless a government cuts off internet access). Information technology is also reshaping the basis of power, driving government accountability, even in nondemocratic regimes. These technologies offer attributes that, in principle, can level the playing field within and across countries. Yet the benefits could just as easily become concentrated in the hands of elites and powerful countries, leaving only crumbs in the hands of poorer households and nations.

These technologies also carry profound dangers and could take us down a dark path, destroying trust, enabling speculation and fraud, and worsening societal and economic inequities. There are few checks in place, with regulation lagging far behind their potential to cause harm. More disturbingly, business titans in these fields have shown a willingness to put profit above fundamental tenets of decency and societal welfare, unleashing innovations without safeguards, or in some cases hiding behind the guise of free speech when it suits their interests.

Technological innovations are undeniably improving standards of living in countless ways, making it easier to fulfill essential human needs while also facilitating and enhancing the benefits of cooperation. At the same time, the malign effects of technology are deepening rifts between economies, societies, and individuals. Surely humanity, for all its flaws, will come to see the value in bridging these divides and moving together toward a future of greater stability and prosperity.

This hope is being undermined by fundamental differences in values and visions of how economies, societies, and political systems should be organized—differences that lie at the heart of both the current struggle between the great powers and a larger contest for influence and power. China's rise has revived a broader set of issues that, following the dissolution of the Soviet Union in 1991, had seemed resolved in favor of market-oriented liberal democracies. These deep-rooted differences suggest that we are not simply in a transitional period that will settle into a new and stable equilibrium. We turn to that subject next.

7

Visions for the World

Every kind of socialism is Utopian, most of all scientific socialism. Utopia replaces God by the future. Then it proceeds to identify the future with ethics; the only values are those which serve
this particular future. For that reason Utopias have almost always
been coercive and authoritarian.

— Albert Camus, *The Rebel*

Life, liberty, and the pursuit of happiness constitute the core set
of inalienable rights enshrined in the US Declaration of Independence. The preamble to the US Constitution lists as its first
goal the creation of "a more perfect Union." The founders also
sought to "establish Justice, insure domestic Tranquility, provide
for the common defence, promote the general Welfare, and secure
the Blessings of Liberty to ourselves and our Posterity." The well-
known maxim of the French Constitution is "Liberty, Equality,
Fraternity." Such sentiments represent the quintessence of liberal
democracy.

Yet while the ideals expressed in these documents embody
laudable aspirations, each of these words has become a loaded
term that means different things to different people. A more
fundamental question asks what a country's citizens really care
about when weighing trade-offs between various goals, such as
economic progress, security, and liberty. There is much to suggest
that the vast majority of people want, most of all, to have their
basic economic necessities met, to be given fair opportunities to
succeed, and to lead safe lives free of crime and violence.

It was certainly a compelling proposition that, once a society's basic needs were met and its people's living standards rose beyond a certain level, they would demand more than material well-being. Intangibles such as freedom of expression and assembly, democracy and accountability in government, and liberty in the practice of religion would be listed near the top of what citizens would demand of their governments. But this lofty premise has proven to be an illusion.

There is little evidence that once ordinary citizens are freed of concerns about their essential needs, they are eager to attain these higher-order freedoms, especially if doing so means compromising their security. It is facile to paint this calculation as a spurious dilemma and argue that civil liberties and security are in all cases fully compatible and even mutually reinforcing. That is not the reality faced by people in many countries. Even when the two objectives are not in conflict, citizens often display a visceral preference for policies that prioritize security. After the horrific terrorist attacks of 9/11, it was not just performative security measures at airports that Americans willingly accepted to feel protected; they also acquiesced to more extensive government surveillance and condoned the torture of accused terrorists. Fear works well as a political tool in the hands of some politicians. When Donald Trump spoke of open borders and rampant crime ravaging the US economy and social fabric, his message clearly resonated with a large portion of the US electorate—even if it was not entirely consonant with the facts.

One does not have to look far for evidence of what really matters to the citizens of countries where the choice is starker. Examples abound of leaders who have pulled their countries back from the brink of chaos, but at the cost of forsaking fair treatment under the law and even certain civil liberties, including freedoms of association and expression. Some of these liberties come to be viewed by ordinary people as luxuries that only the elites, whether domestic or foreign, care about. Despite their use of strong-arm tactics, such leaders often attract extraordinary and persistently high levels of public support, especially given the dark days that preceded their rule, which are imprinted in the memories of their citizenry.

Paul Kagame, who has been president of Rwanda since 2000, restored his country after the ravages of civil war and brutal genocide, overseeing its transition to a relatively prosperous and safe nation. *The New York Times*, which declared the capital city, Kigali, the envy of Africa, describes the transformation: "Smooth streets curl past gleaming towers that hold banks, luxury hotels and tech startups.... Tourists fly in to visit Rwanda's famed gorillas. Government officials from other African countries arrive for lessons in good governance. The electricity is reliable. Traffic cops do not solicit bribes. Violence is rare." And yet, Kagame is criticized in the article for having achieved this stunning transformation with "harsh methods that would normally attract international condemnation." The article goes on to note that many of Kagame's opponents and critics have been jailed or even died under murky circumstances, while free speech has been curtailed.

Or consider Nayib Bukele, the president of El Salvador. He was lauded in the international media for having achieved a seemingly impossible feat—decimating the vicious gangs that had turned El Salvador into one of the world's most violent places. But he also stood accused of having "jailed thousands of innocent people, suspended key civil liberties indefinitely and flooded the streets with soldiers," not to mention "violating the constitution by seeking re-election." The tactics Bukele employed to end two decades of uncontrolled gang violence included jailing some seventy-five thousand people with little due process and instituting a state of emergency. The results have been stunning— killings plunged (the homicide rate fell by 75 percent in just three years, according to one estimate), people returned to the streets, and children could play in parks once again.

It is no wonder that such leaders win enormous public support from their populations, who see coercive tactics that result in the loss of civil liberties as a small price to pay for safety and political stability. Harrumphing from foreign quarters—whether well-intentioned Western media or nongovernmental organizations advocating for certain rights—is often brushed off by much of the populace, whose concerns are far more rudimentary and immediate. "Making streets safer through methods that are blatantly at odds with democracy," as one analyst put it in describing El Salvador's transformation, neatly sums up the trade-off.

These examples highlight deeper considerations, going beyond simple economic power and influence, in determining the nature and characteristics of a new world order. There is little to suggest that the arc of human development will inexorably bend toward liberal, market-oriented democracies—once regarded as the epitome of civilization, both for facilitating the economic progress needed to fulfill essential human needs and for promoting the high-minded ideals that have inspired many a revolutionary movement.

A key manifestation of a country's economic and geopolitical ascendancy is its ability to sway the rest of the world to embrace a particular form of economic, political, and social organization. Much like a parent passing down both good and bad traits to their children—a prospect that causes much mortification among my own offspring—countries can similarly transmit their values to other countries and their citizens.

The tussle underway between China and the United States is ultimately about much more than just economic power, based on measures like GDP, or indirect control of territory that both countries seek to bring under their influence. Rather, it is a competition over values, which in turn reflect their respective visions of an ideal world. The Communist Party of China exercises an iron grip on the country's economic, legal, and political systems.

The United States and other Western economies, by contrast, view governance as enabling, rather than directly controlling, their economic and legal systems, with governments serving at the pleasure of their citizens.

Indeed, the shake-up of the world order is really about whose economic, political, and social values will become the norm that others will aspire to and be judged by. This matters not only for bragging rights but because it has practical consequences: The interests of countries that share similar economic and political structures tend to be closely aligned. It is no accident that democracies frequently find themselves on the same side of most global matters, while de facto autocracies, no matter their ostensible forms of government, often band together. The lines between the two forms of government have become hazier in recent years, though, with even the leaders of some democracies adopting authoritarian postures. Great-power competition is thus shifting, and the process is leading to global realignments that will lock in instability, rather than representing a simple transition to a new, stable equilibrium.

One way to think about alternative visions is to ask whether it is the individual, the community, or society as a whole whose interests should take precedence. In an ideal world, these interests would be aligned—everyone gains or loses together. In the more practical world we live in, however, the priorities of different individuals are often in conflict. The organization of economic and political systems helps mediate these conflicts, generating outcomes that are better in the aggregate than what could be achieved without any coordination.

A basic set of questions that determines the optimal structure of such systems includes which outcomes are considered desirable, how their relative merits should be assessed, and what criteria should be used to evaluate the success of a given system. The answers invariably involve value judgments. Is the loss of political freedom a worthwhile price to pay for economic progress? Is democracy, which tends to favor redistributive policies that have short-term benefits but could harm long-term growth, a luxury that poor countries can afford? These dilemmas were once considered false choices, buoyed by the belief that democracy and free markets would ultimately prevail in maximizing economic progress as well as other aspects of human welfare. The dramatic economic success of China and the concomitant decline of many Western powers has undermined confidence in such beliefs.

Moreover, with true democracies under threat, the distinctions between alternative forms of economic and political organization are blurring, with important consequences for the structure of the world order. One possible result is that, rather than aspiring to higher standards, economic and political systems may gravitate toward the lowest common denominator, such as democracies that nominally give citizens the right to vote but protect incumbency and offer few viable alternatives for voters seeking change. The instinct that drives insecure political leaders to tighten their control often leads to greater rigidity, which breeds instability and, in some cases, prompts more aggressive postures toward other countries.

An additional source of instability is that the fabric of liberal democracy, supplemented by free markets, is itself showing signs of fraying. Democratic processes have put in power leaders like Donald Trump in the United States, Recep Teyyip Erdogan in Türkiye, and Viktor Orbán in Hungary, who have promptly and deliberately undermined democratic institutions in their countries. These are among the more extreme examples, but many major democracies—including Brazil, India, Mexico, Poland, and others—have elected leaders who attack cherished institutions, especially the judiciary and the free press, that attempt to restrain their exercise of absolute power. Even in cases where such leaders serve only brief tenures, the damage they inflict on institutions is long-lasting and difficult to reverse.

Thus, one question that has become increasingly pertinent in the Trump era—during which other fake populists have taken power around the world—is whether the small-d democratic project is sustainable. More pointedly, are democracies doomed to being warped over time? As a political model, liberal democracy seems to work better in relatively homogeneous societies with shared aspirations. Otherwise, tribalism of one sort or another tends to take hold.

Besides, the combination of democracy and free markets, once seen as the paragon to which all countries should aspire, now appears to suffer from intrinsic fragilities that undermine it from within. Chief among these is the tendency of free markets to be characterized by self-reinforcing inequality, which can lead to political capture, allowing the wealthy to tilt government policies in their favor.

In short, the world is now beset by two dynamics that threaten to lock in instability rather than usher in a new equilibrium. The first involves a competition between alternative economic and political models, with dueling visions likely to keep instability at a boil. The second plays out along a spectrum, where market-oriented liberal democracies at one end are themselves convulsed by the adverse interaction between market forces and open democracy, and by the uneven impacts of globalization and technological change. With the range of choices unsettled and in flux, it is difficult to envision a stable outcome or a viable resolution of the doom loop.

Economic Models

Free-market capitalism was long seen as the ideal form of economic organization. Characterized by open and unfettered competition, it ostensibly enables individuals to pursue the best outcomes for themselves and, through their uncoordinated but collective efforts, deliver optimal results for the economy as a whole. Market mechanisms support this process by allocating financial, human, and other resources to their most productive uses. The government's role is limited to maintaining the rule of law, especially by protecting property rights and settling contractual disputes, essential underpinnings of well-functioning markets. Communism—or, in its weaker form, socialism—assigns a greater role to the government in managing the economy, not just through regulations but also through direct control of much, if not all, of the industrial sector and financial system. Neither of these extreme models works particularly well in its pure form.

Free-market fundamentalists see government regulation as unnecessary, intrusive, and even detrimental, arguing that it blocks competition and innovation. In their view, open competition allows for the optimal allocation of resources through prices that adjust freely in response to supply and demand. The underlying logic is that, as long as consumers have access to relevant information, they will make carefully considered and beneficial choices. Goods and services that meet consumers' needs and desires will thrive; others will shrivel away. Even the provision of information need not be mandated by governments. If a merchant offers too little to facilitate informed decisions, then consumers will turn away, giving providers a natural incentive to be more transparent.

Such an idealized world does not exist. Several obstacles prevent markets from working as smoothly as envisioned. Consider the availability of choices. Choices are good, and more of them should increase human welfare—in principle. A wider range of options allows consumers to find products that better align with their preferences, whether they're shopping for toothpaste or a car. Undesirable options can be discarded or ignored, so at worst more choices might leave us no better off, but surely they cannot make things worse.

Market economies offer consumers a dizzying array of choices in products ranging from potato chips to health care plans to investment options. Faced with so many options, the fear of making the wrong choice can be paralyzing, potentially deterring someone from making any decision at all. So people turn to information filters—online ratings, consumer reviews, magazines that test and rank vacuum cleaners, consumer-oriented websites that analyze health care plans. However, the proliferation of these filters, some of dubious quality, only adds to the confusion, creating a need for yet another layer of metainformation filter. These informational frictions, or the limitations of humans' information-processing abilities, especially when faced with information overload or a glut of choices, can have negative consequences. Consumers may prioritize familiarity over quality, making it harder for newer and better products to stand out in the marketplace.

Even when markets function well, they do not necessarily promote the common good. This is encapsulated in the principle of negative externalities (a concept we have already encountered in the context of a country's policies that adversely affect other countries). When an individual or a company takes action that imposes costs on others or on society as a whole, without bearing those costs themselves, everyone is left worse off. Releasing pollutants into nearby waterways rather than disposing of them properly might save a company money, but the detrimental consequences for the community can outweigh the benefits enjoyed by the company and its shareholders.

Another concern is that the market for a particular product or service can be dominated by one firm (a monopoly) or a small group of firms. A dominant firm can initially keep prices artificially low to dissuade competition; once it has cornered the market, it can inflate prices. This is especially true in industries such as utilities (electricity, gas, water), which require enormous investments, making it difficult for new companies to break into the market. Even Google's dominance in web search, which allows it to dictate terms to advertisers and users, shows how competition can evaporate in some unregulated markets.

Such failures of free markets to work well on their own necessitate nonmarket remedies. For instance, it is widely accepted that a government should implement antitrust regulations to limit the formation of monopolies, as well as regulations to curb the pricing power of monopolies in industries where competition is difficult, including utilities. In practice, though, these regulations often bring unintended consequences.

Regulations meant to foster fair competition can sometimes become barriers to entry for new firms, hindering competition. Laws requiring even small-scale businesses to acquire licenses—often a costly and time-consuming process—can discourage entrepreneurship. Barriers to entry limit competition, and successful firms can sometimes use their growing dominance to squelch competition. In their book *Saving Capitalism from the Capitalists*, University of Chicago economists Raghuram Rajan and Luigi Zingales make the case that many successful corporations use their size and clout to thwart competition, not only by undercutting fledgling competitors but also by influencing regulations to their advantage.

Even in economies committed to free-market principles, the government thus plays an important role in ensuring that markets function as intended.

Alternative forms of economic organization—where the government rather than markets plays a central role—have been largely repudiated by the relative success of capitalism and the failure of communism to deliver the goods. Mao Zedong's collectivization of Chinese agriculture and industry in the 1960s resulted in an economic disaster. Even in the more moderate form of socialism, outcomes have been abysmal. India's emphasis on *swadeshi* or self-sufficiency, which, as noted earlier, was a reaction to the exploitation of the country's resources by British rulers prior to India's independence in 1947, not only kept India from opening up to foreign trade and capital but also encouraged early governments to emphasize state involvement in the economy. The state-owned banking system directed resources to industries that the government prioritized, often favoring large, unprofitable state-owned enterprises. Onerous bureaucratic requirements further stifled private enterprise. As a result, India experienced low growth for the first few decades after independence.

Market economies, by contrast, cemented their rising economic power in the 1970s and 1980s. The collapse and splintering of the Soviet Union, followed by the unraveling of its decrepit communist economies in 1991, seemed to settle the matter once and for all in favor of the free-market model. This outcome was affirmed by the performance of former Soviet-bloc countries, like Hungary and Poland, that embraced capitalism and saw their GDPs grow more rapidly than in countries that did not. India's performance also fits this pattern. It was only after various market-oriented reforms were introduced starting in the 1990s that the government's direct involvement began to recede, allowing private enterprise to flourish and enabling the economy to register higher growth.

Still, as the imperfections of markets have become increasingly obvious over time, a question lingers: Might alternative economic models deliver better outcomes? A case can be made, for instance, for allowing forms of economic organization to evolve with an economy's progress. The concept of infant industry protection has a long and checkered history in development economics. The idea is that low-income countries must protect their nascent industries— through trade barriers and other import restrictions—until they are ready to stand up to global competition. This approach brings its own costs, as it typically limits foreign investors' access to those industries, thereby hindering new firms' ability to tap into foreign funding and denying them the benefits of foreign technology transfers.

By the beginning of this millennium, a broad consensus had emerged in academic and policymaking circles that, while not all government intervention is necessarily harmful, the relatively free operation of market forces offers, on balance, many advantages and the best chance of economic success. However, China's remarkable progress, built on a model of state-led capitalism, has upended the narrative. The exact proportion of industry accounted for by state enterprises, and the degree of indirect state involvement in enterprises not directly controlled by the Chinese government, are tricky to measure accurately. In any event, it is clear that in China, the government plays a much bigger role in the economy—and even in financial markets, through state-owned banks—than is typical in market economies.

This extensive state intervention has hardly been an unqualified success. It has resulted in a massive misallocation of resources, with Chinese households' considerable savings funneled through a banking system that has failed to channel those funds to their most productive uses. Instead, inefficient state-owned enterprises have received, and continue to receive, a disproportionate share of bank loans.

None of this has stopped China's astonishing economic rise. In 2024, annual GDP (measured in dollar terms) was fifteen times larger than in 2000. In inflation-adjusted terms, China's economy grew by more than 8 percent annually over this period, an extraordinary run with no precedent in recent economic history.

There are questions about the reliability of Chinese data, especially indicators of month-to-month or quarter-to-quarter changes in variables such as industrial output. Academic research on the matter is actually split on whether China's official statistics have overstated or understated GDP growth since 2000. In any event, anyone visiting China over the last two decades has witnessed its transformation from a low-income to a middle-income economy. Although this change is much more evident in urban areas, no part of the country has been untouched by a substantial increase in living standards.

China's dynamism gave rise to predictions that its economy would become the largest in the world sometime in this decade or next, putting the ultimate stamp of validation on its economic model. That progress stalled after 2020, but it may yet return as a defining theme in the coming years.

The allure of free markets and private enterprise remains strong—even in a command economy. It is now broadly accepted that even though markets do not always allocate resources perfectly, a state-led approach can lead to worse outcomes. Yi Gang, a respected Chinese economist who was then the deputy governor of China's central bank, put it succinctly at a 2015 press conference: "We should believe, respect, revere, and conform with the market."

One must recognize that, for all its shortcomings, a command economy offers one advantage: In certain types of crisis episodes, it gives the government more direct control over markets and financial systems, which can be helpful in staving off collapse.

I base this observation on how the financial systems of the United States, the eurozone, the United Kingdom, Japan, and most other advanced economies—all regarded as sophisticated and well regulated—cracked and nearly fell apart during the global financial crisis of 2007–2009. By contrast, the state-dominated banking systems of countries like China and India held up much better. Long seen as stuck in old ways of doing business and resistant to financial innovation, these systems and their regulators demonstrated that what seemed to be vices were in fact virtues, at least in a crisis.

China, which bounced back quickly and sharply from what had seemed like a global recession, is a case in point. The Chinese government's extensive involvement in the economy and financial system gives it more direct control, rendering monetary and fiscal policy stimulus more effective in periods of economic stress. Most importantly, through its direct support of affected sectors, the government can subdue economic and financial risks, preventing them from cascading and reinforcing each other. After all, when most of the major lending banks and borrowing corporations are under state control, repayment of loans can be postponed until times are better. In Western economies, by contrast, the failures of banks and the bankruptcies of companies that relied on them for loans fed off each other in a downward spiral. China's state-led economy is built to withstand such massive shocks better than market economies, as the government can quickly marshal a broad range of economic and noneconomic responses that go beyond traditional macroeconomic policy tools. Mechanisms that facilitate government support of specific industries and financial institutions are baked into China's economic system.

This is hardly intended as a commendation of China's economic system; it is rather an acknowledgment that, in exceptional times, and usually only in those times, a command economy offers certain virtues. Extensive government intervention breeds inefficiencies in good times but can serve as an effective backstop during prospective crises. One question worth careful consideration is whether a middle path—avoiding the extremes of a pure market economy and an entirely state-dominated one—might offer greater efficiency and stability.

This discussion suggests that the visions driving the structures of competing economic systems are separated by a wide gulf. In practice, however, some commonalities emerge in the operations of these systems, reflecting the inadequacies of both extremes. Surprisingly, a curious if incomplete convergence is taking place between market economies, where the government is playing a bigger role, and command economies, where market mechanisms are gaining somewhat freer rein.

The model of capitalism underpinned by free and unfettered markets is giving way to greater governmental control, even in countries like the United States that purport to be free-market havens. The global financial crisis led to a significant increase in government and central bank involvement in economies and, especially, in financial markets. Some free-market devotees argue that it was government involvement in US mortgage markets, through the implicit backing of government-sponsored enterprises such as Fannie Mae and Freddie Mac (which guarantee mortgages, allowing banks to sell them to investors), that fueled speculative activity and ultimately precipitated the crash. Whatever the merits of that argument, the reality is a growing tendency toward even greater government involvement.

In early 2023, the stability of the US banking system, reinforced by regulatory changes put in place in the aftermath of the global financial crisis, unexpectedly seemed in jeopardy. The prominent midsized Silicon Valley Bank collapsed, followed by Signature Bank and then First Republic Bank. These were not fundamentally unsound banks, but concerns over their sturdiness, which spread like wildfire through social media, triggered a surge of deposit withdrawals that brought them down. Fearing widespread bank runs, the US Treasury Department, the Federal Reserve, and the Federal Deposit Insurance Corporation took the unprecedented step of jointly announcing that virtually all deposits in these banks would temporarily be covered by deposit insurance. This averted the risk of financial panic and sent a clear signal that the government and the Fed would intervene whenever any bank seemed under threat.

In principle, financial systems in the United States and other Western economies are run by the private sector, with little direct government involvement. However, despite banking titans touting their autonomy (not to mention their extraordinary acumen), they all flourish under the implicit guarantee that governments and central banks will protect them from the consequences of their recklessness. Bigger banks, whose failure would harm the economy more, have reason to feel especially secure in this guarantee, which encourages them to take greater risks.

At the other extreme sits China, where much of the banking system remains state-owned. In principle, this has long meant that the entire system was implicitly backed by the government. The government wisely recognized this as a problem, as it gave

depositors no incentive to choose well-run banks over those offering merely convenience or higher interest rates, while giving
banks every incentive to take undue risks. To address this, China
instituted an explicit deposit insurance scheme in 2015. Premium
rates for each bank would be based on the quality of its assets and
liabilities, with banks that had made riskier loans paying more.
Small deposit accounts would be fully insured, but large deposits—
usually held by wealthy individuals or major corporations—would
not. These depositors have the wherewithal to evaluate their banks'
balance sheets and have strong incentives to impose discipline by
moving money out of a bank if they sense trouble.

This scheme closely mirrors deposit insurance systems in
Western economies. Skeptics rightly questioned, though, whether
the government would ever actually allow a major bank to fail.

In any event, both the Chinese and US banking systems now
feature explicit deposit insurance. More importantly, both are
protected by an implicit government guarantee that makes it unlikely a major bank in either country will be allowed to collapse.
Most other countries' banking systems operate under similar
assumptions.

While industrial policy has fallen out of fashion among the in-
telligentsia, governments of all stripes have continued to use it,
often while insisting they are doing no such thing. As we saw in
the chapter on globalization, governments use policies favoring
specific industries in ways that serve as trade barriers, inhibiting
international trade and financial integration. In its various forms,
industrial policy is expanding direct government involvement in
the economy beyond the traditional roles of maintaining the rule
of law and providing a regulatory environment where competition can flourish and improve overall welfare. In doing so, such
policies alter the relationship between markets and the state.

China's "dual circulation" policy and India's "Make in India"
initiative target similar objectives: boosting domestic industries

and increasing self-reliance by protecting specific sectors from foreign competition and giving them financial and other support. Even advanced economies, once seen as champions of free trade and open markets, are jumping on the bandwagon. The Biden administration, for example, took steps—ostensibly to preserve US technological supremacy and promote domestic investment in green and emerging technologies—that included subsidizing certain industries and protecting them from foreign competition. The Inflation Reduction Act of 2022 offers subsidies and tax breaks to incentivize the domestic production of electric vehicles and renewable energy components. This particular legislation riled even America's European allies, who took exception to it for threatening their manufacturing industries by violating long-standing norms that limit direct government support for favored sectors. The CHIPS and Science Act (also enacted in 2022) similarly provides incentives for semiconductor firms to set up manufacturing facilities in the United States and bans outsourcing to "China and other countries of concern."

The Biden administration's approach to integrating domestic, foreign, and international economic policies was articulated in a speech by then–National Security Advisor Jake Sullivan in April 2023. He described the administration's industrial strategy as one that "identifies specific sectors that are foundational to economic growth, strategic from a national security perspective, and where private industry on its own isn't poised to make the investments needed to secure our national ambitions. It deploys targeted public investments in these areas that unlock the power and ingenuity of private markets, capitalism, and competition to lay a foundation for long-term growth." He also explained that restrictions on exports, investments, and transfers of technology to China were aimed at "protecting our foundational technologies with a small yard and high fence." In a subsequent article in *Foreign Affairs*, Sullivan responded to criticism of this new US industrial policy, arguing that public investments were "not about picking winners and losers or bringing globalization to an end. They enable rather than replace private investment. And they enhance the United States' capacity to deliver inclusive growth, build resilience, and protect national security."

French President Emmanuel Macron, in a speech delivered at the Sorbonne in April 2024, explicitly laid out an agenda for accelerating industrial policy in Europe, something he noted had been considered a "dirty word" when he gave a similarly expansive speech at the same venue seven years earlier. He added that Europe had since begun to overcome its "technological and industrial naïveté," but that decisive steps were still needed to lay the foundation for greater technological and industrial sovereignty.

In short, despite all their paeans to the unfettered functioning of markets and the efficiency and stability it is said to deliver, governments overseeing free-market economies have in fact become quite interventionist. At the other end, leaders of many command economies have come to understand that market principles and free enterprise are essential to achieving their economic goals.

Such admittedly limited convergence in practice between competing visions remains far from sufficient to foster a cooperative environment among the adherents of rival economic systems. What these practices in fact demonstrate is that countries championing each vision are grappling with internal flaws, even as they attempt to steer the rest of the world toward their preferred models.

Furthermore, government intervention through industrial policy highlights how competition between major powers, rather than being constructive, can precipitate a race to the bottom by encouraging measures that provide narrow, short-term advantages at the expense of longer-term shared benefits. State intervention, while not inherently bad, in this case seeks to promote domestic industries deemed worthy of support, often based more on political than economic considerations, shielding them from foreign competition. This reduces the benefits of sharing technology across national borders and the innovation and efficiency gains that come from open competition between corporations. Such developments will only lead to worse economic and political outcomes if, instead of adopting best practices from each other, countries with competing economic systems try to outdo each other with policies that ultimately constrain growth and dynamism. In short, this particular aspect of convergence between free-market and command economies—which seems like it ought to bring countries together through shared governing philosophies—is no recipe for a more stable world order.

There is one dimension along which neither economic system has delivered, and that is in equality of opportunity. By most measures, household income and wealth inequality have risen sharply in the United States in recent decades. Although the Chinese economy has produced less inequity, it has risen there, too. In both societies, the poor might envy the rich, but it is a reasonable bet that they are more rankled by unfair rules that privilege richer households, allowing them to accumulate additional wealth while others fall further behind. Moreover, the sense that opportunities for economic advancement are limited, with the benefits of globalization and technological advancement redounding mainly to the rich and offering mostly crumbs to the rest of society, fuels resentment everywhere.

The Chinese government, recognizing the potential of this discontent to stir social unrest, introduced the Common Prosperity Policy around 2021. The policy, which was first referenced in a speech by Xi Jinping and subsequently took more concrete form, was clearly intended to signal that the government would rein in the accumulation of excessive private-sector wealth and put in place measures to ensure that the benefits of growth would be more evenly distributed. In the United States, Donald Trump has effectively argued that the political and economic elites—groups that he is, as luck would have it, a prominent member of—have stacked the deck against ordinary people, denying them opportunities to climb the economic ladder while gaining an increasing share of the benefits of growth.

One could thus argue that economic systems at both ends of the spectrum have delivered unsatisfactory outcomes that have boiled over, undermining confidence in the efficacy and stability of their respective political systems as well. The cracks in these political structures are becoming increasingly evident, revealing a surprising brittleness.

Political Models

The trope of a benevolent despot who has the best long-term interests of her people at heart and rules with a firm but even hand is appealing—but rarely, if ever, consistent with reality. In any event, official monarchies where the monarch holds more than titular powers are now virtually nonexistent. Democracy has become the norm, although this leaves open the question of what form it should take and whether it truly gives voice to the people or merely serves as a fig leaf for an authoritarian leader to claim popular support.

In parts of ancient Greece, referendums that allowed the citizens, however narrowly defined (citizenship was once limited to free men), to voice their views were seen as the most efficient way to manage a society. By their very definition, plebiscites are intended to give plebians—common people—the power to determine their own destinies, rather than leaving decisions to a privileged political class. Of course, referendums and plebiscites are not practical for every policy matter and can foster a tyranny of the majority in systems lacking other checks and balances. Other political systems have evolved to take the place of direct democracy.

At one end of the political spectrum is representative liberal democracy, in which elected officials make policy decisions on behalf of their constituents and are held to account through periodic elections. Various forms of democracy, each with its own advantages and flaws, have evolved through a combination of popular preferences, historical circumstances, and even chance. The Singapore model, for instance, blends benevolent paternalism with little tolerance for serious dissent, even if elections are contested, open, and a means of ensuring accountability.

At the other end of the spectrum are governments characterized by single-party rule, which usually transmute into societies where personal freedoms are subjugated to the will of the state. The degree to which freedoms of association and expression are tolerated can vary among such societies, though the label "authoritarianism" is usually reserved for leaders who consistently stifle dissent and impose their will in all major aspects of public life.

Much of this discussion of political systems ultimately devolves into one about the structure of a country's institutions. A strong institutional framework provides a system of checks and balances and distributes power across different arms of government. Democracy also offers a corrective mechanism over time—one that can be cathartic. The ability to exercise power at the ballot box, regardless of one's economic or social station, can be a powerful escape valve for popular frustration. Moreover, it is the most effective mechanism for ensuring that a leader stays responsive to the needs and aspirations of her people.

In countries that practice parliamentary democracy, such as India and the United Kingdom, there are in effect two branches of government: elected legislatures that create and implement laws, and judiciaries that interpret the laws and ensure they are applied consistently and fairly. In presidential democracies like the United States, there are three separate branches of government: Legislatures create laws, which are administered by an executive branch led by a separately elected president, with the judiciary again interpreting the laws. In both types of democracies, the separate branches act as restraints on each other's powers.

A free press is arguably an institution in its own right, keeping the others in check by exposing uncomfortable truths. Even in an open democracy, it is hardly the case that all journalists and news outlets act on pristine motives, are incorruptible, or prioritize the search for truth above all else. The competitive motive plays an important role, however, by rewarding journalists who uncover stories that require both extensive sleuthing and well-connected sources willing to spill the beans. In countries like the United States and the United Kingdom, the press includes publications and outlets that are economically and socially conservative, those that are professedly liberal, and many that endeavor to adopt a more balanced approach. At a minimum, press autonomy helps keep governments relatively honest. In countries where the press functions as an organ of government propaganda, officials and those with political connections can carry out their business, which is often at odds with the best interests of broader society, under the cover of darkness.

A robust institutional framework serves as the foundation for a well-functioning society. Whether other mechanisms can substitute for the checks and balances in a democracy remains an open question. Chinese government officials will tell you that the system's built-in incentives for demonstrating competence ensure that allegiance to and oversight by the Communist Party of China improve rather than blunt the effectiveness of government, with no need for further checks and balances. In many democracies, not least the United States, institutions ranging from the judiciary to the central bank to the press have suffered immense damage over the last decade. As a result, much of the world is either far from or drifting away from what was once considered a sound institutional framework, a shift that will ultimately affect not just individual nations but the global order as well.

The only excitement generated by elections in some parts of the world is in seeing how close to 100 percent support the winners will receive when votes are tallied. Russia's Vladimir Putin and North Korea's Kim Jong Un regularly rack up large majorities; the real questions are what emboldens the rest of the electorate, and what happens to them after they vote against their leaders. In 2014, Comrade Kim won a 100 percent victory in a North Korean election that had the nation "seething with election atmosphere," according to official reports, in which every registered elector voted, "except for those on foreign tour or working in oceans." To be fair, other elections are more competitive. When Putin won Russia's 2024 presidential election with 88 percent of the vote, his margin was only about 84 percentage points over his closest rival's share. Ebrahim Raisi's 2021 election as president of Iran was an even narrower squeaker of a victory, with his 62 percent share yielding a margin of barely 55 percentage points over his nearest opponent (who, incidentally, received fewer votes than "invalid votes," which largely consisted of Iranians turning in blank ballots to protest the lack of suitable candidates).

It is striking that even autocrats with a lock on power feel compelled to go through the motions of conducting exercises in democracy. Surely it is not to empower their populations, who no doubt resent being forced to vote for leaders who do not serve their interests. Is the charade meant for global consumption—to project an image of domestic political support and thereby gain greater credibility on the world stage? Perhaps staging elections gives autocrats a sense of superiority, allowing them to claim that they consistently have the support of most of their electorate, while their counterparts in Western democracies often eke out slim majorities and are at the mercy of their electorates every few years. Perhaps the behavior suggests that, despite the opprobrium directed at democracy, it remains the standard by which a political system's legitimacy is measured.

Democracies and the institutions that support them have in recent years seemed to lack resilience. Why are democracies fragile if, despite their flaws and occasional periods of turmoil, they remain the most effective form of political organization for meeting people's needs and aspirations? Perhaps the superiority of democracy over authoritarian regimes is a mirage rather than a durable reality, an assumption rather than an axiom. This leads to some deeper questions, ones we must revisit: What do people in modern societies aspire to, and how do they weigh differing objectives against one another?

Freedom, Accountability, and Legitimacy

Whatever the theoretical merits of various forms of political organization, it is ultimately the results that count. Using this yardstick yields some interesting perspectives when evaluating political systems.

There is impeccable logic behind the idea that economic progress and rising living standards will drive a growing thirst for intangible goods, such as genuine democracy—the power to choose leaders and hold them accountable—as well as freedoms of speech, association, and the practice of religion. After all, true fulfillment lies not in the pursuit of material ends, which can perhaps never be fully satisfied, but in a superior quality of life that goes beyond the merely corporeal. Yet there is little evidence that this idealized view has any basis in fact.

Consider one narrow but important aspect of freedom of expression: the liberty to call one's national leader a rank idiot, whether or not the statement is grounded in fact. This is a powerful freedom, one that cannot be taken for granted in many countries. In China, state-run media constantly extol the glories of the country and, particularly, its leader. One would be hard pressed to find a single statement suggesting that the great leader might be less than perfect in his actions or pronouncements. This is not to say that such sentiments are not expressed in online forums, chats among friends, or even on the sidelines of economic and financial conferences—or that Western media never fawn over their leaders. Many media outlets in the United States view Donald Trump as a savior who can do no wrong. But even Fox News sometimes takes him to task for not delivering on his promises—though usually because they believe that his immigration, economic, and social policies are insufficiently in line with right-wing desires.

Some of these freedoms are arguably priceless, yet they become part of a bargain that citizens seem prepared to accept. In truth, the public often appears quite willing to trade off such intangible benefits if they can be assured of greater economic prosperity and political stability. Ordinary people often put up little resistance when asked to give up a wide range of rights if they can be assured of essentials like safety and a decent standard of living. The degree of unstinting popular support for many leaders who come to power through democratic means but then hack away at the institutions that bolster democracy bears testament to this.

There are countries where public dissent is not altogether quashed but remains purely symbolic, as the political and economic elites combine forces to ensure that no viable threat emerges to challenge the stability of the system. In other countries, a stifling police state is seen as the price of safety and security.

It is remarkable to some observers, especially in Western societies, how untroubled people in other societies seem by this trade-off between rudimentary human liberties on one hand and economic well-being, public safety, and political stability on the other. As an entrepreneur in Shanghai once put it to me (using more colorful language), "All that people here want is to be left alone to pursue their ambitions to attain a decent standard of living and ensure the security and safety of their families. All businessmen want is to have the government off their backs and make money."

One evening a few years ago, a Chinese friend and I were on a postdinner jaunt on a crowded street just off the Shanghai Bund, the city's bustling financial district and a tourist magnet. As someone in the throng brushed against me, I instinctively cradled my phone to my chest, eliciting a chuckle from my friend. He said that one thing he was proud of as a Chinese citizen was that you could walk around any city in China at whatever time of day or night without worrying about your safety or that of your possessions. Whether this sentiment reflects reality or results from the effective suppression of news about crime is not entirely clear. There are certainly deterrents: In addition to the (de facto) lack of a presumption of innocence in the legal system, a criminal's entire family can in some cases suffer the burden of punishment. In ancient China, the notion of a "family penalty" was widespread, with an entire family subject to punishment or even execution if the crime was deemed serious enough, such as counterfeiting currency or rebelling against the emperor. That tradition persists to this day in somewhat weaker form, with the penalty taking the form of family stigma.

My friend, who was educated and had worked in the United States and generally espoused liberal values on most matters, acknowledged that his confidence in the absence of petty crime in China stemmed from the overwhelming presence of government surveillance. The unspoken subtext was that a police state does have its upsides. Admittedly, even I found it liberating to walk around without worrying about stumbling into the wrong neighborhood or being robbed—a fear I would have in practically any major US or European city. And it certainly is worth reflecting on whether the price of freedom justifies the risk of being robbed or, worse, shot with a firearm.

In July 2023, on my first post-COVID trip to China, I left Washington, DC, at a time when Canadian wildfires had befouled the air along the East Coast of the United States, creating dangerous, smog-like conditions in the capital. Much like the air in Beijing, I glumly thought to myself as I boarded my flight, recalling the smog that had been a pervasive feature of the city during my previous visits. Upon landing in Beijing, I was pleasantly surprised to behold clear skies and distant mountains, sights usually reserved for occasions like the Olympics or other major international events, when the government would shut down industrial activity around the city. Occasionally, weather conditions helped briefly clear the air. What was striking this time was that the clean air persisted through my stay.

Inquiring into this unexpected improvement, I learned that it was the result of concerted efforts by the Beijing government to clean up the air. These included relocating many polluting factories away from the city's vicinity and limiting gasoline-fueled vehicles on the road through alternate-day driving based on license plate numbers (the proliferation of electric vehicles has helped, too).

The contrast with the pollution in New Delhi, which has worsened by the year as central and local governments shy away from taking the needed drastic measures, was stark. On a trip to Delhi in the fall of 2023, my throat and eyes were irritated after a short walk outside my hotel, with the smog-filled air casting a pall even though it was a sunny day. Natural and human factors make things worse in the winter. Celebrations of the Hindu festival of Deepavali (or Diwali), which commemorates the mythical king Rama's victory over the evil Ravana, involve setting off firecrackers—not in an organized, central way but with every household lighting its own share.

This brings back fond memories of my youth. As Diwali season drew near, I'd spend my time at school not working on assigned math problems but carefully calculating how to optimize the total sonic output from the various firecrackers I could purchase with my allotted funds. I contemplated a wealth of options, each with varying degrees of auditory power—"atom bombs," "hydrogen bombs," red and green string firecrackers, and, most exciting of all, rockets, which were shot out of glass bottles and followed unpredictable trajectories, often veering off course and imperiling anyone in the vicinity.

For a time, my family lived in a complex consisting of sixteen apartments. My buddies and I competed to see who would be the first to set off a firecracker on Diwali morning. On one occasion, I beat the others by lighting one at four a.m. (Oddly, none of the neighbors ever complained about being subject to a loud blast at that ungodly hour.) The real action, fortunately, started at dawn. Other than the sheer volume from the explosion of a fearsome atom bomb, the best way to make the younger kids and girls squeal in terror was to light a firecracker's fuse while holding it, and then throw it in the air at the last possible instant so it would explode midflight. Not for the faint of heart, though I did survive such foolhardiness with my limbs intact.

You can well imagine how the firecrackers become a major source of pollution, with practically every family participating in the joyous Diwali celebrations. This would be true in any city, of course, but the cold air of Delhi causes the smoke to settle in. And it is only made worse by farmers in adjoining states who burn their fields as an economical way to clear detritus from their fall planting in preparation for spring crops. The government apparently lacked the gumption to take on the farmers, a powerful lobby, or to compel Hindus, who form the backbone of support for the Modi government, to celebrate Diwali in a more environmentally friendly fashion.

So the people of Delhi, the capital of the fifth-largest economy in the world and an aspiring major world power, suffer. While air quality readings are especially awful in the winter months, they are appalling year round. The poor breathe in the pollutants all the time. The well-off have air conditioners, air filters, and purifiers, but they too can hardly escape the foul air altogether. It is well documented that numerous health problems and shorter lifespans are the consequence. And yet, remarkably, the people don't rise up against a government that is failing them.

The citizens of India are hardly unique in this regard. People in the United States have become inured to gun-related fatalities, even those that affect children. Many public schools in the country have metal detectors and armed officers for security, with places of education turned into fortresses. In her high school years, my younger daughter, like other children around the country, regularly experienced the trauma of live-shooter drills. And yet, most of us parents blithely go about our lives, hoping desperately that our kids' school will not be the scene of the next tragedy, without rising up en masse against the spineless politicians who stubbornly oppose even the mildest gun control measures and put our precious children at risk for their own petty ends.

In principle, democracy holds elected officials accountable to their citizens. But the structure of some democracies—particularly the way election districts, procedures, and rules are set up—can lead to outcomes that do not reflect the views of the majority. In the United States, there have been multiple instances where a president is elected by winning a majority of the electoral college votes, despite failing to secure a majority of the votes cast by ordinary citizens. Legislation often serves the interests of a narrow group of people or businesses with outsize influence, gained through financial contributions to key members of Congress. Thus, for all its virtues, representative democracy does not always deliver the accountability and outcomes that citizens expect from a system designed to respond to their desires and promote their interests.

Autocrats, by contrast and at least in principle, are less beholden to special interests because they do not need to spend money on reelection campaigns. Even a despot interested mainly in self-preservation can see the benefits of a system that generates economic success and maintains social stability. Indeed, there is a strong incentive for a despot to behave benevolently and focus on longer-term objectives, unlike a politician in a democracy, who must cater to constituents' immediate interests. The shorter time frames driven by the election cycle might push the politician to advocate for policies that are less conducive to achieving better long-term outcomes.

This is by no means an argument for the superiority of autocratic forms of government. Rather, it is a cri de coeur to restore the institutional frameworks, including those of democracy itself, that are necessary for a republic to thrive. These frameworks are essential to ensure that outcomes align with the majority's interests while protecting the rights of minorities on any given issue. Otherwise, the ideal of democracy will continue to shrivel.

Open and democratic governments build trust by sharing bad news, even if they would rather focus on the good news or, at a minimum, put a positive spin on all news. In contrast, many authoritarian governments adopt the tack that it is best for the populace not to be given bad news. While this tactic becomes harder to sustain in the internet age, access to online information can still be restricted in many ways.

China, in particular, has made concerted attempts to control the flow of unflattering information. The government regularly suppresses or limits the availability of official data that paints the economy or the country in a negative light. When fertility rates recently started falling, raising concerns about a shrinking labor force, the government stopped releasing those data. When youth unemployment surged in 2023, the government discontinued publishing those figures as well. It later began releasing revised unemployment data, presenting supposed "improvements" that showed lower youth unemployment rates, but those numbers are seen as less credible (even though the methodology for gathering the data has in fact been improved in some ways). Other data, such as measures of consumer confidence and financial market performance, have also been subject to blackouts.

Of course, every government tries to put a positive spin on economic data. Still, wiping out unfavorable statistics, coupled with censorship and repression of negative sentiment, hardly inspires confidence. In fact, it can cast doubt even on seemingly good news. When Chinese Premier Li Qiang announced at the World Economic Forum summit in Davos in January 2024 that China's economy had exceeded its 5 percent growth target for 2023—despite mounting concerns about the state of the economy—the claim was (rightly) met with skepticism.

Such skepticism toward official narratives of current events is unfortunately no longer unique to countries with nondemocratic governments, and with good reason. Andreas Georgiou, who was the head of the Greek statistical agency during 2010–2015 (and is a former IMF colleague of mine), was criminally charged by the Greek government and convicted of slander and breach of duty—for having had the temerity to expose the government's misrepresentations in budget data provided to the European Union. The Trump administration's gutting of the US federal government, which has slashed funding and staffing at statistical agencies, will inevitably undermine the reliability of and trust in US economic data, once considered the gold standard for the rest of the world.

In theory, the freer flow of information in open societies, combined with the presence of trusted arbiters to assess the quality of that information, allows for a better-informed citizenry. But that principle has given way to a harsher reality: The challenges posed by disinformation and misinformation are in some ways even greater in open societies, as we saw in the chapter on technology.

Countries like India and the United States, with long traditions of press freedom, have not been spared from direct government attacks, led by leaders such as Modi and Trump, against media sources critical of official policies. Trump's invocation of "fake news" whenever confronted with evidence of his lies or policy missteps proved surprisingly effective in undercutting the credibility of media sources holding him to account, while his own credibility suffered little among his followers. Thus, in short order, the proliferation of online and nontraditional sources of information—amplified by social media—has led to fragmentation of the information landscape and the decay of trust in traditional media. This, in turn, has contributed to the erosion of confidence in an array of institutions once seen as pillars of liberal democracy.

In November 2016, the Modi government sent shockwaves through the Indian economy and society. With no advance notice, it imposed a surprise overnight demonetization—wiping out the value of high-denomination banknotes—as a strike against corruption and the black market economy. These banknotes were seen as key facilitators of illegitimate activities, although they also played a significant role in legitimate commerce. The move unleashed chaos in an economy that was still largely cash-driven, hurting economic growth.

My family and I landed in India a few weeks later on vacation. At the upscale hotels where we stayed, we had the privilege of exchanging foreign currency for the equivalent of 500 rupees (roughly $7) per day in cash. Others had a much harder time getting their hands on cash for daily transactions. The less well-off, most of whom had no bank accounts, suffered far more than those who did. Surely this should have caused huge political blowback against Modi, especially among the poor.

Hardly. Most of my friends and family members in India supported Modi's move, even as they freely criticized the lack of preparation. It took the central bank, which had also been caught off guard, several months to circulate enough new currency. Perhaps the people in my circles were well off and less dependent on cash than most Indians. Yet remarkably, over the two weeks I was there, every cab driver we encountered in several cities had only praise for Modi. More than one mentioned that their families back in their villages were struggling even more with the disruption. Still, they lauded "Modi Sir" for his bold strike against corruption.

This bombshell of demonetization landed in India on the same day as another bolt from the blue halfway across the globe: the election of Donald Trump as US president. As I tried to understand and process the convulsions that hit both the United States and India that fateful day in November 2016—and which continue to reverberate—one unifying thread came into sharp focus. How could so many decent people hold their noses and vote for Trump? And how could so many poor and middle-class people in India accept such a big disruption to their daily lives and yet sing Modi's praises?

What we were hearing on two continents was, perhaps in part, a loud and piercing cry of frustration against endemic corruption. Trump and Modi heard that cry and responded, and large swaths of the public embraced them. In India, the masses seemed to finally have hope that the government was willing to tackle corruption head-on by wiping out some of the ill-gotten wealth of corrupt elites. Ordinary citizens were willing to overlook the enormous temporary difficulties in their day-to-day lives because Modi had given them hope that a cancer bedeviling their existence would be cut out.

In the United States, how could a man who bragged about paying no federal income taxes for many years and "brilliantly" using tax loopholes to enrich himself possibly sell himself as a credible corruption fighter? Trump benefited from the public's perception that economic and political elites need not break laws to enrich themselves; they simply modify or bend the rules to their advantage, as Trump himself did. Even without overt or blatant corruption, these elites walk away with most of the benefits flowing from globalization, technological change, and other disruptive forces hitting economies worldwide. Trump's message—that the only fix was to blow up the system rather than relying on the elites to reform a system they thrive on—resonated with many voters. Although Trump profited from the system, which should have eroded his credibility on the issue, even a minuscule possibility of drastic change based on his rhetoric was apparently more attractive to many Americans than the alternative, where they saw no significant change on the horizon.

Even President Xi Jinping of China, less constrained by the need to respond to an electorate, has drawn enormous popular support with his anticorruption campaign. Xi's slogan of taking on corrupt "tigers and flies"—high-ranking officials and low-level bureaucrats—seems to have resonated well with the public. His approach had an added political edge: He mostly targeted tigers, including a few powerful provincial bosses who were not closely allied with him.

One of Xi's most prominent takedowns was of Bo Xilai, a powerful and charismatic politician who had gained prominence as the party chief of Chongqing city and a member of the Politburo, the group of top officials who oversee the government. Bo was arrested in 2012 and eventually sentenced to life in prison following his conviction on charges of embezzlement, taking bribes, and abuse of power in an attempt to stifle criminal allegations against his wife. This tawdry affair was seen mainly as an unmistakable signal that any senior party official with an independent power base and questionable loyalty to Xi needed to be on guard. Still, the notion that even powerful officials were not immune to corruption charges restrained the avarice of the "flies" and even "ants"—lower-level party cadres—and emboldened ordinary people to call out petty corruption.

Modi, by contrast, took a hammer to the wealth of the corrupt in every political party, including his own. Postmortems of Modi's demonetization scheme paint it as a fiasco, not just in terms of the economic disruption it caused, but also due to the lack of follow-through to change the incentives that foster corruption, especially the intrusive role of the state in most aspects of the economy. The move mostly affected unsophisticated corrupt officials—those who collected their payoffs in envelopes or bagfuls of cash—rather than the more sophisticated ones who had stashed their ill-gotten wealth in offshore bank accounts.

For all its evident flaws, though, Modi's gambit was a political masterstroke. Once the dust settled, he had garnered more credibility to push forward with economic reforms. He could plausibly argue that he had the common man's interests in mind, rather than just those of the powerful, when he proposed those reforms. Similarly, Trump's rhetorical approach to taking on the establishments of both parties (draining the swamp!) clearly resonated with a broad swath of voters in the United States, notwithstanding Trump's own blatant corruptibility. Even Xi's bare-knuckled approach seems to have played well in the Chinese hinterlands, though his motives might have had more to do with cementing his hold over the Communist Party of China apparatus than with actually tackling corruption.

Democracies that simply institutionalize corruption through the legislative process can lose legitimacy. Throwing out the bastards every four or five years through the ballot box certainly has a cathartic effect. But the sense that all this does is bring in a new set of bastards while leaving the game stacked in favor of the economic and political elites has severely disruptive consequences, as has become apparent around the world in what were once vibrant democracies. This trend has not only highlighted the inherently unstable dynamics of democracies but has also given a leg up to alternative forms of government.

Promoting a Vision

The battle for supremacy between competing visions of economic, social, and political organization is being waged on multiple fronts, with differing tactics employed by the combatants. Leading by example has traditionally been an effective way to promote a particular vision of the economic and political system,

demonstrating that a specific combination is optimal for delivering economic progress and social stability. Increasingly,
though, the key players are taking an activist approach, propa-
gating their visions while attempting to disguise their flaws. The
American approach is essentially built on the belief in American exceptionalism—We know what is good for you and for the
world. The Chinese approach is different—We will not preach to
you, but we will give you money and other forms of support on
our terms if you buy into our vision. With China's economic and
military prowess catching up to those of the United States, the
battle lines have become more clearly drawn.

Rather than facing a clear set of choices, each with its own advantages, the rest of the world is confronted with highly muddled,
mediocre options. The systems epitomized by each of the two
leading powers have been beset by turmoil as their internal flaws
and inconsistencies rise to the surface. Thus, rather than providing stable anchors, each system is fomenting both internal and
global instability, while the competition between them is proving
more destructive than constructive. The two systems seem locked
in a race to the bottom, characterized by less open and democratic
governments, the erosion of the rule of law, and greater government involvement in the economy. The consequence has been the
loss of a lodestar for well-intentioned citizens and leaders, as the
ideal of free-market liberal democracy crumbles, dragging the stability of the world order down with it.

Is a resolution to what seems like an inexorable slide into chaos
possible? There is an answer—one that has undergirded human
progress and, in the past, brought stability and prosperity to society. The solution lies in halting the decay of, and reinforcing, domestic and global institutions. Accomplishing this will take bold,
principled leaders and engaged citizens. The solution is clear, but
the path to attaining it is not.

8

Reclaiming Order from Disorder

The animal is both prey and a guide.... The hunter who follows the animal, keeping his eye on one single point, fails to notice he is venturing into the unknown. This is how discovery is made: by following the call of another being that is constantly escaping, remaining always in view, but can never be reached. Whereas that which is discovered is already around, already behind—and is almost no longer visible.

—Roberto Calasso, *The Celestial Hunter*

The contours of the world economic and financial order are being reshaped by a variety of forces, including national policies, technological developments, and political cycles. Economic, political, and geopolitical factors are fueling a doom loop, breeding turmoil rather than stability, disarray rather than order. Each of these factors—including the more even distribution of economic might, the restructuring of multilateral organizations, the ascendance of middle powers, the formation of new alliances, and technological advances—has both stabilizing and destabilizing implications.

It is not foreordained that negative currents will dominate, but breaking out of the doom loop will take herculean effort. Despite perceptions that humanity is being swept along by forces beyond its control, leaders, policymakers, and ordinary citizens can—and should—play active roles in shaping how these forces are created and play out.

The outcomes will depend in large part on how well institutional guardrails—checks and balances, the rule of law, a free press—function at both the national and global levels. On this score, we have reason to be concerned. The weakening of national institutions has gone hand in hand with the warping of democracy, while the erosion of the global institutional framework has generated destructive competition between countries and fomented greater instability in international relations.

The combination of free markets, globalization, and democracy has proven vulnerable to perversion by power-grabbing business and political elites. This mix has turned toxic in many countries, leaving significant portions of their populations feeling disenfranchised and excluded from opportunities for economic advancement, and rendering them vulnerable to the siren songs of false prophets.

The fraying of institutions has facilitated the ascendance of self-proclaimed populists, who ostensibly protect the interests of common citizens while actually undermining them. Some of these mercenary politicians are adept at eliciting the powerful emotion of fear, especially of the other (immigrants, foreign governments), to perpetuate their own power at the cost of stoking and deepening social and political schisms. And it is these very rabble-rousers upon whose shoulders would fall the unenviable task of rejuvenating national and global institutions. They are clearly loath to take on this responsibility, preferring instead to grind down institutions that expose their fallacies and check their power.

Sliding down this path toward a world wracked by conflict and instability seems unavoidable. In fact, though, none of it is inevitable. It will take extraordinary determination to reverse this downward spiral and reinvigorate institutions to keep destructive demagogues out of power, or at least to check their power, and to harness all the good that humanity is capable of. And it will take enlightened leaders as well as concerted efforts from each of us, as citizens of our countries and of the world, to counterbalance the various malign forces in our societies and to fashion a harmonious and prosperous future.

The Uncertain Arc of History

Nations and civilizations have historically experienced cycles in which an existing order becomes fragile and eventually gives way to a new one that promises greater stability and less conflict. In 1992, on the heels of the dissolution of the Soviet Union, the political scientist Francis Fukuyama boldly proclaimed the "end of history." It appeared that Western liberal democracy had triumphed decisively in the Cold War and would foster a durable new world order. That hope has been dashed.

We can no longer cling to the consoling but implausible belief that the tumult around us simply reflects a temporary rocky phase in a transition from chaos to stability, with fragmentation of the world order eventually giving way to cohesion. The outcome is particularly uncertain as the world economy is simultaneously gripped by forces that promote equalization—emerging-market countries are growing and catching up to the more affluent, advanced economies—and those that exacerbate inequality, with many poorer countries receding even further into the margins of the world economy while rising inequality fuels dissatisfaction within many countries.

Persistent imbalances, especially the narrowing but still large gap in per capita incomes between emerging-market and advanced economies, have frustrated efforts to find cooperative solutions to issues such as climate change. This lack of cooperation further destabilizes global relations as the areas of conflict between established and rising powers expand and as the global institutional framework frays from the pressures it faces from all sides, eroding its effectiveness, legitimacy, and relevance.

Chronicles of many ancient civilizations reveal a recurring pattern: Extreme concentrations of wealth and power among elites typically lead to collapse, with regeneration far from assured. When economic and political systems are captured by elites to the detriment of the broader population, they eventually come apart. The rot sets in from within and is difficult to reverse, largely because those responsible for the rot have every incentive to preserve the status quo. We see evidence of this pattern in the two major powers vying for global supremacy. Both the United States and China are exhibiting versions of these inauspicious dynamics, heightening insularity and hypernationalism while diminishing their willingness to seek cooperative solutions.

Is there a natural arc of history that will eventually bend toward greater global cohesion? One would hope so—even in relatively normal times but particularly when humanity faces a major calamity. An encouraging example surfaced during the 2007–2009 financial crisis, when the G20—a disparate group of countries, as we have seen—came together at a moment when the global financial system teetered on the brink and the world economy was at risk of devastation. The collective response—printing more money and ramping up government spending—was perhaps not the heaviest lift. Nevertheless, the will to act in concert may have helped, at least marginally, to reassure consumers and businesses that governments (and central banks) were working to fix things—and not at cross-purposes.

Whether this spirit of cooperation can be reinvigorated in the face of today's looming crises—or whether crisis will result from its very absence—is the question of the hour. Changes in the worldwide distribution of economic power, particularly China's emergence as a major player, have so far generated conflict rather than cohesion. Factors that should promote stability, including the benefits to be gained from economic collaboration, have been overwhelmed by the perception that every dimension of the quest for global power is a zero-sum game.

The promise of the G20 and the complications it has faced in recent years stand as metaphors for both the importance of global cooperation and the difficulties that make it so elusive. Against the background of raging geopolitical tensions and a world economy beleaguered by immense challenges, such groups need to find common ground, at least on issues where interests clearly align. Doing so would bolster efforts to address longer-term challenges like climate change and short-term imperatives such as debt restructuring for highly indebted low-income countries, whose long-suffering populations subsist at the margins of survival. Swirling questions about the cohesion and potency of the G20—amid elevated economic and geopolitical tensions between advanced and emerging-market economies, and even between some countries within each group—highlight the trials facing such coalitions.

Democracy and Free Markets

In March 2024, South Korea proudly hosted the Third Summit for Democracy, a high-profile international event whose main theme was preserving democracy for future generations. Nine months later, South Korean President Yoon Suk Yeol declared martial law, suspending civil rights and limiting the powers of courts and government agencies. This was a stunning development in a country viewed as having shaken off a troubled past and, in recent decades, having built strong democratic institutions, ones thought to be unshakable despite deep political divides in Korean society. Two weeks after martial law was imposed, it was rescinded, and the president was impeached with support from members of his own party. In short, the institutions held and the corrective mechanisms worked.

There was, of course, an even more prominent test of a country's institutions at the beginning of the decade. The insurrection that took place in Washington, DC, on January 6, 2021, pushed the US institutional framework disconcertingly close to a breaking point. This stain on American democracy was instigated by then-President Donald Trump, who actively sought to thwart the peaceful transfer of power to his successor, Joe Biden. In that moment, long-standing and seemingly unshakable institutions were nearly subverted, with many senior members of the Republican Party condoning the attempt. It has become painfully obvious that even once-robust democracies can see their own leaders erode the foundations of their institutions from within. Trump's reelection in 2024 demonstrates that such actions can bear minimal political cost, even in a country once held up as the paragon of democracy and institutional strength. Trump's second term has already damaged core American institutions, especially the rule of law, to an extent that will be difficult to fix.

These two instances highlight the fragility of representative democracy. Such frailness is puzzling, especially if one views this political system as the product of a long period of experimentation and evolution. After all, democracies have an intrinsic advantage in being directly responsive to the needs of their citizens. Democracy provides a check on the power of leaders, enables course corrections when needed, and gives citizens a voice in determining their own futures and those of their societies. There have been far too many examples in recent years, though, of democracies being subverted and the institutions supporting them proving brittle. The combination of representative democracy and unchecked market forces has clearly failed to deliver on citizens' aspirations for feasible paths to economic prosperity and security from both domestic and external strife.

Still, no realistic substitute exists for free markets as a system for channeling resources effectively to maximize productivity and overall economic welfare. This creates a conundrum for which market forces provide no easy solution. Income and wealth inequality inevitably arise in a system that thrives on entrepreneurial activity, risk-taking, and innovation. Yet it is not these measures of inequality but the lack of opportunities for economic mobility that frustrates those who feel left behind. Their alienation is worsened by the widespread perception that the costs and benefits of the constant churn in firms, industries, and entire sectors—essential for keeping economies dynamic—are distributed unfairly.

Globalization, for example, wiped out textile and toy manufacturing in the United States while workers in high-tech sectors prospered—changes that on the whole were good for American consumers and the country's economic growth. However, the costs of disruptions accompanying such changes in economic structure tend to fall most heavily on those least able to bear the burden, while the benefits go to those who are already privileged, particularly corporate executives and, more broadly, well-educated and highly skilled workers. A system that creates winners and losers is not intrinsically bad, unless the losers have no safety net to catch them when they fall and, worse still, feel they have no realistic path to achieving, or regaining, economic security.

These weaknesses in the dominant paradigm of market-oriented liberal democracies mattered less when no viable alternative was in sight. In the 1990s, it seemed that with some marginal fixes, this paradigm would become pervasive, set the standard for all countries, and dominate the world order. That vision did not last.

China's remarkable rise as an economic power has seemingly refuted the premise that democracy, free markets, and strong institutions are essential for rapid economic progress. One could argue (and many have) that China has found workarounds—for instance, a meritocratic system that rewards government officials for competency and keeps them accountable to citizens—allowing it to adopt the best elements of democracy while discarding those it finds less savory. Similarly, state-led capitalism might keep the undesirable aspects of free markets at bay while providing room for private enterprise to flourish.

For much of China's recent ascendance, it has been a compelling proposition that the country's apparent strength masks underlying fragility, a comforting notion for true believers in economic and political orthodoxy. It is not hard, after all, to point to the many deficiencies and risks in the growth model that delivered such success (and many have done so). Still, China's exceptional economic achievements have led many countries to view its economic and political models as a reasonable alternative.

When I headed the IMF's China division in the early 2000s, a fascinating period when China was opening up parts of its economy to the world, my team's annual reports on the country highlighted a range of risks, including high levels of local government and corporate debt, a decrepit banking system, and excessive reliance on state-owned companies and their wasteful investments to propel growth. Each report sagely concluded that China could get by that year and perhaps the next without any of these issues crashing the economy. But without substantive reforms to tackle the problems head-on, and with the risks therefore ballooning over time, economic disaster was in the cards. To this day, IMF and other organizations' reports on China express similar sentiments. Time and again, the day of reckoning has seemed imminent, but the government has managed to navigate the economy away from disaster, even when it was at the threshold.

Now, finally, the China model seems to have hit its limits (perhaps!). Various problems in the Chinese economy have come to a head in the post-COVID period, with slowing growth exposing intrinsic weaknesses that were successfully papered over during the previous three decades of high growth. A shrinking labor force and an inefficient financial system have fueled growing concerns about the economy's long-term prospects. The property market, once a mainstay of the economy, is unraveling, with overbuilding and diminished government support causing prices to tumble. Of greatest consequence, the rigid political and institutional structure seems to be eroding the long-standing confidence of Chinese households and private entrepreneurs in the government's ability to address these challenges. In short, cracks are becoming visible in the model, reducing its attractiveness to other countries that are considering how to orient their own economies and political systems.

The failures of various political and economic models in their present forms leave countries bereft of aspirational goals and instead exert a gravitational pull, drawing them toward the lowest common denominator. This could lead to a hybrid of the less desirable features of each model, propelling a downward spiral toward lower standards. Resisting this pull and aiming for higher standards across political and economic dimensions will require much greater effort in many areas.

Principles for a Better World

The world is a far different place now than it was at the beginning of the millennium. History would have taken a different turn if European integration, especially the eurozone project that was initiated in 1999, had succeeded in fostering economic and political cohesiveness among its members and ushering in a surge of dynamism. The United States would now face a rival equal in economic might and grounded in similar values. Instead, Europe has floundered, and China, a nation that embraces few Western values, has risen to become the United States' main economic, geopolitical, and military rival. These changes are just the leading edge of broader, dramatic shifts in the locus of economic and other forms of power.

Various groups of countries must adjust to the realities of a shifting and unsettled world order. Advanced economies can no longer count on having their way in global affairs or on the unquestioned supremacy of their economic and political structures. China and many other emerging-market countries, meanwhile, are hitting the limits of their nondemocratic political arrangements and state-dominated economies. Resolving the tensions between these competing models seems to call for both cooperation and constructive competition.

An important hurdle for countries and their leaders is the need to separate issues on which they share interests from those that inherently spur conflict, so that cooperation on the former does not fall victim to tensions and disputes over the latter. On issues such as tackling climate change and improving the workings of globalization, the major powers ought to align their goals, even if their strategies for addressing these problems differ markedly. Of course, in the Trump era, some issues, such as climate change, will hardly take center stage, but even in this period not all avenues of collaboration are automatically shut off.

China and the United States, in particular, should find ways to separate the mutually beneficial aspects of their relationship from those, such as the quest for regional hegemony, in which they unavoidably compete head to head. They must recognize that allowing conflicts in some areas to overwhelm their policy agendas risks turning positive-sum games like trade into negative-sum outcomes that damage both their economies and the world at large.

Grand bargains are out of fashion, but they might have to be revived to reconcile competing considerations, not only the tensions between short-term and long-term interests within countries, but also the divergent aims between countries. For example, every country, and the world as a whole, would benefit from pursuing international trade and financial integration. Yet these gains can be subverted if the inevitable costs and disruptions fall disproportionately on some segments of society, particularly less-skilled workers and lower-income households. Democracies, most of all, need to buffer households from these burdens or risk trading off long-term societal gains for the illusory benefits of short-term job stability. Trump's use of tariffs, supposedly to protect American jobs from unfair foreign competition, illustrates such misguided policies—ones that will ultimately hurt the US economy in both subtle and direct ways.

Similarly, globalization will not work well if some countries violate the rules governing cross-border trade by erecting import barriers or using subsidies to give their industries an unfair competitive advantage in domestic and international markets. Both the United States and China have adopted variants of these practices, subverting trade in the process. The Trump administration's aggressive use of tariffs and its disengagement from the World Trade Organization—a reaction to China's abuse of the organization's rules—undermine an institution and a set of rules that benefited both countries.

Navigating these impediments will necessitate greater trust—both between governments and between citizens and their governments—along with mechanisms to bolster that trust. The institutions responsible for designing and maintaining these mechanisms must adapt to new realities and support a rapidly shifting world order. For instance, multilateral financial institutions like the IMF should not impose harsh terms on small countries seeking assistance while applying different standards to wealthier economies like Greece or large ones like Argentina. If the IMF rails against China's nonmarket policies, it must criticize with equal force the protectionism and undisciplined fiscal and monetary policies of the United States and other advanced economies.

Moreover, the IMF and World Bank cannot maintain their legitimacy in a world where economic power is shifting rapidly to emerging-market countries while these institutions remain bound by historical structures and dominated by advanced economies. These and other global institutions are clearly in need of reform. It will take foresight and courage for advanced countries to cede some of their legacy power and for emerging-market countries to show that they will wield their new power responsibly.

Middle powers such as India and Indonesia find themselves in a challenging position amid great-power competition, yet they must not retreat into their shells or shirk their responsibility to play a constructive role on the global stage. Attempts to shield their economies from geopolitical turbulence by remaining neutral in some cases while pursuing narrow, short-term interests in others may seem like a winning strategy. But this approach will not promote global economic and geopolitical stability, which is essential for their own prosperity.

The Role of the State

With the archetype of liberal, free-market-oriented democracies under threat, the distinctions between alternative forms of economic and political organization are becoming blurrier, with important consequences for the structure of the world order. At a basic level, this distinction reflects the role the state plays in any economy. Direct government intervention hinders the operation of free markets, but so does the lack of effective oversight needed to ensure fair competition and to restrain corporate actions that improve profitability at the expense of the greater good. Striking the right balance is essential but poses a perennial challenge, particularly in areas of rapidly evolving technological innovation like digital currencies and AI. The solution is not the withdrawal of the state from the economy, but rather a more nuanced approach to how and where it plays an active role.

Governments must be involved with, but not interfere in, the functioning of markets. In practice, this means regulators should avoid picking sides between firms or technologies, leaving that to market forces. But they must establish transparent and clear legal frameworks that allow firms to operate in a stable and predictable environment. If Google provides a better search engine than Microsoft or Yahoo, it should not be restrained from expanding its market share. But if Google uses its market power to shut down rivals or undercut them through nefarious means, then the government should step in. Governments have a crucial role in harnessing and managing new technologies for the broader benefit of humanity, ensuring that these advancements serve the common good rather than benefiting specific groups or countries at the expense of others. They must leave space for innovation and the risks that come with it, while limiting the broader fallout from such risks, particularly for economically vulnerable households.

Governments must be efficient in providing services but also show heart by ensuring an adequate safety net for households facing economic hardship due to disruptions such as job losses, catastrophic health events, or extreme weather. Governments can use technology to better support their most vulnerable citizens, thereby garnering public support for their policies. Mobile phone–based financial technologies can give even low-income households easy access to digital payments and basic banking services to manage their financial affairs. Expanding financial access helps citizens become more integrally connected to their country's economic success, making it easier for them to accept the short-term disruptions caused by reforms that bring long-term societal benefits.

Policy actions taken by governments often have far-reaching consequences, and even the best intentions can go awry. When a system is beset by multiple problems, trying to fix one in isolation can sometimes result in worse outcomes. An interesting example comes from China, where the government and financial regulators in recent years have sought to reduce their frequent direct involvement in stock markets, whether to prop up prices or cool off excessive speculation, depending on the circumstances. The official mantra is that markets should be left alone to find the right prices for stocks, even if that means more severe price volatility. However, reforms designed to improve corporate governance, beef up auditing and accounting procedures, and encourage greater corporate transparency have not kept pace with those intentions. As a result, the Chinese stock market often resembles a casino rather than a vibrant marketplace for trading financial assets.

The solution is not a return to government intervention, but the harder work of building a regulatory and institutional framework that allows markets to function well.

Course corrections in response to changing circumstances and policy errors are inescapable in any economy, no matter its size or complexity and no matter how competent and farsighted its public officials. Such flexibility is a hallmark of a government that is accountable to its people—through both the ballot box and the more immediate feedback provided by a free press—and that has the capability to reshape and adjust policies.

A government that is not seen as accountable and nimble has two choices. It can enhance its capacities in both areas by plugging gaps in the institutional framework. Alternatively, it can tighten its grip by stifling accountability and feedback mechanisms. For obvious reasons, the latter approach is highly tempting, especially because it improves the odds of short-term survival for the government that adopts it. This approach, however, makes a government more rigid and therefore more brittle.

As countries become increasingly interconnected, developments that affect a single nation's fortunes cannot be addressed in isolation. Financial and technological developments, which are rapidly transforming our lives even as they pose enormous risks to the economic and social fabric, are a primary case in point.

Technology can play a positive role in expanding resources and reducing the potential for conflict, both within and between countries. However, trusting technology to police itself can lead to destructive outcomes. For instance, despite its promise of democratizing finance, the blockchain technology behind Bitcoin has mainly facilitated financial speculation and illicit commerce. On the flip side, other cryptocurrencies, such as stablecoins, are improving the speed and lowering the cost of both domestic and cross-border payments, benefiting consumers, small businesses, and economic migrants sending remittances to their home countries. Similarly, although AI poses risks to entire job categories and could cause massive disruptions in labor markets, it can also enhance human life in many ways big and small, from improving traffic flow to creating new medicines.

A cooperative approach and a willingness to abide by a common set of rules are indispensable for enjoying the fruits of technological change while limiting its adverse effects. Cryptocurrencies and AI know no borders, and no country can realistically expect to wall itself off from their effects. But it cannot be just the largest and most financially sophisticated economies at the table, with their needs being the main focus when international rules are written. Coordinated regulation needs to account for cross-country differences in regulatory expertise and the varying risks countries face, recognizing that smaller and less-developed countries are highly vulnerable to disruption.

These arguments highlight the critical role that strong institutional frameworks can play in fostering an environment where governments can effectively carry out their duties, maintain the trust of citizens and businesses, and promote constructive international cooperation.

Institutions Rule—or Ought To

Robust institutions form the bedrock of democracies and a salutary world order. Both domestic and international institutions need to be revamped—and in some cases rebuilt—to ensure their legitimacy and credibility. This requires setting high standards of inclusion, fairness, consistency, and transparency in the formulation and enforcement of rules. Putting these high-minded ideals into practice is a demanding task, especially in a world where practically every institution of democracy and global governance is under attack.

Consider one of the critical elements of any country's institutional framework: a judiciary that provides consistent interpretations of laws and acts as an independent branch of government, keeping the powers of the other branches in check. This is essential for economic prosperity and social stability. In most democracies, judges are appointed by elected representatives, which keeps courts accountable to the public, even if indirectly, but also exposes them to the wrath of leaders who chafe at restraints on their power. The perception that judges, even at the apex of the judicial system, interpret laws based on personal political views rather than the intent and spirit of those laws has eroded the legitimacy of this critical branch of government—even in countries like the United States, not to mention fledgling democracies.

Similarly, long-term stability depends on a free press to uncover the missteps and malfeasance of government officials, which can harm the citizens they are sworn to serve. The power of the free press has been weakened rather than fortified by the combination of free speech and technology. Social media platforms, which have given a megaphone to purveyors of misinformation and disinformation, along with attacks from public officials who want to elude accountability, have eroded trust in traditional news outlets and wiped out common agreement on facts. Conspiracy theories can now spread widely and rapidly, not only undermining trust in governments and official agencies but even impeding their ability to function at critical times. After Hurricane Helene in September 2024, the US Federal Emergency Management Agency had to pause its relief work due to threats against its employees; a few residents in the affected areas had bought into long-standing rumors that the agency was confiscating supplies meant for hurricane victims, setting up internment camps, and prioritizing help for nonwhite people.

Governments faced with the torrent of misleading information spread through social media will find it difficult to choke off channels that compete with more reliable information sources. AI adds to the challenge of distinguishing fact from fiction—or worse, from distorted versions of reality that appear plausible and are therefore especially pernicious. Government efforts to constrain the flow of information, even if propagated by demonstrably ill-intentioned actors who should rightfully be reined in, will only stoke distrust.

The answer, unsatisfactory as it seems, calls for governments to become more transparent, explaining their policies in ways that resonate with citizens, and acknowledging and correcting the defects that emerge in both policy design and implementation. Trust is built, slowly but surely, only through greater openness about both successes and failures, and by communicating a clear sense of direction and purpose in policymaking.

The forces impairing domestic institutions are also corroding the structures of global governance established by the United States and other Western nations after World War II. These institutions, and their authority to set and enforce rules of the game, are especially important for smaller and less powerful countries, which are otherwise buffeted by a lack of predictable guidelines for engaging with others. The crisis of legitimacy extends beyond the IMF and World Bank. Other institutions, including the United Nations and the World Trade Organization, are also becoming weaker amid growing recognition that powerful countries often use them to advance their own interests and ignore commonly accepted rules when it is inconvenient to follow those rules. Demagogues have successfully blamed these institutions for domestic economic woes and social instability, claiming they do not represent the interests of common citizens. The result has been rising hostility toward and disengagement from these institutions at the urging of such politicians.

In short, the institutional frameworks that support well-functioning democracies and a stable global order are being undermined by a confluence of malevolent forces. Perhaps the most corrosive of these is the widespread perception that, in their present form, domestic and international institutions are managed by and primarily serve the interests of privileged individuals and countries.

Civic Engagement and Leadership

Clearly, many daunting challenges need to be acknowledged and addressed before the institutional framework—and with it the social fabric—deteriorates to a point where it can no longer be patched up or reinforced, making collapse unavoidable.

A starting point for any remedy is the recognition that the average citizen in every country desires and deserves, above all, a stable and safe society with realistic prospects for a decent standard of living and equal opportunity. In a world that is increasingly interconnected, achieving this requires greater cooperation, even between countries. An unstable world wracked by conflict serves no one, particularly when each country faces enormous internal challenges that can only be confronted through collaborative effort.

What is the path to more fruitful cooperation and better outcomes for humankind? The answer has many parts, but at its root lies the power of common citizens: to demand positive change, elect leaders who share that vision, and strengthen institutions, both domestic and global, that foster collegiality over conflict.

Citizens must demand leadership that delivers on these goals and repudiate leaders who, wielding disinformation and division as their tools, prey on our fears and baser instincts. We must strive to put in power leaders committed to long-term improvements in people's lives and capable of managing the difficult transitions away from economic, political, and legal systems that have outlived their usefulness. Choices made by governments and politicians are ultimately driven by the will of the people. While it may be unfair to blame citizens for the bad choices of their leaders, there is no excuse for failing to hold those leaders to account. In troubling times, democracy demands more than casting a vote on Election Day (as essential as that is). It is the engagement and eternal vigilance of citizens that ultimately determine the contours of domestic and international policies.

The world needs more compelling visions—both for countries and for humanity at large—that speak to common needs and aspirations. Personalities matter, and it is clear that many populist and authoritarian leaders find traction because their messages resonate in a world rife with uncertainty and turmoil. It will take informed, courageous, and inspiring leaders to craft narratives that appeal to the hopes of citizens rather than stoke their fears and darker impulses.

Effective leaders must also help citizens, who may prioritize security and immediate economic concerns, recognize where their deeper interests lie. It is difficult, for instance, to ask a country's citizens to support military activities—even if they are intended to block territorial aggression elsewhere or prop up democracies—if those citizens do not agree that their immediate safety and security are at stake, particularly if they believe that their basic needs will suffer when financial and other resources are redirected to the battlefield.

In the United States, the isolationist wing of the Republican Party, which was loath to support Ukraine's defense against Russian incursion, has gained significant public support. The facile narrative that the money and armaments given to Ukraine drained US resources without delivering tangible returns began to prevail against what ought to have been the more compelling imperative of maintaining a stable world order in the face of brazen aggression by an authoritarian leader. Similarly, the Trump administration's hostility toward the US Agency for International Development was driven by an unwillingness to recognize that the agency's disbursements saved untold lives at minimal cost and generated goodwill toward the United States in many corners of the world. In the hands of demagogues, the use of taxpayers' money, expressed in concrete numbers, stands little chance of being justified to the public if the payoffs are unclear, in the distant future, or difficult to quantify.

Visionary leaders must convince their citizens that their policies can align short-term and long-term objectives, as well as domestic and global interests, and that any trade-offs bringing disruption and costs are transitory and worth the overall benefits. In other words, leaders need to inspire and lead their constituents rather than pander to their fears. Acknowledging citizens' fears about change and disruption, however, and developing plans to mitigate the ill effects are part of the process of building trust.

Not only government leaders but also business and community leaders must play crucial roles in this process. To be successful, leaders of major corporations are tasked with balancing the needs of shareholders, customers, employees, and other stakeholders. The sensitivity of stock market returns to quarterly or annual earnings can cause executives to emphasize short-term considerations, particularly if their compensation structures and job security hinge on stock prices. This setup can diminish their willingness to take a longer view on business decisions.

Corporate executives must recognize—and act on—their broader societal and political responsibilities, for they have the power to effect significant change. They can promote progress by influencing politicians to implement policies that generate more equitable economic outcomes and to build bridges with other countries rather than tear them down. Support for such policies need not be driven purely by altruism; it requires the foresight to see that corporations themselves would ultimately benefit. Economic and geopolitical stability, after all, are good for business; they not only reduce risk in the production and distribution of goods and services but also encourage consumers to spend more freely.

Community leaders—including local elected officials, heads of community organizations and advocacy groups, even educators and religious leaders—can play useful roles in building and maintaining connections among members, despite differences in economic status, social outlooks, and political leanings. Building empathy and a sense of shared interests can also help promote civic engagement, a key driver of change. It is our obligation as citizens to actively engage with the political process not only at the local and national levels but also within our communities, no matter their size. Doing so takes effort, both to become better informed and to put the broader interests of the community and nation above our narrow individual concerns. This requires not so much a sacrifice as it does a better understanding of how our personal interests are in fact congruent with those of our communities and the world at large.

Leaders come and go, economic power waxes and wanes, and alliances form and splinter. Strong institutional frameworks, at the levels of individual communities, nations, and the global stage, are essential for maintaining stability and prosperity through these cycles. We must enshrine core principles like fairness, transparency, and flexibility as foundational elements to ensure that our institutions retain legitimacy among all members, while evolving, adapting, and staying relevant amid changing circumstances.

None of this will be easy. Yet we have little choice but to rise to the challenge, because the stakes, for ourselves and the generations to come, are far too high. To secure a better future, one where order rather than chaos reigns, we must break out of the doom loop rather than allow it to become our destiny.

Acknowledgments

I received helpful comments on various drafts of this book's material from Brahima Coulibaly, Eric Helleiner, Harold James, Marek Kamiński, Peter Katzenstein, Jonathan Kirshner, Sarah Kreps, Nicholas Mulder, Victor Nee, Thomas Pepinsky, Raghuram Rajan, Rachel Beatty Riedl, Meg Rithmire, Aditi Sahasrabuddhe, JP Schutte, Melanie Sisson, Jessica Chen Weiss, and Ethan Wu. I benefited from presentations of early drafts of portions of the material at a lecture at Boston University, a book workshop at the Einaudi Center at Cornell University, and a seminar at the Brookings Institution. I am particularly grateful to Glenn Altschuler for his detailed comments on and edits of some key parts of the text.

Cornell University and the Brookings Institution have been extraordinarily supportive of my work over the years, and I am grateful to both institutions for this support. I have benefited enormously from my distinguished colleagues at both Cornell and Brookings, who have been generous with their time and insights. Many of my colleagues who are not explicitly acknowledged here have played important roles in shaping my thinking on the topics covered in this book.

I am grateful to a band of excellent and dedicated research assistants who helped with background research, fact-checking, and editing: Vidya Balaji, Sharan Banerjee, Justin Black, Felipe De Bolle, Ava Lee, Joanne Lee, Micere Mugweru, Karen Petrosyan, Jay Philbrick, Yuvika Prasad, Caroline Smiltneks, and Ethan Wang. William Barnett edited the text and, as usual, not only fixed my syntax but also improved how I formulated many ideas. Kelley Blewster's edits substantially enhanced the quality of my prose, rendering it clearer and more accessible. Melissa Veronesi ably shepherded the book through various stages of production.

I am indebted to Emily Taber, my editor at Hachette, who saw promise in an inchoate proposal and provided invaluable guidance and advice that helped shape what had been a great many words expressing disparate ideas into a book with a coherent theme.

This book is dedicated to the memories of my beloved canine companion, Mozart, who kept me company on many long walks, and Roberto Calasso, whose writing I have long cherished and admired. My wonderful daughters, Berenika and Yuvika, keep me grounded and make it all worthwhile. And now it is Argos, my new puppy, who keeps me on my toes.

This book would not exist without the confidence boost my wife and soulmate, Basia, provided when, hesitantly, I first floated a (far less coherent) idea for a book, and her constant encouragement as I labored over the actual writing of it. She read and critiqued multiple drafts of the manuscript and has declared this book more readable than any of my previous efforts, generously noting that I seem to be getting better at this. That is the best endorsement I could hope for.

Bibliography

Acemoglu, Daron, and Simon Johnson. 2023. *Power and Progress: Our Thousand-Year Struggle over Technology and Prosperity.* London: Basic Books.

Acemoglu, Daron, and James A. Robinson. 2013. *Why Nations Fail: The Origins of Power, Prosperity, and Poverty.* New York: Crown Currency.

Agarwal, Isha, Wentong Chen, and Eswar Prasad. 2024. "Beyond the Fundamentals: How Media-Driven Narratives Influence Cross-Border Capital Flows." NBER Working Paper 33159.

Agrawal, Ajay, Joshua Gans, and Avi Goldfarb. 2018. *Prediction Machines: The Simple Economics of Artificial Intelligence.* Boston: Harvard Business Review Press.

Alfaro, Laura, and Davin Chor. 2023. "Global Supply Chains: The Looming 'Great Reallocation.'" NBER Working Paper 31661.

Allison, Graham T. 2017. *Destined for War: Can America and China Escape Thucydides's Trap?* Boston: Houghton Mifflin Harcourt.

Autor, David. 2024. "Applying AI to Rebuild Middle Class Jobs." NBER Working Paper 32140.

Autor, David H., David Dorn, and Gordon H. Hanson. 2016. "The China Shock: Learning from Labor-Market Adjustment to Large Changes in Trade." *Annual Review of Economics* 8: 205–40.

Azhar, Azeem. 2021. *The Exponential Age: How Accelerating Technology Is Transforming Business, Politics, and Society.* New York: Diversion Books.

Beltran, Daniel O., Maxwell Kretchmer, Jaime Marquez, and Charles P. Thomas. 2012. "Foreign Holdings of U.S. Treasuries and U.S. Treasury Yields." Unpublished manuscript. Washington, DC: Board of Governors of the Federal Reserve System.

Bergsten, C. Fred. 2022. *The United States Versus China: The Quest for Global Economic Leadership.* Cambridge, UK: Polity Press.

Bernanke, Ben S. 2017. *The Courage to Act: A Memoir of a Crisis and Its Aftermath.* New York: Norton.

Blinder, Alan S. 2018. *Advice and Dissent: Why America Suffers When Economics and Politics Collide*. New York: Basic Books.

Blustein, Paul. 2025. *King Dollar: The Past and Future of the World's Dominant Currency*. New Haven, CT: Yale University Press.

Bremmer, Ian. 2023. *The Power of Crisis: How Three Threats—and Our Response—Will Change the World*. New York: Simon and Schuster.

Bremmer, Ian. 2018. *Us vs. Them: The Failure of Globalism*. New York: Portfolio Penguin.

Brooks, Stephen G., and William C. Wohlforth. 2023. "The Myth of Multipolarity." *Foreign Affairs*, April 18.

Brunnermeier, Markus K., Harold James, and Jean-Pierre Landau. 2016. *The Euro and the Battle of Ideas*. Princeton, NJ: Princeton University Press.

Calasso, Roberto. 2010. *Ardor*. Translated by Richard Dixon. 2014. New York: Farrar, Straus and Giroux.

Calasso, Roberto. 2016. *The Celestial Hunter*. Translated by Richard Dixon. 2020. New York: Farrar, Straus and Giroux.

Camus, Albert. 1992 [1951]. *The Rebel: An Essay on Man in Revolt*. Translated by Anthony Bower. New York: Vintage.

Cassidy, John. 2025. *Capitalism and Its Critics*. New York: Farrar, Straus and Giroux.

Clausing, Kimberly A. 2019. *Open: The Progressive Case for Free Trade, Immigration, and Global Capital*. Cambridge, MA: Harvard University Press.

Condon, Bradly J. 2010. "Lost in Translation: Plurilingual Interpretation of WTO Law." *Journal of International Dispute Settlement* 1 (1): 191–216.

Dalio, Ray. 2021. *Principles for Dealing with the Changing World Order: Why Nations Succeed or Fail*. New York: Simon and Schuster.

DeLong, James Bradford. 2022. *Slouching Towards Utopia: An Economic History of the Twentieth Century*. New York: Basic Books.

Deming, David J., Christopher Ong, and Lawrence H. Summers. 2025. "Technological Disruption in the Labor Market." NBER Working Paper 33323.

Doepke, Matthias, Anne Hannusch, Fabian Kindermann, and Michèle Tertilt. 2022. "The Economics of Fertility: A New Era." NBER Working Paper 29948.

Economy, Elizabeth C. 2022. *The World According to China*. Cambridge, UK: Polity Press.

Eichengreen, Barry J. 2011. *Exorbitant Privilege: The Rise and Fall of the Dollar*. Oxford, UK: Oxford University Press.

Eichengreen, Barry, Arnaud Mehl, and Livia Chiţu. 2017. *How Global Currencies Work: Past, Present, and Future*. Princeton, NJ: Princeton University Press.

El-Erian, Mohamed A. 2017. *The Only Game in Town: Central Banks, Instability, and Avoiding the Next Collapse*. New York: Random House.

Fukuyama, Francis. 1992. *The End of History and the Last Man*. New York: Free Press.

Gamble, John King, and Charlotte Ku. 1993. "Choice of Language in Bilateral Treaties: Fifty Years of Changing State Practice." *Indiana International and Comparative Law Review* 3 (2): 233–64.

Goldberg, Pinelopi K., and Tristan Reed. 2023. "Is the Global Economy Deglobalizing? If So, Why? And What Is Next?" *Brookings Papers on Economic Activity* (Spring): 347–96.

Gourinchas, Pierre-Olivier, and Hélène Rey. 2007. "From World Banker to World Venture Capitalist: U.S. External Adjustment and the Exorbitant Privilege." In *G7 Current Account Imbalances: Sustainability and Adjustment*, edited by Richard H. Clarida. Chicago: University of Chicago Press.

Grabel, Ilene. 2022. "Post-American Moments in Contemporary Global Financial Governance." In Katzenstein and Kirshner, *The Downfall of the American Order?*

Grabel, Ilene. 2018. *When Things Don't Fall Apart: Global Financial Governance and Developmental Finance in an Age of Productive Incoherence*. Cambridge, MA: MIT Press.

Haass, Richard. 2021. *The World: A Brief Introduction*. New York: Penguin Books.

Helleiner, Eric. 2021. *The Neomercantilists: A Global Intellectual History*. Ithaca, NY: Cornell University Press.

Helleiner, Eric. 2014. *The Status Quo Crisis: Global Financial Governance After the 2008 Meltdown*. Oxford, UK: Oxford University Press.

Helleiner, Eric, and Jonathan Kirshner, eds. 2009. *The Future of the Dollar*. Ithaca, NY: Cornell University Press.

Hesse, Hermann. 2007. *Siddhartha: An Indian Poem*. Translated by Susan Bernofsky. New York: Modern Library.

Hill, Fiona. 2021. *There Is Nothing for You Here: Finding Opportunity in the Twenty-First Century*. New York, NY: Mariner Books.

Hirschman, Albert O. 1971. *A Bias for Hope: Essays on Development and Latin America*. New Haven, CT: Yale University Press.

Hirschman, Albert O. 2013 [1971]. "Political Economics and Possibilism." In *The Essential Hirschman*, edited by Jeremy Adelman. Princeton, NJ: Princeton University Press.

Jaishankar, Subrahmanyam. 2020. *The India Way: Strategies for an Uncertain World*. Gurugram, India: HarperCollins Publishers India.

James, Harold. 2014. *Making the European Monetary Union*. Cambridge, MA: Harvard University Press.

James, Harold. 2023. *Seven Crashes: The Economic Crises That Shaped Globalization*. New Haven, CT: Yale University Press.

Jin, Keyu. 2023. *The New China Playbook: Beyond Socialism and Capitalism*. New York: Viking.

Katzenstein, Peter J. 2026. *Entanglements in World Politics: The Power of Uncertainty*. Cambridge, UK: Cambridge University Press.

Katzenstein, Peter J., and Jonathan Kirshner, eds. 2022. *The Downfall of the American Order?* Ithaca, NY: Cornell University Press.

Katzenstein, Peter J., and Lucia A. Seybert. 2018. *Protean Power: Exploring the Uncertain and Unexpected in World Politics*. Cambridge, UK: Cambridge University Press.

Kennedy, Paul M. 1989. *The Rise and Fall of the Great Powers: Economic Change and Military Conflict from 1500 to 2000*. New York: Random House.

Kindleberger, Charles P. 1981. "Dominance and Leadership in the International Economy: Exploitation, Public Goods, and Free Rides." *International Studies Quarterly* 25 (2): 242–54.

Kirshner, Jonathan. 2014. *American Power After the Financial Crisis*. Ithaca, NY: Cornell University Press.

Kirshner, Jonathan. 2022. *An Unwritten Future: Realism and Uncertainty in World Politics*. Princeton, NJ: Princeton University Press.

Kissinger, Henry A. 2012. *On China*. New York: Penguin Press.

Kissinger, Henry A., Eric Schmidt, and Daniel P. Huttenlocher. 2021. *The Age of AI: And Our Human Future*. Boston: Little, Brown and Company.

Kose, Ayhan M., Eswar S. Prasad, Kenneth Rogoff, and Shang-Jin Wei. 2006. "Financial Globalization, A Reappraisal." *International Monetary Fund Staff Papers* 56 (1): 8–62.

Kose, Ayhan M., Eswar S. Prasad, and Ashley D. Taylor. 2011. "Thresholds in the Process of International Financial Integration." *Journal of International Money and Finance* 30 (1): 147–79.

Kreps, Sarah. 2025. *Tech Titans: Navigating the Policy Landscape from Nuclear Weapons to Artificial Intelligence*. Oxford, UK: Oxford University Press.

Ku, Hyejin, and Asaf Zussman. 2010. "Lingua Franca: The Role of English in International Trade." *Journal of Economic Behavior and Organization* 75 (2): 250–60.

Landes, David S. 1999. *The Wealth and Poverty of Nations: Why Some Are So Rich and Some So Poor*. New York: Norton.

Lee, Kai-Fu. 2018. *AI Superpowers: China, Silicon Valley and the New World Order*. Boston: Houghton Mifflin Harcourt.

Leonhardt, David. 2023. *Ours Was the Shining Future: The Story of the American Dream*. New York: Random House.

Levitsky, Steven, and Daniel Ziblatt. 2018. *How Democracies Die*. New York: Penguin Random House.

Li, David Daokui. 2024. *China's World View: Demystifying China to Prevent Global Conflict*. New York: Norton.

Luce, Edward. 2017. *The Retreat of Western Liberalism*. New York: Atlantic Monthly Press.

Mahbubani, Kishore. 2022. *Has China Won? The Chinese Challenge to American Primacy*. New York: PublicAffairs.

Mohsin, Saleha. 2024. *Paper Soldiers: How the Weaponization of the Dollar Changed the World Order*. New York: Portfolio Penguin.

Mulder, Nicholas. 2022. *The Economic Weapon: The Rise of Sanctions as a Tool of Modern War*. New Haven, CT: Yale University Press.

Nash, Ogden. 1995. *Selected Poetry of Ogden Nash*. New York: Black Dog and Leventhal.

North, Douglass C. 1991. "Institutions." *Journal of Economic Perspectives* 5 (1): 97–112.

North, Douglass C., and Robert Paul Thomas. 1973. *The Rise of the Western World: A New Economic History*. Cambridge, UK: Cambridge University Press.

Nye, Joseph S. 2015. *Is the American Century Over?* Cambridge, UK: Polity Press.

Nye, Joseph S. 2004. *Soft Power: The Means to Success in World Politics*. New York: PublicAffairs.

O'Neil, Shannon K. 2022. *Globalization Myth: Why Regions Matter*. New Haven, CT: Yale University Press.

O'Neill, Barry, and Bezalel Peleg. 2000. "Reconciling Power and Equality in International Organizations: A Voting Method from Rabbi Krochmal of Kremsier." *Jewish Political Studies Review* 12: 67–81.

Paulson, Henry M. 2016. *Dealing with China: An Insider Unmasks the New Economic Superpower*. New York: Twelve.

Pearson, Margaret M., Meg Rithmire, and Kellee Tsai. 2023. *The State and Capitalism in China*. Cambridge, UK: Cambridge University Press.

Pepinsky, Thomas, and Jessica Chen Weiss. 2021. "Washington Should Avoid Ideological Competition with Beijing." *Foreign Affairs*, June 11.

Pirsig, Robert M. 1975. *Zen and the Art of Motorcycle Maintenance: An Inquiry into Values*. New York: Bantam Books.

Posner, Eric A., and Alan O. Sykes. 2014. "Voting Rules in International Organizations." University of Chicago, Public Law Working Paper No. 458.

Pottinger, Matt, and Mike Gallagher. 2024. "No Substitute for Victory." *Foreign Affairs*, April 10.

Prasad, Eswar S. 2014. *The Dollar Trap: How the U.S. Dollar Tightened Its Grip on Global Finance*. Princeton, NJ: Princeton University Press.

Prasad, Eswar S. 2021. *The Future of Money: How the Digital Revolution Is Transforming Currencies and Finance*. Cambridge, MA: Belknap Press of Harvard University Press.

Prasad, Eswar S. 2016. *Gaining Currency: The Rise of the Renminbi*. New York: Oxford University Press.

Prasad, Eswar S. 2023. "Has China's Growth Gone from Miracle to Malady?" *Brookings Papers on Economic Activity* 1: 243–70.

Prasad, Eswar S. 2024. "Top Dollar: Why the Dominance of America's Currency Is Harder than Ever to Overturn." *Foreign Affairs*, June 18.

Pritchett, Lant, and Lawrence H. Summers. 2014. "Asiaphoria Meets Regression to the Mean." NBER Working Paper 20573.

Pushkin, Alexander. 1995. *Eugene Onegin: A Novel in Verse*. Translated by James E. Falen. Oxford, UK: Oxford University Press.

Quah, Danny. 2024. "Economic Principles for a New World Order of Multipolarity and Multilateralism." Unpublished manuscript, National University of Singapore.

Rachman, Gideon. 2022. *The Age of the Strongman: How the Cult of the Leader Threatens Democracy Around the World*. New York: Other Press.

Rajan, Raghuram G. 2010. *Fault Lines: How Hidden Fractures Still Threaten the World Economy*. Princeton, NJ: Princeton University Press.

Rajan, Raghuram G. 2020. *The Third Pillar: How Markets and the State Leave the Community Behind*. New York: Penguin Books.

Rajan, Raghuram, and Rohit Lamba. 2024. *Breaking the Mold: India's Untraveled Path to Prosperity*. Princeton, NJ: Princeton University Press.

Rajan, Raghuram G., and Luigi Zingales. 2004. *Saving Capitalism from the Capitalists: Unleashing the Power of Financial Markets to Create Wealth and Spread Opportunity*. Princeton, NJ: Princeton University Press.

Reinhart, Carmen, and Kenneth Rogoff. 2011. *This Time Is Different: Eight Centuries of Financial Folly*. Princeton, NJ: Princeton University Press.

Riedl, Rachel Beatty, Paul Friesen, Jennifer McCoy, and Kenneth Roberts. 2025. "Democratic Backsliding, Resilience, and Resistance." *World Politics* 1: 151–78.

Riedl, Rachel Beatty, Dan Slater, Joseph Wong, and Daniel Ziblatt. 2020. "Authoritarian-Led Democratization." *Annual Review of Political Science* 23: 315–32.

Rithmire, Meg. 2023. *Precarious Ties: Business and the State in Authoritarian Asia*. Oxford, UK: Oxford University Press.

Roach, Stephen. 2022. *Accidental Conflict: America, China, and the Clash of False Narratives*. New Haven, CT: Yale University Press.

Roberts, Anthea, and Nicolas Lamp. 2021. *Six Faces of Globalization: Who Wins, Who Loses, and Why It Matters.* Cambridge, MA: Harvard University Press.

Rodrik, Dani. 2012. *The Globalization Paradox: Democracy and the Future of the World Economy.* New York: Norton.

Rogoff, Kenneth. 2025. *Our Dollar, Your Problem: An Insider's View of Seven Turbulent Decades of Global Finance, and the Road Ahead.* New Haven, CT: Yale University Press.

Roubini, Nouriel. 2022. *Megathreats: Ten Dangerous Trends That Imperil Our Future, and How to Survive Them.* New York: Little, Brown and Company.

Rubin, Robert E. 2023. *The Yellow Pad: Making Better Decisions in an Uncertain World.* New York: Penguin.

Rushdie, Salman. 2023. *Victory City.* New York: Random House.

Sanger, David E., and Mary K. Brooks. 2024. *New Cold Wars: China's Rise, Russia's Invasion, and America's Struggle to Defend the West.* New York: Penguin Books.

Sen, Amartya. 1981. *Poverty and Famines: An Essay on Entitlement and Deprivation.* Oxford, UK: Oxford University Press.

Shambaugh, David. 2025. *Breaking the Engagement: How China Won and Lost America.* Oxford, UK: Oxford University Press.

Sisson, Melanie W. 2024. *The United States, China, and the Competition for Control.* Abingdon, UK: Routledge.

Slaughter, Anne-Marie. 2005. *A New World Order.* Princeton, NJ: Princeton University Press.

Smith, Gary. 2018. *The AI Delusion.* Oxford, UK: Oxford University Press.

Solzhenitsyn, Aleksandr. 1975. "Words of Warning to America." *Imprimis*, September.

Tavlas, George. 1991. "On the International Use of Currencies: The Case of the Deutsche Mark." *Essays in International Finance*, March.

Tegmark, Max. 2017. *Life 3.0: Being Human in the Age of Artificial Intelligence.* New York: Knopf.

Tooze, Adam. 2021. *Shutdown: How Covid Shook the World's Economy.* New York: Viking.

Tucker, Paul. 2022. *Global Discord: Values and Power in a Fractured World Order.* Princeton, NJ: Princeton University Press.

Vidal, Gore. 2002. *The Decline and Fall of the American Empire.* Tucson, AZ: Odonian Press.

Wallace, Jeremy L. 2022. *Seeking Truth and Hiding Facts: Information, Ideology, and Authoritarianism in China.* New York: Oxford University Press.

Weiss, Jessica Chen. 2022. "The China Trap: U.S. Foreign Policy and the Perilous Logic of Zero-Sum Competition." *Foreign Affairs*, August 18.

Wohlforth, William C. 1999. "The Stability of a Unipolar World." *International Security* 24 (1): 5–41.

Wolf, Martin. 2023. *The Crisis of Democratic Capitalism.* New York: Penguin Press.

Wolf, Martin. 2015. *The Shifts and the Shocks: What We've Learned—and Have Still to Learn from the Financial Crisis.* London: Penguin Books.

Zakaria, Fareed. 2025. *Age of Revolutions: Progress and Backlash from 1600 to the Present.* New York: Norton.

Notes

Introduction: Disorder

The epigraph comes from Calasso, *Ardor*, 27.

For a timeline of the dissolution of the Soviet Union, see "The Collapse of the Soviet Union," The Office of the Historian, US Department of State, accessed March 2025, https://history.state.gov/milestones/1989-1992/collapse-soviet-union. The calculations in this section are based on national and world GDP, all measured in US dollars at market exchange rates, taken from the World Bank's World Development Indicators database, accessed June 2025, https://datatopics.worldbank.org/world-development-indicators/.

For a summary of the effects of China's WTO accession on its economy and that of the United States, see "What Happened When China Joined the WTO?" Council on Foreign Relations, last updated February 6, 2025, https://education.cfr.org/learn/reading/what-happened-when-china-joined-wto#.

Dimensions of Power

The per capita income comparison is based on data from the IMF DataMapper, accessed June 2025, www.imf.org/external/datamapper/NGDPDPC@WEO/USA?zoom=USA&highlight=USA.

Data on greenhouse gas emissions can be found at J. Friedrich, M. Ge, A. Pickens, and L. Vigna, "Interactive Chart," World Resources Institute, last updated March 2, 2023, www.wri.org/insights/interactive-chart-shows-changes-worlds-top-10-emitters; and "GHG Emissions of All World Countries," European Commission, 2023 report, https://edgar.jrc.ec.europa.eu/report_2023#emissions_table.

New Technologies: Panacea or Peril?

The discussion in this section draws on Prasad, *The Future of Money*.

1. Dimensions of Power

This exchange from *Game of Thrones* takes place in the first episode of season two, "The North Remembers." A clip can be found on YouTube, accessed April 5, 2025, www.youtube.com/watch?v=zdRJybJ047I.

Data on GDP (total and per capita; at market and PPP exchange rates) come from the IMF's World Economic Outlook database, accessed June 2025, www.imf.org /en/Publications/SPROLLs/world-economic-outlook-databases.

Even using PPP exchange rates, the average per capita income of middle-income countries is about one-quarter that of high-income countries. Data on per capita GDP at PPP exchange rates is available at the World Bank's Open Data portal: https://data.worldbank.org/indicator/NY.GDP.PCAP.PP.CD. In 2022, the average annual per capita incomes (in US dollars, based on PPP exchange rates) for various country groups were as follows: high income 62,231; middle income 15,407; low income 2,314; sub-Saharan Africa 4,639.

Data on greenhouse gas emissions come from J. Friedrich, M. Ge, A. Pickens, and L. Vigna, "Interactive Chart," World Resources Institute, last updated March 2, 2023, www.wri.org/insights/interactive-chart-shows-changes-worlds-top-10-emitters.

Economic Power

Details about the International Comparison Program methodology and data on purchasing power parities is available at World Bank's programs page, accessed March 2025, www.worldbank.org/en/programs/icp. Information regarding the PPP exchange rates is available at OECD's data explainer webpage, accessed March 2025, www.oecd.org/en/data/insights/data-explainers/2024/06/purchasing-power -parities---frequently-asked-questions-faqs.html.

Renminbi to US dollar spot exchange-rate data are available at Federal Reserve Economic Data (FRED): https://fred.stlouisfed.org/series/EXCHUS. Calculations are based on monthly exchange rates (averages of daily exchange rates) in December 2000 and December 2024.

For data on export shares, see UN Trade and Development webpage, accessed March 2025, https://unctad.org/topic/trade-analysis/chart-10-may-2021. See also OECD's Trade in Value-Added (TiVa) database, accessed March 2025, www.oecd.org /en/topics/sub-issues/trade-in-value-added.html. Data on countries' shares of global manufacturing are derived from World Population Review, accessed March 2025, https://worldpopulationreview.com/country-rankings/manufacturing-by-country.

For evidence on the negative correlation between income levels and fertility, see G. Vandenbroucke, "The Link Between Fertility and Income," Federal Reserve Bank of St. Louis, December 13, 2016, www.stlouisfed.org/on-the-economy/2016/decccm ber/link-fertility-income. Doepke et al., "Economics of Fertility," find that this correlation is less evident in recent years and argue that government and social policies can affect the correlation. The replacement rate is defined at "Fertility rates," OECD, accessed March 2025, https://data.oecd.org/pop/fertility-rates.htm.

Data on global fertility rates is available at the World Bank's Open Data portal, accessed February 2025, https://data.worldbank.org/indicator/SP.DYN.TFRT.IN.

Also see Valentina Romei, "Falling Birth Rates Raise Prospect of Sharp Decline in Living Standards," *Financial Times*, January 15, 2025.

See FRED, accessed March 2025, https://fred.stlouisfed.org/series/LFWA64TTJPM647S for data on Japan's working-age population. For estimates of China's labor force, see the World Bank's Open Data portal, accessed March 2025, https://data.worldbank.org/indicator/SL.TLF.TOTL.IN?locations=CN; and the data available on Statista, accessed March 2025, www.statista.com/statistics/282134/china-labor-force/.

US population and migration data are from the US Census Bureau, accessed February 2025, www.census.gov/data/tables/time-series/demo/popest/2010s-state-total.html; and A. Knapp, "Net Migration Between the U.S. and Abroad," US Census Bureau, December 30, 2019, www.census.gov/library/stories/2019/12/net-international-migration-projected-to-fall-lowest-levels-this-decade.html, respectively. For data on the foreign-born labor force in the United States, see "Immigration Is Surging, with Big Economic Consequences," *The Economist*, April 30, 2024; and data from the Bureau of Labor Statistics, accessed March 2025, www.bls.gov/news.release/pdf/forbrn.pdf. China's net migration rate is shown at the World Bank's Open Data portal, accessed March 2025, https://data.worldbank.org/indicator/SM.POP.NETM?locations=CN.

For data on the ratio of beneficiaries to the labor force, see the Social Security Administration History webpage, accessed March 2025, www.ssa.gov/history/ratios.html.

The statement from the Forty-Eighth Meeting of the IMFC by the representative of Saudi Arabia, Finance Minister Mohammed Aljadaan, is available at the IMF's Annual Meetings webpage, accessed March 2025, https://meetings.imf.org/en/2023/Annual/Statements.

US energy independence is shown in "Is the US Energy Independent?," USAFacts, last updated May 14, 2023, https://usafacts.org/articles/is-the-us-energy-independent/.

For more information on rare earth minerals, see Bradley Van Gosen, Philip Verplanck, Keith Long, Joseph Gambogi, and Robert Seal, *The Rare-Earth Elements: Vital to Modern Technologies and Lifestyles* (US Geological Survey, 2014), https://pubs.usgs.gov/publication/fs20143078.

Countries with substantial rare earth reserves are listed at M. Pistilli, "Rare Earth Reserves: Top 8 Countries," Nasdaq, February 5, 2025, www.nasdaq.com/articles/rare-earths-reserves-top-8-countries. For data on the share of China's control over rare earth minerals and its processing capacity, see G. Baskaran, "Could Africa Replace China as the World's Source of Rare Earth Elements?," Brookings Institution, December 29, 2022, www.brookings.edu/articles/could-africa-replace-china-as-the-worlds-source-of-rare-earth-elements/. For data on America's reliance on mineral imports, China's export restrictions on critical minerals, and Biden's tariffs, see "Geopolitical Perspectives: Critical Minerals," J. P. Morgan Strategy Research, June 10, 2024, https://markets.jpmorgan.com/research/email/scx/7g02dsml/Xi02ErEa7aRyHiJAylXX6A/GPS-4717568-0.

For discussions about Africa's mineral wealth, see Baskaran, "Could Africa Replace China?"; Dorina A. Bekoe, Sarah A. Daly, Stephanie M. Burchard, Sydney N. Deatherage, and Erin L. Sindle, *Rare Earth Elements in Africa: Implications for U.S. National and Economic Security* (Institute for Defense Analyses, 2022), https://apps.dtic

.mil/sti/trecms/pdf/AD1204908.pdf; and UNEP's webpage regarding their work in Africa, accessed March 2025, www.unep.org/regions/africa/our-work-africa.

For data on the DRC's wealth of resources and conflict minerals, see Oluwole Ojewale, *Mining and Illicit Trading of Coltan in the Democratic Republic of Congo* (ENACT, 2022), https://enact-africa.s3.amazonaws.com/site/uploads/2022-05-03 -research-paper-29-rev.pdf.

For more details on the resource curse and possible explanations, see Natural Resource Governance Institute, *The Resource Curse* (2015), https://resourcegovernance .org/sites/default/files/nrgi_Resource-Curse.pdf. For Kaunda's quote, see M. L. Ross, "The Political Economy of the Resource Curse," *World Politics* (January 1999), https:// tinyurl.com/bdf8repj; and World Bank, *What Would It Take for Zambia's Copper Mining Industry to Achieve Its Potential* (2011), https://openknowledge.worldbank.org /server/api/core/bitstreams/2357f133-5123-57f6-9ef4-eb08b908583b/content.

For more on Guyana's growth and inflation, see Gaiutra Bahadur, "Is Guyana's Oil a Blessing or a Curse?," *New York Times*, March 30, 2024.

Military Muscle

For data on military expenditures and cross-country comparisons, see the World Bank's Open Data portal, accessed March 2025, https://data.worldbank.org /indicator/MS.MIL.XPND.CD; SIPRI Military Expenditure Database at https:// milex.sipri.org/sipri; and "The United States Spends More on Defense than the Next 9 Countries Combined," Peterson Foundation, last updated April 22, 2024, www.pgpf.org/blog/2024/04/the-united-states-spends-more-on-defense-than-the -next-9-countries-combined. China's military budget for 2024 is reported in Clement Tan, "China Boosts Military Spending," CNBC, March 4, 2024. For PPP exchange rates, see the IMF DataMapper, accessed March 2025, www.imf.org/external /datamapper/PPPEX@WEO/OEMDC/ADVEC/WEOWORLD/TWN.

For an inventory of estimated global nuclear warheads, see K. Davenport, "Nuclear Weapons: Who Has What at a Glance," Arms Control Association, January 2025, www.armscontrol.org/factsheets/Nuclearweaponswhohaswhat. Also see John O'Sullivan and Oli Smith, "Map Shows All Countries with Nuclear Weapons as Iran Attack 'Minutes Away,'" *Irish Star*, April 16, 2024.

Intangible Power

The "only game in town" reference comes from El-Erian, *The Only Game in Town*. For reporting on political attacks on the Indian and Brazilian central banks' leaderships, see Amy Kazmin and Simon Mundy, "India's Central Bank Governor Urjit Patel Resigns Amid Tense Stand-Off," *Financial Times*, December 10, 2018; and Bryan Harris, "Brazil's Ruling Workers' Party Seeks to Gag Central Bank Chief," *Financial Times*, June 19, 2024, respectively.

For more information about how the People's Bank of China operates under strict oversight by the State Council, see Cheng Leng and Sun Yu, "China Sidelines Its Once Venerated Central Bank," *Financial Times*, December 25, 2023. For a discussion of

China's lack of judicial independence, see J. A. Cohen, "'Rule of Law' with Chinese Characteristics: Evolution and Manipulation," *International Journal of Constitutional Law* (September 2021), https://academic.oup.com/icon/article/19/5/1882/6365813; and the report about the events of 2023 in China by Human Rights Watch, accessed March 2025, www.hrw.org/world-report/2024/country-chapters/china.

On the topic of uncertainty, see Katzenstein and Seybert, *Protean Power*; and Katzenstein, *Entanglements*. See Kirshner, *Unwritten Future*, for related work.

For an estimate of BTS's economic impact, see Yu Young Jin, "BTS Ponders Its Future, and South Korea's Economy Warily Takes Note," *New York Times*, June 17, 2022. For data on Korea's cultural content exports, see K. Hyelin, "Content Sector," Korea.net, January 5, 2023, www.korea.net/NewsFocus/Culture/view?arti cleId=226990. For more on measuring the impact of the Korean wave, see Jimmyn Parc, *Measuring the Impact of Hallyu on Korea's Economy* (Korea Economic Institute of America, 2021), https://keia.org/wp-content/uploads/2021/10/KEI_Koreas -Economy_2021_211019_Parc_2.pdf.

Data about the world's most spoken languages, based on estimates for 2025, come from "What Is the Most Spoken Language?," Ethnologue, www.ethnologue.com /insights/most-spoken-language/.

See Gamble and Ku, "Choice of Language," and Condon, "Lost in Translation," on the subject of treaties; and Ku and Zussman, "Lingua Franca," on the relationship between adoption of English as the lingua franca and trading volumes.

Agarwal, Chen, and Prasad, "Beyond the Fundamentals," show that media narratives affect institutional investor portfolio allocations in China.

For a discussion of soft power, see Nye, *Soft Power*.

The Exercise of Power

Then again, this outcome, which resulted when Daenerys Targaryen unleashed the full force of her fearsome fire-breathing dragon, Drogon, on King's Landing and pulverized it despite Cersei's sign of surrender, should perhaps be taken as a validation of Cersei's proposition about power. See *Game of Thrones*, season eight, episode five, "The Bells."

For a catalog and one perspective on US interventions in Latin America, see J. Coatsworth, "United States Interventions," *ReVista*, May 15, 2005, https://revista.drclas.har vard.edu/united-states-interventions. For more on US involvement in Bosnia, see Sarah E. Garding, *Bosnia and Herzegovina: Background and U.S. Policy* (Congressional Research Service, 2019), https://crsreports.congress.gov/product/pdf/R/R45691.

Data from the Lowy Institute are available at "The Power Gap," Asia Power Index, 2024 edition, https://power.lowyinstitute.org/power-gap/.

The discussion in this section draws extensively on Prasad, *Gaining Currency*.

Details about the Silk Road Fund are available at its official website, accessed March 2025, www.silkroadfund.com.cn/enweb/.

In addition, from 2008 to 2021, the China Development Bank and the Export-Import Bank of China provided roughly half a trillion dollars in development finance to foreign governments. See the Global China Database of Boston

University's Global Development Policy Center: www.bu.edu/gdp/2023/12/19/gdp-center-round-up-2023-global-china-database-updates/.

Xi's remarks can be found at Yunbi Zhang, "Spokeswoman: China's Aid to Africa Never Offers Blank Promises," *China Daily*, December 10, 2015; and http://en.cabc.org.cn/?c=policys&a=view.

For data on China's investment abroad, see "China Global Investment Tracker," American Enterprise Institute, accessed March 2025, www.aei.org/china-global-investment-tracker/. For information on China's control over Ecuador's oil exports, see Clifford Krauss and Keith Bradsher, "China's Global Ambitions, Cash and Strings Attached," *New York Times*, July 24, 2015.

For more information on Xi's visit to Pakistan, see Katharine Houreld, "China and Pakistan Launch Economic Corridor Plan Worth $46 Billion," Reuters, April 20, 2015. For his promises to Africa, see "China Pledges $60bn to Develop Africa," BBC, December 4, 2015.

The pushback against China's investments in Sri Lanka is reported in Shihar Aneez, "China's 'Silk Road' Push Stirs Resentment and Protest in Sri Lanka," Reuters, February 2, 2017; and "Protest over Hambantota Port Deal Turns Violent," Al Jazeera, January 7, 2017.

President Sirisena's quote is reported in "Sri Lankan President Thanks China for Strong Assistance, Support," Xinhua, August 11, 2017. Rajapakshe's quote is reported in Philip Wen, "China's Lending Comes Under Fire as Sri Lankan Debt Crisis Deepens," *Wall Street Journal*, January 18, 2022.

Fuziah Salleh is the Malaysian politician quoted in the text. The statements are reported in Hannah Beech, " 'We Cannot Afford This': Malaysia Pushes Back Against China's Vision," *New York Times*, August 20, 2018.

For two perspectives on China's foreign aid, see Pierre Mandon, *Has Chinese Aid Benefited Recipient Countries* (IMF, 2022), www.elibrary.imf.org/view/journals/001/2022/046/article-A001-en.xml; and T. M. Harchaoui, R. K. J. Maseland, and J. A. Watkinson, "How China Strategically Uses Aid to Facilitate Chinese Business Expansion in Africa," *Journal of African Economies* (September 2020), https://academic.oup.com/jae/article/30/2/183/5909730.

For details on the BRI revamp, see "Wang Yi on High-Quality Belt and Road Cooperation," *China News*, March 7, 2024, http://us.china-embassy.gov.cn/eng/zgyw/202403/t20240308_11256435.htm; and S. L. Tan, "China's Evolving Belt and Road Initiative in Southeast Asia," International Institute for Strategic Studies, July 31, 2024, www.iiss.org/online-analysis/online-analysis/2024/07/chinas-evolving-belt-and-road-initiative-in-southeast-asia/.

For information on China's bailing out of indebted nations, see Jessie Yeung, "China Gave Huge Loans to Some Countries. Now It's Spending Billions to Bail Them Out," CNN, March 28, 2023. China's support to South Asian countries is described in Sharon Seah, Joanne Lin, Melinda Martinus, et al., *The State of Southeast Asia: 2024 Survey Report* (Singapore: ISEAS—Yusof Ishak Institute, 2024), www.iseas.edu.sg/wp-content/uploads/2024/03/The-State-of-SEA-2024.pdf.

For details about B3W and PGII, see the following Fact Sheets from the White House: B3W, June 2021, https://bidenwhitehouse.archives.gov/briefing-room/statements-releases/2021/06/12/fact-sheet-president-biden-and-g7-leaders-launch-build

-back-better-world-b3w-partnership/; PGII, June 2022, https://bidenwhitehouse.ar
chives.gov/briefing-room/statements-releases/2022/06/26/fact-sheet-president-biden
-and-g7-leaders-formally-launch-the-partnership-for-global-infrastructure-and-in
vestment/; and PGII, May 2023, https://bidenwhitehouse.archives.gov/briefing-room
/statements-releases/2023/05/20/fact-sheet-partnership-for-global-infrastructure-and
-investment-at-the-g7-summit/. Also see C. Crystal, "The G7's B3W Infrastructure Plan
Can't Compete with China," Council on Foreign Relations, August 10, 2021, www.cfr
.org/blog/g7s-b3w-infrastructure-plan-cant-compete-china-thats-not-point.

The Blue Dot Network is described on the US Department of State's webpage,
accessed March 2025, www.state.gov/blue-dot-network/.

For reporting on the closure of USAID and the implications thereof, see Joanna
Kakissis, Kate Bartlett, Eyder Peralta, and Diaa Hadid, "How the Gutting of USAID
Is Reverberating Around the World: Worry, Despair, Praise," NPR, February 11,
2025. The quotes are taken from Joshua Goodman, "Trump's Foreign Aid Freeze
Could Prove to Be a Boon for the World's Authoritarian Strongmen," Associated
Press, February 4, 2025.

Figures related to the PGII are drawn from the White House Fact Sheet on PGII,
June 2022; and Antony Blinken's remarks at the PGII forum, US Department of
State (archived), September 21, 2023, https://2021-2025.state.gov/secretary-antony
-j-blinken-at-the-u-s-partnership-for-global-infrastructure-and-investment-investor
-forum/.

Balancing Forces Go Rogue

Littlefinger's words of wisdom to Lady Sansa Stark are uttered in *Game of Thrones*,
season five, episode three, "High Sparrow." In a later episode, these words come back
to haunt him.

For data on the world population, see A. Morse, "Population Growth Is Slowing,"
US Census Bureau, November 9, 2023, www.census.gov/library/stories/2023/11
/world-population-estimated-eight-billion.html.

2. Currency Competition

The epigraph comes from Rushdie, *Victory City*, 262.

The quotes from Le Maire, Macron, Lula, Putin, and Yeo are taken from the fol-
lowing articles: Keith Johnson, "The Buck Stops Here: Europe Seeks Alternative to
U.S.-Dominated Financial System," *Foreign Policy*, September 5, 2018; Jamil Anderlini
and Clea Caulcutt, "Europe Must Resist Pressure to Become 'America's Followers,' Says
Macron," *Politico*, April 9, 2023; Joe Leahy and Hudson Lockett, "Brazil's Lula Calls for
End to Dollar Trade Dominance," *Financial Times*, April 13, 2023; Maria Tsvetkova,
"Putin Says U.S. Is 'Parasite' on Global Economy," Reuters, August 1, 2011; William
Pesek, "Fed Fingerprints All Over 'Dollar-Is-Doomed' Talk," *Asia Times*, April 7, 2023.

Javier Milei's quotes are reported in Jack Nicas, "Argentina's Currency Plummets
Under Attack from Far-Right Candidate," *New York Times*, October 10, 2023. For
the shares of Argentina's trade with various trading partners, see "Argentine Trade

Exchange—Year 2023," Ministry of Foreign Affairs, International Trade, and Worship, https://cancilleria.gob.ar/en/cie/news/argentine-trade-exchange-year-2023. Milei's dollarization idea is reported in Jack Nicas, "Argentina Elects Javier Milei in Victory for Far Right," *New York Times*, November 19, 2023.

Data on country shares of global GDP (based on national GDP, measured in current dollars at market exchange rates) are derived from the World Bank's World Development Indicators, https://databank.worldbank.org/source/world-development-indicators. For data on GDP of emerging-market and developing countries, measured in current prices, see IMF DataMapper, accessed March 2025, www.imf.org/external/datamapper/NGDPD@WEO/OEMDC/ADVEC/WEOWORLD.

For varying perspectives on the dollar's role in global finance, and risks to its dominance, see Helleiner and Kirshner, *Future of the Dollar*; Eichengreen, *Exorbitant Privilege*; Prasad, *The Dollar Trap*; Blustein, *King Dollar*; and Rogoff, *Our Dollar, Your Problem*. This chapter draws on Prasad, "Top Dollar."

Currency Dominance

For data on US national debt, see "What Is the National Debt?," Fiscal Data, US Treasury, accessed April 14, 2025, https://fiscaldata.treasury.gov/americas-finance-guide/national-debt/.

Estimates of the US dollar's share of export invoicing are available at "Dollar Dominance Monitor," Atlantic Council, accessed March 2025, www.atlanticcouncil.org/programs/geoeconomics-center/dollar-dominance-monitor/.

Currency shares in global payments are based on the SWIFT Institute's RMB Tracker, January 2024, www.swift.com/our-solutions/compliance-and-shared-services/business-intelligence/renminbi/rmb-tracker/rmb-tracker-document-centre. Six months after striking a deal to conduct trade in their own currencies, a grand total of one minor transaction between Brazil and China was conducted in this manner. See "China, Brazil Strike Deal to Ditch Dollar for Trade," *Barron's*, March 29, 2023; and "China, Brazil Trade in Local Currencies for First Time," Xinhua, October 5, 2023.

The share of US dollar reserves in total global foreign exchange reserves is based on end-2024 data on "allocated reserves," foreign exchange reserves whose currency composition is reported to the IMF. Data are available in the IMF'S Currency Composition of Official Foreign Exchange Reserves (COFER) database, accessed March 2025, https://data.imf.org/cofer. See the appendix to the IMF's 2023 Annual Report, https://cdn.sanity.io/files/un6gmxxl/production/fcf8c6131482fbcfed9a5a9f832259ffaab23132.pdf.

See Section 3 of the European Central Bank's June 2023 report on the International Role of the Euro, www.ecb.europa.eu/pub/ire/html/ecb.ire202306~d334007ede.en.html#toc7. Even some European companies and banks prefer to raise capital in dollars. See Luna Azahara Romo González, *The Drivers of European Banks' US Dollar Debt and Issuance* (Banco De España, 2016), www.bde.es/f/webbde/SES/Secciones/Publicaciones/PublicacionesSeriadas/DocumentosTrabajo/16/Fich/dt1611e.pdf (banks); and information on International Debt Securities available at the BIS Data Portal, accessed March 2025, https://data.bis.org/topics/IDS/tables-and-dashboards/BIS,SEC_C1,1.0 (for corporations; data can be filtered by issuing country and currency of issuance).

Reinhart and Rogoff, *This Time Is Different*, show that a public-debt-to-GDP ratio of more than 90 percent tends to be associated with lower growth. For evidence
of the effects of US Treasury security issuance on US interest rates, see Ben Bernanke, "Remarks by Governor Ben S. Bernanke: The Global Saving Glut and the
U.S. Account Deficit," Federal Reserve Board, March 10, 2005, www.federalreserve
.gov/boarddocs/speeches/2005/200503102/; and Beltran, Kretchmer, Marquez, and
Thomas, "Foreign Holdings of U.S. Treasuries and U.S. Treasury Yields."

For information on central bank swap lines, see B. Steil, E. Harding, and S.
Zucker, "Central Bank Currency Swaps Tracker," Council on Foreign Relations, October 2, 2024, www.cfr.org/article/central-bank-currency-swaps-tracker.

For details on the Foreign and International Monetary Authorities Repo Facility, see Mark Choi, Linda Goldberg, Robert Lerman, and Fabiola Ravazzolo, *The
Fed's Central Bank Swap Lines and FIMA Repo Facility* (Federal Reserve Bank of
New York, 2022), www.newyorkfed.org/medialibrary/media/research/epr/2022/epr
_2022_fima-repo_choi.pdf.

A Mixed Blessing

For a discussion of the deutsche mark and Japanese yen, see Tavlas, "On the International Use of Currencies."

The shares of the deutsche mark and Japanese yen in global foreign exchange reserves can be found in Table 16 of the IMF's 1983 *Annual Report*, www.imf.org/ex
ternal/pubs/ft/ar/archive/pdf/ar1983.pdf; and in Table I.2 of the IMF's 1990 *Annual
Report*, www.imf.org/external/pubs/ft/ar/archive/pdf/ar1990.pdf.

The Perplexing Persistence of Dollar Dominance

See Reinhart and Rogoff, *This Time Is Different*. India's central government finances are shown in Table 4 in International Monetary Fund, *India: 2023 Article
IV Consultation—Press Release; Staff Report; and Statement by the Executive Director
for India* (2023), www.imf.org/en/Publications/CR/Issues/2023/12/18/India-2023
-Article-IV-Consultation-Press-Release-Staff-Report-and-Statement-by-the-542605.

Of the total gross US federal public debt, "debt held by the public," which includes government securities on the Fed's balance sheet, is about 100 percent of GDP,
while the remainder is debt held by "government accounts," mainly the Social Security trust funds. See P. L. Swagel, "Letter Regarding CBO's Long-Term Projections
of Gross Federal Debt," Congressional Budget Office, September 8, 2023, www.cbo
.gov/system/files/2023-09/59512-GrossDebt.pdf; and "What Is the National Debt?"

A profile of a leading proponent of MMT is at Jeanna Smialek, "Is This What
Winning Looks Like?," *New York Times*, February 6, 2022.

The US debt downgrade is reported in Binyamin Appelbaum and Eric Dash,
"S.& P. Downgrades Debt Rating of U.S. for the First Time," *New York Times*, August 5, 2011.

Fitch's announcement of its downgrade of US debt is available at "Fitch Downgrades the United States' Long-Term Ratings to 'AA+' from 'AAA': Outlook Stable,"

Fitch Ratings, August 1, 2023, www.fitchratings.com/research/sovereigns/fitch-down grades-united-states-long-term-ratings-to-aa-from-aaa-outlook-stable-01-08-2023. The implications of the downgrade are discussed in Alan Rappeport and Joe Rennison, "Fitch Downgrades U.S. Credit Rating," *New York Times*, August 1, 2023.

Trump's views on the Fed and his quotes are from Owen Ullmann, "'Over My Dead Body': Janet Yellen Refused to Take a Dive for Trump," *Politico*, September 22, 2022; Howard Schneider, "Analysis: Federal Reserve 'Boneheads' Emerge from Trump Era Unscathed," Reuters, December 16, 2020; James Politi, "Donald Trump's Fed Board Nominee Judy Shelton Fails Crucial Senate Vote," *Financial Times*, November 17, 2020; Katherine Doyle and Jonathan Allen, "Feeling Betrayed, Trump Wants a Second Administration Stocked with Loyalists," NBC News, February 12, 2024.

For details about China's CIPS, see the official introduction on CIPS's website, accessed March 2025, www.cips.com.cn/cipsenmobile/7242/7256/34009/index .html.

SWIFT's governance structure is described on its official website, accessed March 2025, www.swift.com/about-us/organisation-governance. For a discussion of SWIFT's role in international payments, see Marco Cipriani, Linda S. Goldberg, and Gabriele La Spada, *Financial Sanctions, SWIFT, and the Architecture of the International Payments System* (Federal Reserve Bank of New York, 2023), www.newyork fed.org/medialibrary/media/research/staff_reports/sr1047.pdf.

Sanctions against the Central Bank of Syria and the Central Bank of Venezuela are described on the FAQ page of the Office of Foreign Assets Control (OFAC), accessed March 2025, https://ofac.treasury.gov/faqs/225; and https://ofac.treasury.gov /faqs/680, respectively.

See SWIFT's sanctions at www.swift.com/about-us/legal/compliance-0/swift-and -sanctions. For examples of sanctioned firms and individuals, see "Russia-Related Designations and Designations Updates: Issuance of Russia-Related General Licenses," Office of Foreign Assets Control, December 12, 2023, https://ofac.treasury.gov/recent -actions/20231212. Mulder, *Economic Weapon*, discusses the efficacy of sanctions.

The freezing of Russian central bank assets is reported in Alan Rappeport, "U.S. Escalates Sanctions with a Freeze on Russian Central Bank Assets," *New York Times*, February 28, 2022; and Elena Fabrichnaya and Guy Faulconbridge, "What and Where Are Russia's $300 Billion in Reserves Frozen in the West?," Reuters, December 28, 2023.

Yellen's statements are in "Yellen Says Sanctions May Risk Hegemony of US Dollar," *Barron's*, April 16, 2023; and Ben Norton, "Sanctions 'Undermine Hegemony of Dollar,' US Treasury Admits," *Geopolitical Economy Report*, April 17, 2023.

The evolution of reserve holdings can be seen at L. Chiţu, J. Gomes, and R. Pauli, "Trends in Central Banks' Foreign Currency Reserves," *ECB Economic Bulletin*, 2019, www.ecb.europa.eu/press/economic-bulletin/articles/2019/html/ecb.ebart 201907_01~c2ae75e217.en.html. International reserves data are available on the IMF's data portal, accessed March 2025, at https://data.imf.org/irfcl.

For data on debt securities by country and broken down by issuer type, see the BIS Data Portal, accessed March 2025, https://data.bis.org/topics/DSS/tables-and -dashboards/BIS,SEC_C1,1.0.

Feeble Alternatives

For data on GDP, measured in current prices, of the euro area and the United States, see the IMF DataMapper, accessed March 2025, www.imf.org/external/data mapper/NGDPD@WEO/USA/EURO.

Data on the currency composition of global foreign exchange reserves are available in the IMF'S COFER database. The eurozone project is analyzed in James, *Making the European Monetary Union*; and Brunnermeier, James, and Landau, *The Euro and the Battle of Ideas*.

The IMF announcement is available at "Press Release: IMF's Executive Board Completes Review of SDR Basket, Includes Chinese Renminbi," International Monetary Fund, November 30, 2015, www.imf.org/en/News/Articles/2015/09/14/01/49/pr15540. The SDR basket is discussed on the Special Drawing Rights (SDR) fact sheet, International Monetary Fund, accessed March 2025, www.imf.org/en/About/Factsheets/Sheets/2023/special-drawing-rights-sdr.

See B. Steil and E. Harding, "China's Central Bank Is Becoming the Developing World's 'Payday Lender,'" Council on Foreign Relations, October 22, 2024, www.cfr.org/blog/chinas-central-bank-becoming-developing-worlds-payday-lender.

The RMB's share in global payments is taken from the SWIFT Institute's RMB Tracker.

China's currency devaluation is reported in Neil Gough and Keith Bradsher, "China Devalues Its Currency as Worries Rise About Economic Slowdown," *New York Times*, August 10, 2015.

Barry Eichengreen and coauthors document the rise of nontraditional reserve currencies in S. Arslanalp, B. Eichengreen, and C. Simpson-Bell, "The Stealth Erosion of Dollar Dominance and the Rise of Nontraditional Reserve Currencies," *Journal of International Economics*, September 2022, www.sciencedirect.com/science/article/abs/pii/S0022199622000885. For data on the Australian and Canadian dollars' roles in international finance, see the IMF's COFER database; and SWIFT's RMB Tracker.

The proposal for a BRICS currency is reported in Simone Iglesias, "Lula Backs BRICS Currency to Replace Dollar in Foreign Trade," Bloomberg, April 13, 2023.

The discussion of digital currencies draws on Prasad, *Future of Money*, Chapters 4 and 5.

For a discussion of how SDRs can be used by IMF member countries, see IMF's overview of SDRs, accessed March 2025, www.imf.org/en/Topics/special-drawing-right#.

Why the Dollar Will Remain Dominant

Data on US external assets and liabilities are available at "U.S. International Investment Position, Year 2024," U.S. Bureau of Economic Analysis, March 26, 2025, www.bea.gov/data/intl-trade-investment/international-investment-position.

Gourinchas and Rey, "From World Banker to World Venture Capitalist," note that "almost all U.S. foreign liabilities are in dollars, whereas approximately 70 percent of U.S. foreign assets are in foreign currencies."

Data on the United States' international investment position, including foreign assets and liabilities, are available in the BEA's data portal, accessed January 2025, www.bea.gov/data/intl-trade-investment/international-investment-position.

The numbers discussed in this section are taken from "Board-Approved SDR Basket Currency Weights at Past Quinquennial Reviews," International Monetary Fund, accessed February 2025, www.imf.org/-/media/Files/About/Infographics /board-approved-sdr-basket-currency-weights-at-past-quinquennial-reviews.ashx. For the currency composition of the SDR before 1999, see W. Antweiler, "Pacific Exchange Rate Service," Sauder School of Business, University of British Columbia, accessed March 2025, https://fx.sauder.ubc.ca/SDR.php.

Rickety Currency Configurations

For more on the roles of the Chinese and Indian currencies in international finance, see Prasad, *Gaining Currency*; and Radha Shyam Ratho, Ajay Kumar Misra, R. Lakshmi Kanth Rao, et al., *Report of the Inter-Departmental Group (IDG) on Internationalisation of INR* (Reserve Bank of India, 2023), www.rbi.org.in/Scripts/Pub licationReportDetails.aspx?UrlPage=&ID=1244.

3. Globalization: Cohesion or Disarray?

The epigraph comes from Pushkin, *Eugene Onegin*, Chapter 1, Verse 7.

Trump's comments can be found here: "President Trump: 'We Have Rejected Globalism and Embraced Patriotism'," White House Archives, August 7, 2020, https:// trumpwhitehouse.archives.gov/articles/president-trump-we-have-rejected-globalism -and-embraced-patriotism/. His quotes are reported in John McCormick, "Trump Calls Tariffs the 'Most Beautiful Word,'" *Wall Street Journal*, October 16, 2024; and Zachary Basu, "'The Greatest Thing Ever Invented': Tariffs Become Trump's Miracle Cure," Axios, September 25, 2024. Xi Jinping's comments are reported here: "Let the Torch of Multilateralism Light Up Humanity's Way Forward: Special Address by Xi Jinping," Xinhua News Agency, January 25, 2021, https://interpret.csis.org /translations/let-the-torch-of-multilateralism-light-up-humanitys-way-forward -special-address-by-xi-jinping-at-the-world-economic-forum-virtual-event-of-the -davos-agenda/; and Eduardo Baptista and Lucinda Elliott, "As Trump Return Looms, China's Xi at APEC Criticises Protectionism," Reuters, November 16, 2024.

Trump's tariffs on US imports are reported in Ana Swanson and Chris Buckley, "China Counters Trump's Tariffs as Talks Remain in Limbo," *New York Times*, February 4, 2025. The transcript of Ding Xuexiang's speech is available at "Davos 2025: Special Address by Ding Xuexiang," World Economic Forum, January 21, 2025, www.weforum.org/stories/2025/01/davos-2025-special-address-ding-xuexiang -vice-premier-china/.

For a reprise of the Asian Financial Crisis (1997–1998) and Mexican currency crisis (1994–1995), see, respectively, M. Carson and J. Clark, "Asian Financial Crisis," Federal Reserve History, November 22, 2013, www.federalreservehistory.org/essays /asian-financial-crisis; and Edwin M. Truman, *The Mexican Peso Crisis: Implications for International Finance* (Board of Governors of the Federal Reserve System, 1996), www.federalreserve.gov/pubs/bulletin/1996/396lead.pdf.

James, *Seven Crashes*, argues that crashes prompted by a lack of supply lead to greater globalization, while crises triggered by a lack of demand result in less globalization.

For a range of views on how the US-China relationship ought to be managed, see Pepinsky and Weiss, "Washington Should Avoid Ideological Competition with Beijing"; Weiss, "The China Trap"; and Pottinger and Gallagher, "No Substitute for Victory."

Data on global trade is available at "Evolution of Trade Under the WTO: Handy Statistics," World Trade Organization, accessed March 2025, www.wto.org/english /res_e/statis_e/trade_evolution_e/evolution_trade_wto_e.htm.

The Promise and the Reality

For a discussion of succeeding waves of globalization, see P. Vanham, "A Brief History of Globalization," World Economic Forum, January 17, 2019, www.wefo rum.org/stories/2019/01/how-globalization-4-0-fits-into-the-history-of-globaliza tion/. The literature on the potential benefits of globalization and diverse perspectives on the tradeoff between the benefits and costs includes Wolf, *The Shifts and the Shocks*; Rodrik, *The Globalization Paradox*; and Roberts and Lamp, *Six Faces of Globalization*. Kose, Prasad, Rogoff, and Wei, "Financial Globalization, a Reappraisal," discuss an alternative framework for understanding the channels through which financial globalization promotes growth. The discussion of capital flows in this section draws on Prasad, *The Dollar Trap*.

A full list of Apple's suppliers is available at "Supplier List," Apple, accessed March 2025, https://s203.q4cdn.com/367071867/files/doc_downloads/2024/04/Apple-Sup plier-List.pdf.

For a list of US companies that rely on China for a significant share of their revenues, see "US Companies with Highest Exposure to China," Reuters, May 14, 2024. For a regional breakdown of Gucci's and Prada's revenues, see, respectively, Kering's key figures, available on the official website, accessed March 2025, www.kering.com /en/finance/about-kering/#anchor1; and "Prada Group Continues to Deliver Solid Performance," Prada Group, October 30, 2024, www.pradagroup.com/en/news-me dia/press-releases-documents/2024/24-10-30-prada-group-2024-9m-revenue.html.

Financial contagion is discussed in "The Global Consequences of Financial Contagion," Council on Foreign Relations, August 3, 2023, https://education.cfr.org /learn/reading/global-consequences-financial-contagion. Also see Ben Bernanke's famous "Global Saving Glut" speech: "Remarks by Governor Ben S. Bernanke," Federal Reserve Board, March 10, 2005, www.federalreserve.gov/boarddocs/speeches /2005/200503102/.

For an analysis of global capital flows in the immediate aftermath of the global financial crisis, see G. Milesi-Ferretti and C. Tille, "The Great Retrenchment: International Capital Flows During the Global Financial Crisis," *Economic Policy* (August 2014), https://academic.oup.com/economicpolicy/article/26/66/289/2918382; and Elliott James, Kate McLoughlin, and Ewan Rankin, *Cross-Border Capital Flows Since the Global Financial Crisis* (Reserve Bank of Australia, 2014), www.rba.gov.au/publi cations/bulletin/2014/jun/pdf/bu-0614-8.pdf.

Trade Turns into a Zero-Sum Game

The trade data are taken from US Census Bureau, accessed March 2025, www .census.gov/foreign-trade/balance/c5700.html. Calculations are based on US GDP, measured in US dollars at market exchange rates, taken from the World Bank's World Development Indicators database, accessed March 2025, https://databank .worldbank.org/reports.aspx?source=2&country=ARE.

For an overview of the US-China trade relationship, see Karen M. Sutter, *U.S.- China Trade Relations* (Congressional Research Service, 2025), https://crsreports .congress.gov/product/pdf/IF/IF11284.

See Autor, Dorn, and Hansen, "The China Shock." Their estimate of between 2 million and 2.4 million jobs lost implies that the China Shock accounted for about half of manufacturing job losses during the period mentioned. A higher estimate of job losses is offered in R. E. Scott, "Growing U.S. Trade Deficit with China Cost 2.8 Million Jobs Between 2001 and 2010," Economic Policy Institute, September 20, 2011, www.epi.org/publication/growing-trade-deficit-china-cost-2-8-million/.

For a discussion of China's currency management and US commercial interests in China, see Prasad, *The Dollar Trap* and *Gaining Currency*.

The full text of Xi Jinping's speech is available here: Nikkei Asia, "Full Text of Xi Jinping's Speech on the CCP's 100th Anniversary," *Nikkei Asia*, July 1, 2021. For some useful perspectives on the "Century of Humiliation" and its implications for China's current policy, see Alison A. Kaufman, *The "Century of Humiliation" and China's National Narratives* (U.S.-China Economics and Security Review Commission, 2011), www.uscc.gov/sites/default/files/3.10.11Kaufman.pdf.

China's subsidy policies are reviewed in U. Haley and G. Haley, "How Chinese Subsidies Changed the World," *Harvard Business Review*, April 25, 2013, https://hbr .org/2013/04/how-chinese-subsidies-changed; and Keith Bradsher and Matthew L. Wald, "A Measured Rebuttal to China over Solar Panels," *New York Times*, March 20, 2012. Also see "What Happened When China Joined the WTO?," Council on Foreign Relations, February 6, 2025, https://education.cfr.org/learn/reading/what -happened-when-china-joined-wto.

China's zero-COVID policy is reviewed in "What Is China's Zero-COVID Policy and How Does It Work?," Reuters, November 3, 2022. China's ban on iPhone purchases by its government officials is reported in "China's iPhone Ban Accelerates Across Government and State Firms," Bloomberg, December 15, 2023.

The shift in US views on China is reported in Gavin Bade, "DC Slammed Trump's Tariffs. Biden's Decision to Keep Them Draws a Very Different Reaction," *Politico*, May 15, 2024.

Details regarding China's EV sector are given in "China's BYD Prices New Version of Best-Selling EV Lower than Predecessor," Reuters, March 4, 2024; Tom Krisher and Ken Moritsugu, "Small, Well-Built Chinese EV Called the Seagull Poses a Big Threat to the US Auto Industry," Associated Press, May 13, 2024; and Keith

Naughton, "China's Super-Cheap EVs Offer Hope for Average American Buyers," Bloomberg, March 18, 2024.

For a discussion of subsidies enjoyed by Chinese EV producers, see "China's EV Makers Got $231 Billion Aid over 15 Years, Study Says," Bloomberg, June 20, 2024.

For a discussion of China Shock 2.0, see Jacky Wong, "China Shock 2.0 Will Be Different," *Wall Street Journal*, April 11, 2024. For details on US investment restrictions, see U.S. Department of the Treasury, *Provisions Pertaining to U.S. Investments in Certain National Security Technologies and Products in Countries of Concern* (Office of Investment Security, 2024), www.govinfo.gov/content/pkg/FR-2024-11-15/pdf /2024-25422.pdf.

Government Policies Add Risks

For a discussion of Europe's dependence on Russian energy exports and how the sanctions affected Europe, see S. Kardaś, "Conscious Uncoupling: Europeans' Russian Gas Challenge in 2023," European Council on Foreign Relations, February 13, 2023, https://ecfr.eu/article/conscious-uncoupling-europeans-russian-gas-challenge -in-2023/.

China's dual circulation policy is discussed in Kevin Yao, "What We Know About China's 'Dual Circulation' Economic Strategy," Reuters, September 8, 2020. Details about Make in India are available on its official website, accessed March 2025, www .makeinindia.com/.

Modi's Davos speech can be found here: "Prime Minister's Statement on the Subject 'Creating a Shared Future in a Fractured World,'" Ministry of External Affairs, Government of India, January 23, 2018, www.mea.gov.in/Speeches-Statements .htm?dtl/29378/. The WTO estimates that India's average tariff rate on imports was 18 percent in 2022 (the trade-weighted average was lower at 12 percent). Trade and tariff data for WTO members are available in the WTO's data portal, accessed March 2025, at www.wto.org/english/res_e/statis_e/statis_e.htm. See also "India Must Abandon Protectionism," *The Economist*, August 17, 2023.

The texts of the Inflation Reduction Act (H.R. 5376) and the CHIPS and Science Act (H.R. 4346) are available at the website of the US Congress, www.congress .gov/bill/117th-congress/house-bill/5376, and www.congress.gov/bill/117th-congress /house-bill/4346, respectively.

See "The Green Deal Industrial Plan," European Commission, accessed March 2025, https://commission.europa.eu/strategy-and-policy/priorities-2019-2024/european -green-deal/green-deal-industrial-plan_en; and "What's in the EU's Green Industrial Plan," Reuters, March 16, 2023.

How Corporations Are Managing Risk

Calculations of Thailand's share of global GDP, measured in US dollars at market exchange rates, are based on the IMF World Economic Outlook, October 2024, www.imf.org/en/Publications/SPROLLs/world-economic-outlook-databases. Reporting on the impacts of the Thai floods can be found in Eric Savitz, "Thailand Floods

Causing Tech Supply Chain Issues (Updated)," *Forbes*, October 12, 2011; and "Thai Floods Threaten Global Automotive Supply Chain, Japanese Firms Worst Hit," S&P Global, October 14, 2011, www.spglobal.com/marketintelligence/en/mi/country -industry-forecasting.html?id=1065931666. The impact of the floods on global industrial output is discussed in "Counting the Cost of Calamities," *The Economist*, January 14, 2012.

Financial Flows

Biden's August 2023 executive order (14105) is available on the Federal Register's website, www.federalregister.gov/documents/2023/08/11/2023-17449/address ing-united-states-investments-in-certain-national-security-technologies-and-prod ucts-in. The implications of the executive order are reported in Ana Swanson, "Biden to Restrict Investments in China, Citing National Security Threats," *New York Times*, August 8, 2023.

For an analysis of patterns in FDI flows, see Chapter 4 of the IMF's World Economic Outlook, April 2023, www.imf.org/en/Publications/WEO; and Shekhar Aiyar, Jiaqian Chen, Christian H. Ebeke, et al., *Geoeconomic Fragmentation and the Future of Multilateralism* (International Monetary Fund, 2023), www.imf.org/en /Publications/Staff-Discussion-Notes/Issues/2023/01/11/Geo-Economic-Fragmen tation-and-the-Future-of-Multilateralism-527266.

Shifts in supply chains away from China are discussed in "Global Firms Are Eyeing Asian Alternatives to Chinese Manufacturing," *The Economist*, February 20, 2023.

Diversion of trade and investment flows away from China is reported in Rajesh Roy and Yang Jie, "Apple Aims to Make a Quarter of the World's iPhones in India," *Wall Street Journal*, December 8, 2023; and Peter S. Goodman, "Why Chinese Companies Are Investing Billions in Mexico," *New York Times*, February 3, 2023. For formal empirical evidence, see Alfaro and Chor, "Global Supply Chains"; Goldberg and Reed, "Is the Global Economy Deglobalizing?"; and L. Torres and A. Jayashankar, "Mexico Awaits 'Nearshoring' Shift as China Boosts Its Direct Investment," Federal Reserve Bank of Dallas, April 14, 2023, www.dallasfed.org/research/swe/2023 /swe2303.

Too Early to Sound the Requiem

For a survey of the literature on and empirical evidence pertaining to such "threshold conditions," see Kose, Prasad, and Taylor, "Thresholds."

For an official US perspective on China's WTO compliance, see "USTR Releases Annual Report on China's WTO Compliance," Office of the United States Trade Representative, January 20, 2025, https://ustr.gov/about-us/policy-offices /press-office/press-releases/2025/january/ustr-releases-annual-report-chinas-wto -compliance.

4. Rules of the Game

The epigraph comes from Hesse, *Siddhartha*, 121–122.

EU regulations are explored in Nick Jardine, "Guess Which of These Crazy EU Laws Are Actually Real," *Business Insider*, December 16, 2011. EU standards on bananas can be found at "Commission Regulation (EC) No 2257/94 Laying Down Quality Standards for Bananas," European Commission, September 16, 1994, https://eur-lex.eu ropa.eu/LexUriServ/LexUriServ.do?uri=CONSLEG:1994R2257:20060217:EN:PDF. Also see "Council Regulation (EEC) No 404/93 on the Common Organization of the Market in Bananas," EUR-Lex, last updated June 5, 2008, https://eur-lex.europa.eu /EN/legal-content/summary/bananas.html.

The text of the Cutting Red Tape on Child Care Providers Act of 2024 is available here: www.congress.gov/bill/118th-congress/house-bill/10015/text. This article points out that the legislation addresses a nonexistent regulation: Nathan J. Robinson, "Why Is a Democratic Representative Claiming It's Illegal to Peel Bananas in a Daycare?," *Current Affairs*, November 21, 2024. For more on the public's response to EU regulations, see Jon Henley, "Is the EU Really Dictating the Shape of Your Bananas?," *The Guardian*, May 11, 2016.

For details about Japan's surrender, see "Surrender of Japan (1945)," National Archives, accessed March 2025, www.archives.gov/milestone-documents/surrender -of-japan#. The formation of the Bretton Woods system is described in "Bretton Woods-GATT, 1941–1947," US Department of State, Office of the Historian, accessed March 2025, https://history.state.gov/milestones/1937-1945/bretton-woods. For information on GATT, see "Fiftieth Anniversary of the Multilateral Trading System," World Trade Organization, accessed March 2025, www.wto.org/english /thewto_e/minist_e/min96_e/chrono.htm. The WTO was established in 1995, building on GATT, which was signed by twenty-three countries in 1947.

To learn more about North Korea's trade with China, see A. Durkin, "North Korea-China Trade Ties," Hinrich Foundation, September 29, 2017, www.hinrich foundation.com/research/tradevistas/sustainable/north-korea-china-trade/; and N. Watts, "North Korea's Illicit Trade with China and Russia," *Georgetown Journal of International Affairs* (March 2020), https://gjia.georgetown.edu/2020/03/25/business -as-usual-unusually-north-koreas-illicit-trade-with-china-and-russia/.

A description of the WTO's role, structure, and membership roster are available on WTO's official website, accessed June 2025, www.wto.org/english/thewto_e/thewto_e .htm. For details on how Washington disrupted the WTO's functioning, see Ana Swanson, "Trump Cripples W.T.O. As Trade War Rages," *New York Times*, December 8, 2019.

For information on the ICJ, see its official website, accessed March 2025, www.icj -cij.org/court.

A list of IMF senior management positions can be found at the IMF's website, www.imf.org/en/About/senior-officials.

Global Governance Is a Matter of Life and Death

Prime Minister Modi's quote comes from "PM Addresses Meeting of Foreign Minister of G20," Press Information Bureau, Prime Minister's Office, March 2, 2023, https://pib.gov.in/PressReleaseIframePage.aspx?PRID=1903533.

The challenges low-income countries faced in vaccine accessibility are reported in Ashleigh Furlong, "Why 'Equal Access' to Coronavirus Vaccines Is Failing Poor Countries," *Politico*, January 20, 2021; "How Rich Countries and Pharmaceutical Corporations Are Breaking Their Vaccine Promises," UNAIDS, October 21, 2021, www.unaids.org/en/resources/presscentre/featurestories/2021/october/20211021 _dose-of-reality; and J. Bouey, "Global Health Data Sharing: The Case of China and the Two Coronavirus Pandemics," RAND, November 22, 2021, www.rand.org/pubs /commentary/2021/11/global-health-data-sharing-the-case-of-china-and-the.html.

US and Chinese climate change mitigation efforts are discussed in Tom Kertscher, "US Versus China: Which Nation Is Doing More to Address Climate Change?," PolitiFact, March 27, 2023. China's impact on emissions is analyzed in "Here's How China Can Achieve Economic Growth Without Increasing Carbon Emissions," World Economic Forum, May 10, 2021, www.weforum.org/agenda/2021/05/china -decoupling-gdp-growth-rising-emissions-climate-change-economics/.

A discussion of financial contagion can be found at "The Global Consequences of Financial Contagion," Council on Foreign Relations, last updated August 3, 2023, https://education.cfr.org/learn/reading/global-consequences-financial-contagion.

Rules About Rulemaking

An overview of Jean-Jacques Rousseau's *The Social Contract* is available at Jonathan Bennett's website Early Modern Texts, 2017, www.earlymoderntexts.com/assets /pdfs/rousseau1762.pdf. Rousseau's key argument is that freedom can exist only within a framework of laws created by the collective will of the people.

The count of the IMF's original members includes Denmark, which did not have a government-in-exile but was invited to send an official to attend in his personal capacity. See IMF's webpage, accessed March 2025, www.imf.org/en/About. Dates of entry into IMF membership can be found at the same website, www.imf.org/external /np/sec/memdir/memdate.htm. Italy became a member in 1947; Germany and Japan did so in 1952. See IMF's timeline at www.imf.org/en/About/Timeline.

The World Bank, which was also created at the Bretton Woods conference, had 38 members when it began operations in 1946. It now has 189 members. See "Getting to Know the World Bank," World Bank, July 26, 2012, www.worldbank.org/en /news/feature/2012/07/26/getting_to_know_theworldbank. Information about the G7's formation and history can be found at "The History of the G7," Press and Information Office of the Federal Government of Germany, accessed March 2025, www .bundesregierung.de/breg-en/service/the-history-of-the-g7-397438. The G6 held their first meeting in 1975; the group was expanded to include Canada in 1976.

Individual countries' voting shares at the IMF are shown at "IMF Members' Quotas and Voting Power, and IMF Board of Governors," International Monetary Fund, last updated June 16, 2025, www.imf.org/en/About/executive-board/members-quotas. For more information about the Bretton Woods conference, see "Bretton Woods and the Birth of the World Bank," World Bank, accessed March 2025, www.worldbank.org /en/archive/history/exhibits/Bretton-Woods-and-the-Birth-of-the-World-Bank. Calculations of shares of global GDP are based on data on national and world GDP, all measured in US dollars at market exchange rates, taken from "World Economic Outlook Database, October 2024," IMF, www.imf.org/en/Publications/SPROLLs/world -economic-outlook-databases.

Hungary's actions to block EU aid to Ukraine are described in Matina Stevis-Gridneff and Steven Erlanger, "Hungary Blocks Ukraine Aid After E.U. Opens Door to Membership," *New York Times*, December 14, 2023; and Jorge Liboreiro, "EU Countries Voice Exasperation over Hungary's Vetoes on Ukraine Aid," Euronews, May 27, 2024.

The IMF's governance is described at B. S. Coulibaly and K. Derviş, "The Governance of the International Monetary Fund at Age 75," Brookings Institution, July 1, 2019, www.brookings.edu/articles/the-governance-of-the-international-monetary -fund-at-age-75/.

My proposal for the IMF is summarized in E. Prasad, "Getting the International Monetary Fund's Groove Back," Brookings Institution, October 30, 2008, www .brookings.edu/articles/getting-the-international-monetary-funds-groove-back/. Alternative voting rules are analyzed in O'Neill and Peleg, "Reconciling Power and Equality in International Organizations"; and Posner and Sykes, "Voting Rules in International Organizations."

For details on the Stability and Growth Pact, see the EUR-Lex online database, accessed March 2025, https://eur-lex.europa.eu/EN/legal-content/glossary/stability -and-growth-pact.html.

Discussions about deviations from the pact are at "Stability and Growth Pact," European Commission, accessed March 2025, https://economy-finance.ec.europa.eu /economic-and-fiscal-governance/stability-and-growth-pact_en; Mark Tran, "France and Germany Evade Deficit Fines," *The Guardian*, November 25, 2003; and "Launching an Excessive Deficit Procedure," European Commission, https://economy-finance .ec.europa.eu/economic-and-fiscal-governance/stability-and-growth-pact/corrective -arm-excessive-deficit-procedure/launching-excessive-deficit-procedure_en.

For an overview of the eurozone debt crisis, see M. Ray, "Euro-Zone Debt Crisis," *Britannica Money*, last updated April 1, 2025, www.britannica.com/topic/euro-zone -debt-crisis.

For more on the Brexit vote and timeline, see "Brexit," *Britannica*, last updated April 23, 2025, www.britannica.com/topic/brexit.

The price range for crude oil is based on data since 1980 for Brent and West Texas Intermediate Crude Oil contracts, available at FRED, accessed March 2025, https:// fred.stlouisfed.org/series/DCOILWTICO. For reporting on negative oil prices, see Stanley Reed and Clifford Krauss, "Too Much Oil: How a Barrel Came to Be Worth Less than Nothing," *New York Times*, April 20, 2020; and Vikas Bajaj, "What Negative Oil Prices Mean and How the Impact Could Last," *New York Times*, April 22, 2020.

Governing the International Financial System

For details on the conditions typically attached to IMF loans, see IMF's Conditionality webpage, accessed March 2025, www.imf.org/en/About/Factsheets/Sheets /2023/IMF-Conditionality. For a critical evaluation of IMF lending policies, see

Independent Evaluation Office of the International Monetary Fund, *The IMF's Exceptional Access Policy* (2024), https://ieo.imf.org/en/Evaluations/Completed/2024-1212-imfs-exceptional-access-policy.

Details about IMF governance are at "IMF Executive Directors and Voting Power," International Monetary Fund, last updated April 12, 2025, www.imf.org/en/About/executive-board/eds-voting-power; and the overview webpage of the World Bank, last updated April 5, 2023, www.worldbank.org/en/about/leadership/directors.

IMF quotas and voting shares (which are nearly but not quite the same) can be found at "IMF Quota and Governance Publications," International Monetary Fund, last updated September 20, 2024, www.imf.org/external/np/fin/quotas/pubs/.

The IMF quota formula is available at "What Are IMF Quotas?," International Monetary Fund, last updated December 2023, www.imf.org/en/About/Factsheets/Sheets/2022/IMF-Quotas.

The IMF provides recent data and implications of those data for quotas at "Updated IMF Quota Data—July 28 2022," International Monetary Fund, November 9, 2022, www.imf.org/external/np/fin/quotas/2022/0728.htm.

The announcement of the creation of a new deputy managing director position at the IMF in July 2011 and the appointment of a Chinese national, Zhu Min, to that position is available at "Press Release: IMF Managing Director Christine Lagarde Proposes Appointment," International Monetary Fund, July 12, 2011, www.imf.org/en/News/Articles/2015/09/14/01/49/pr11275. The informal agreement between Europe and the United States regarding leadership positions at the IMF and World Bank is discussed in Martin A. Weiss, *Selecting the World Bank President* (Congressional Research Service, 2023), https://crsreports.congress.gov/product/pdf/R/R42463.

For an overview of the BIS, see its official website, accessed March 2025, www.bis.org/about/index.htm. For information about the Basel Committee on Banking Supervision, see "The Basel Committee—Overview," Bank of International Settlements, accessed March 2025, www.bis.org/bcbs/index.htm.

The BIS meeting schedule is described at "The Basel Process—Meetings," Bank of International Settlements, accessed March 2025, www.bis.org/about/meetings.htm. For information on committees that the BIS supports, see "About Committees and Associations," Bank of International Settlements, accessed March 2025, www.bis.org/stability.htm. The quote is based on my notes from a personal conversation.

China Makes Its Move

Africa's and Latin America's largest trade partners can be tracked using the World Bank's World Integrated Trade Solution tool, accessed March 2025, https://wits.worldbank.org/CountryProfile/en/Country/SSF/Year/LTST/TradeFlow/EXPIMP#.

For an overview of China's role in and contributions to the WTO, see WTO's website, accessed March 2025, www.wto.org/english/thewto_e/countries_e/china_e.htm.

Information on the EBRD is available at Martin A. Weiss, *European Bank for Reconstruction and Development (EBRD)* (Congressional Research Service, 2022), https://crsreports.congress.gov/product/pdf/IF/IF11419. The agreement establishing the EBRD is available at EBRD, *Political Aspects of the Mandate of the EBRD,* accessed April 14, 2025, www.ebrd.com/downloads/about/aspects.pdf. For an official description of China's electoral system, see "China's Electoral System," website of the People's Republic of China (English-language version), accessed April 14, 2025, english .www.gov.cn/archive/china_abc/2014/08/23/content_281474982987216.htm.

For information on the member countries and future prospects of the AIIB, see the members page of its official website, accessed March 2025, www.aiib.org/en /about-aiib/governance/members-of-bank/index.html; and "The State of the Asian Infrastructure Investment Bank," *U.S.-China Nexus Podcast*, Georgetown Initiative for U.S.-China Dialogue on Global Issues, April 3, 2024, https://uschinadialogue .georgetown.edu/podcasts/the-state-of-the-asian-infrastructure-investment-bank.

For information on the AIIB's governance structure, see "How We Are Organized," Asian Infrastructure Investment Bank, accessed March 2025, www.aiib.org/en/about -aiib/governance/index.html; and www.inclusivedevelopment.net/china-global-pro gram/china-global-newsletter-edition-5/.

A recent controversy that summarizes this perception and the AIIB's official response to it is summarized in Joe Cash, "AIIB Says Review Finds Chinese Communist Control Charge Unfounded," Reuters, July 7, 2023.

The first summit was held by the initial four BRIC countries in 2009. South Africa was added to the group in 2010. See the World Bank's World Development Indicators for data on GDP and population by country, accessed March 2025, https:// databank.worldbank.org/source/world-development-indicators.

The declaration from the 2012 BRICS summit is available at "Fourth BRICS Summit: Delhi Declaration," BRICS Information Centre, March 29, 2012, www .brics.utoronto.ca/docs/120329-delhi-declaration.html. Extensive information about the BRICS, including about their summits and communiqués, can be found at the BRICS Information Centre, accessed March 2025, www.brics.utoronto.ca/.

The Contingent Reserve Arrangement is described in "BRICS Countries Signed Contingent Reserve Arrangement (CRA)," People's Bank of China, July 16, 2014, www.pbc.gov.cn/english/130721/2875046/index.html; and "Treaty for the Establishment of a BRICS Contingent Reserve Arrangement," BRICS Information Centre, July 15, 2014, www.brics.utoronto.ca/docs/140715-treaty.html.

For details about the New Development Bank, see the About and Shareholding pages on its official website, accessed March 2025, www.ndb.int/about-ndb/; and www.ndb.int/about-ndb/shareholding/.

For reporting on the NDB's membership expansion, see "BRICS Countries Launch New Development Bank in Shanghai," BBC News, July 21, 2015; and www .ndb.int/about-ndb/history/.

The launch of the BRICS Bank and its collaboration with the AIIB are discussed in Brenda Goh, " 'BRICS' Bank Launches in Shanghai, to Work with AIIB," Reuters, July 21, 2015.

Refashioning the Rules-Based System

Trump's executive order initiating the US withdrawal from the WHO is available at "Withdrawing the United States from the World Health Organization," White

House, January 20, 2025, www.whitehouse.gov/presidential-actions/2025/01/with drawing-the-united-states-from-the-worldhealth-organization/.

Trump's views on NATO are summarized in Michael Hirsh, "Trump's Plan for NATO Is Emerging," *Politico*, July 2, 2024.

5. Middle Powers and Alliances

The epigraph comes from Pirsig, *Zen and the Art of Motorcycle Maintenance*, 175.

For more on India's imports of Russian oil, see Curtis Williams, "India Plans to Keep Buying Cheap Russian Oil, Oil Minister Says," Reuters, September 18, 2024; and "How India's Imports of Russian Oil Have Lubricated Global Markets," *The Economist*, April 11, 2021.

The opposition politician's comments and Jaishankar's response are reported in "EAM Jaishankar's Response to RJD MP Major Jha," *Economics Times*, December 9, 2022, 2:18–2:32, https://economictimes.indiatimes.com/news/india/eam-jaishan kars-response-to-rjd-mp-manoj-jha-i-plead-guilty-/videoshow/96112298.cms. For a positive take on Jaishankar's remarks, see " '2014 Was a Watershed': S Jaishankar Gives a Befitting Reply to RJD MP's Remarks on India's Foreign Policy Approach After BJP Came to Power in 2014," OpIndia, December 9, 2022.

My interaction with Minister Jaishankar took place at the Kautilya Economic Conclave 2023, Plenary Session 11 (Closing Plenary Session), New Delhi, October 22, 2023. A video, including the question and answer period, is available at: www.youtube .com/watch?v=ooR6VKP-9Mg. Question: 53:23–54:24; answer: 1:08:12–1:11:21. Also see "Remarks by EAM, Dr. S. Jaishankar at the Closing Plenary Session of the Kautilya Forum," Ministry of External Affairs, Government of India, October 22, 2023, www .mea.gov.in/Speeches-Statements.htm?dtl/37206/Remarks_by_EAM_Dr_S_Jaishankar _at_the_closing_plenary_session_of_the_Kautilya_Forum.

Challenging Choices

For a modern take on the Thucydides trap, see Allison, *Destined for War*; and G. Allison, "Thucydides's Trap," Belfer Center for Science and International Affairs, accessed March 2025, www.belfercenter.org/thucydides-trap/overview-thucydides-trap.

Trump's desire to take over Greenland is reported in David Sanger and Michael Shear, "Trump Floats Using Force to Take Greenland and the Panama Canal," *New York Times*, January 7, 2025. Rubio's statement is taken from "Trump Interest in Buying Greenland 'Not a Joke,' Rubio Says," Reuters, January 30, 2025. Trump's threat to pull the United States out of NATO is discussed in "Trump Confirms He Threatened to Withdraw from NATO," Atlantic Council, August 23, 2018, www.atlanticcouncil .org/blogs/natosource/trump-confirms-he-threatened-to-withdraw-from-nato/.

The Fed's swap lines are discussed in "Central Bank Liquidity Swaps," Board of Governors of the Federal Reserve System, accessed March 2025, www.federalreserve .gov/monetarypolicy/bst_liquidityswaps.htm. India's unsuccessful attempt to secure a swap line is discussed in Prasad, *The Dollar Trap*. A list of swap lines is available at B. Steil, E. Harding, and S. Zucker, "Central Bank Currency Swaps Tracker,"

Council on Foreign Relations, October 2, 2024, www.cfr.org/tracker/central-bank
-currency-swaps-tracker.

An overview of India's *swadeshi* movement is in N. Pai, "A Brief Economics History of Swadeshi," *Indian Public Policy Review* (July 2021), www.ippr.in/index.php/ippr/ar ticle/view/53. China's economic reforms and integration into the global trading system are discussed in J. A. Dorn, "China's Post-1978 Economic Development and Entry into the Global Trading System," Cato Institute, October 10, 2023, www.cato.org/publica tions/chinas-post-1978-economic-development-entry-global-trading-system.

Switzerland's neutrality is discussed in "The Ukraine War Led to a Head-Spinning Shift in European Neutrality," *Washington Post*, April 6, 2023.

For information on ECOWAS, see its official website at https://ecowas.int/; and "Confidence and Security Building Measures: Economic Community of West African States (ECOWAS)," Bureau of Political-Military Affairs, U.S Department of State, June 26, 2000, https://1997-2001.state.gov/global/arms/bureau_pm/csbm /fs_000626_ecowas.html. Recent political turmoil in ECOWAS is discussed in N. Obasi, "What Turmoil in ECOWAS Means for Nigeria and Regional Stability," International Crisis Group, March 29, 2024, www.crisisgroup.org/africa/west-africa /nigeria-sahel/what-turmoil-ecowas-means-nigeria-and-regional-stability.

India Hedges Its Bets

For more on the Non-Aligned Movement, see "Non-Aligned Movement (NAM)," Nuclear Threat Initiative, accessed March 2025, www.nti.org/education-center/trea ties-and-regimes/non-aligned-movement-nam/.

Piyush Goyal's quotes are reported in Lee Ying Shan, "India Rules Out Joining World's Largest Trade Deal, Accuses China of 'Very Opaque' Trade Practices," CNBC, September 23, 2024.

For data on US financial assistance to Pakistan, see "Aid to Pakistan by the Numbers," Center for Global Development, accessed January 2025, www.cgdev.org/page /aid-pakistan-numbers.

For a comparison of India's post-COVID economic performance relative to other major economies, see R. Biswas, "India Seizes Crown of Fastest Growing G20 Economy," S&P Global, December 8, 2023, www.spglobal.com/marketintelligence /en/mi/research-analysis/india-seizes-crown-of-fastest-growing-g20-economy-dec23 .html. The US response to India's stance on the war in Ukraine is reported in Jonathan Lemire and Jennifer Haberkorn, "Biden Is Happy to Throw Modi an Esteemed Dinner. And Bite His Lip About Human Rights," *Politico*, June 22, 2023. Also see the US-India joint statement, available at "Joint Statement from the United States and India," U.S. Embassy and Consulates in India, June 22, 2023, https://in.usem bassy.gov/joint-statement-from-the-united-states-and-india/.

For information about India's G20 Presidency and the communiqué (New Delhi G20 Leaders' Declaration), see Ministry of External Affairs, *G20 New Delhi Leaders' Declaration* (Government of India, 2023), www.mea.gov.in/Images/CPV /G20-New-Delhi-Leaders-Declaration.pdf. The Leaders' Declaration is analyzed in "Experts React: Did India's G20 Just Crack the Code for Diplomatic Consensus?," Atlantic Council, September 10, 2023, www.atlanticcouncil.org/blogs/new

-atlanticist/experts-react-did-indias-g20-just-crack-the-code-for-diplomatic-consen sus/. For more on the joint declaration on Ukraine, see Vikas Pandey and Soutik Biswas, "G20: How Russia and West Agreed on Ukraine Language," BBC, September 10, 2023.

The Rest of the Middle

Territorial disputes between China and the Philippines are summarized in Center for Preventive Action, "Territorial Disputes in the South China Sea," Council on Foreign Relations, September 17, 2024, www.cfr.org/global-conflict-tracker/conflict /territorial-disputes-south-china-sea.

Lee Kuan Yew's speech is available at "Singapore Government Press Statement," National Archives Singapore, June 15, 1966, www.nas.gov.sg/archivesonline/data /pdfdoc/lky19660615.pdf.

Data on Singapore's GDP is available in the World Bank's Open Data portal, accessed June 2025, https://data.worldbank.org/indicator/NY.GDP.MKTP.CD?lo cations=SG.

Kausikan's comments are reported in www.straitstimes.com/opinion/no-sweet -spot-for-spore-in-us-china-tensions. This article is archived on the Wayback Machine internet archive at https://web.archive.org/.

Vietnam's trade data are available in the webpage on Vietnam by the Observatory of Economic Complexity (OEC), accessed March 2025, https://oec.world/en/profile /country/vnm. Vietnam's policy is described in Tom O'Connor, "America's Favorite Communists Are on the Frontlines of a US-China Rivalry," *Newsweek*, September 10, 2023; and Linh Pham, "Vietnam Releases Defense White Paper, Reaffirming No Military Alliance," *Hanoi Times*, November 26, 2019.

The Spratly Islands dispute between China and the Philippines is discussed in Emily Feng, "On a Remote Island, a Test of Wills Between the Philippines and China," NPR, April 11, 2024. For information on the US-Philippines Mutual Defense Treaty, see E. Albert, "The U.S.-Philippines Defense Alliance," Council on Foreign Relations, October 21, 2016, www.cfr.org/backgrounder/us-philippines-de fense-alliance. The Trump presidency's implications for the Philippines are discussed in Raissa Robles, "US Aid Freeze Sparks Fears Philippines Will Become 'Bargaining Chip' in Trump's China Talks," *South China Morning Post*, January 29, 2025.

Macron's speech is available at "Emmanuel Macron: Europe—It Can Die. A New Paradigm at the Sorbonne," Groupe d'études géopolitiques, April 26, 2024, https:// geopolitique.eu/en/2024/04/26/macron-europe-it-can-die-a-new-paradigm-at-the -sorbonne/.

Macron's dissolution of the French Parliament is reported in Sylvie Corbet and Samuel Petrequin, "Macron Dissolves the French Parliament and Calls a Snap Election After Defeat in EU Vote," Associated Press, June 9, 2024. The results of the French election are reported in Hanne Cokelaere and Victor Goury-Laffont, "France Election Results 2024: Who Won Across the Country," *Politico*, July 7, 2024. Jaishankar's quote about Europe appears in Patrick Wintour, "Why US Double Standards on Israel and Russia Play into a Dangerous Game," *The Guardian*, December 26, 2023.

For a discussion of Africa's demographics, see Jackie Cilliers, *Demographics* (ISS African Futures, last updated 2025), https://futures.issafrica.org/thematic/03-demo graphic-dividend/; and A. Stanley, "African Century," *Finance and Development Magazine*, IMF, September 2023, www.imf.org/en/Publications/fandd/issues/2023 /09/PT-african-century.

For annual GDP of Nigeria and South Africa, see World Bank's Open Data portal, accessed March 2025, https://data.worldbank.org/indicator/NY.GDP.MKTP .CD?locations=NG-ZA.

Details about the African Continental Free Trade Area are available on its official website, accessed March 2025, https://au-afcfta.org/about/. The agreement covers all fifty-five members of the African Union: "Member States," African Union, accessed March 2025, https://au.int/en/member_states/countryprofiles2. Whether Africa has fifty-four or fifty-five countries is a matter of dispute, with the status of Western Sahara ambiguous.

The findings about the effects of climate change on Africa come from the World Meteorological Association's 2023 report, available at "Africa Suffers Disproportionately from Climate Change," World Meteorological Organization, September 4, 2023, https://wmo.int/media/news/africa-suffers-disproportionately-from-climate-change.

Lula's quote on the dollar is from Joe Leahy and Hudson Lockett, "Brazil's Lula Calls for End to Dollar Trade Dominance," *Financial Times*, April 13, 2023. Lula's quote about the US embargo on Cuba is from "Brazil's President Calls U.S. Economic Embargo on Cuba 'Illegal,' Condemns Terrorist List Label," Reuters, September 16, 2023.

Milei's quote appears in "Milei: 'We Must Strengthen Strategic Alliance with United States,'" *Buenos Aires Times*, May 4, 2024.

Argentina's activation of the swap line is reported in Manuela Tobias, "China Lets Argentina Tap Extra $6.5 Billion from Swap Line," Bloomberg, October 18, 2023.

China's reactions to Milei's actions are reported in Natalie Liu, "Milei's Government Pays IMF Without Tapping China Currency Swap," Voice of America, December 24, 2023.

Atrophying Alliances

The aftermath of the 2018 G7 summit is reported in David Ljunggren and Roberta Rampton, "Trade War Turns Canada's G7 Summit into Six-Plus-Trump," Reuters, June 4, 2018; Yuko Takeo, Natalie Obiko Pearson, and Jana Randow, "U.S. Isolated at 'G-6 Plus 1' as Divisions Sap Western Alliance," Bloomberg, May 31, 2018; and www.brookings.edu/articles/trump-just-blew-up-the-g-7-now-what/.

The Trump and Navarro quotes are taken from "G7 Summit Ends in Disarray over Tariffs," BBC, June 10, 2018; and Brent D. Griffiths, "Navarro: 'Special Place in Hell' for Trudeau," *Politico*, June 10, 2018. Navarro later apologized for his language but did not retract his sentiments.

The African Union and EU statements are taken from "Theme of the Year 2023: 'Acceleration of AfCFTA Implementation,'" African Union, 2023, https://au.int/en /theme/2023/acceleration-of-afcfta-implementation; and Directorate-General for

Communication, *A Short Guide to the EU* (European Commission, 2021), https://op.europa.eu/webpub/com/short-guide-eu/en/, respectively.

For details about the TPP, see "Overview of TPP," Office of the United States Trade Representative, accessed December 2024, https://ustr.gov/tpp/overview-of-the-TPP.

Clinton's and Trump's views on the TPP are reported in Jacob Pramuk, "Clinton and Trump Can Agree on at Least One Thing," CNBC, August 11, 2016. The Obama administration's abandonment of TPP ratification is reported in William Mauldin, "Obama Administration Gives Up on Pacific Trade Deal," *Wall Street Journal*, November 16, 2016.

Trump's withdrawal from the TPP is reported in Peter Baker, "Trump Abandons Trans-Pacific Partnership, Obama's Signature Trade Deal," *New York Times*, January 23, 2017. For a discussion of the tariff threats directed at Canada and Mexico, see Ana Swanson, Alan Rappeport, and Colby Smith, "Trump Will Hit Mexico, Canada and China with Tariffs," *New York Times*, January 31, 2025.

Trump's sentiments about NAFTA are reported in "Trump Calls NAFTA 'One of the Worst Deals Anybody in History Has Ever Entered Into,'" *Washington Post*, August 29, 2017. His threat to pull out of NATO is discussed in "Trump Confirms He Threatened to Withdraw from NATO," Atlantic Council, August 23, 2018, www.atlanticcouncil.org/blogs/natosource/trump-confirms-he-threatened-to-withdraw-from-nato/.

The USMCA is discussed in Alan Rappeport, "What's in a Name Change? For Those Saying U.S.M.C.A., a Mouthful," *New York Times*, October 2, 2018.

For a discussion of the RCEP, see P. A. Petri and M. Plummer, "RCEP: A New Trade Agreement That Will Shape Global Economics and Politics," Brookings Institution, November 16, 2020, www.brookings.edu/articles/rcep-a-new-trade-agreement-that-will-shape-global-economics-and-politics/.

The IPEF is described in "Indo-Pacific Economic Framework for Prosperity (IPEF)," Office of the United States Trade Representative, accessed December 2024, https://ustr.gov/trade-agreements/agreements-under-negotiation/indo-pacific-economic-framework-prosperity-ipef. US pullback from the negotiations on the trade pillar is reported in Gavin Bade, "How Sherrod Brown Rattled Biden's Summit Agenda," *Politico*, November 14, 2023.

Putin's participation at the Johannesburg Summit is discussed in Mogomotsi Magome, "South African Leader Says That Arresting Putin If He Comes to Johannesburg Next Month Would Be 'War,'" Associated Press, July 18, 2023.

For additional commentary on the BRICS, see Oliver Stuenkel, "BRICS Faces a Reckoning," *Foreign Policy*, June 22, 2023. India's and China's differing goals for the BRICS are analyzed in Hung Tran, "China and India Are at Odds over BRICS Expansion," Atlantic Council, August 8, 2023.

The BRICS expansion is discussed in Sumayya Ismail, "'A Wall of BRICS': The Significance of Adding Six New Members to the Bloc," Al Jazeera, August 24, 2023.

Modi's quote is reported in Geeta Mohan, "6 Countries to Join BRICS from 2024, PM Congratulated for Chandrayaan-3 Success," *India Today*, August 24, 2023.

The response of Türkiye to the proposal for NATO expansion is discussed in Paul Levin, "The Turkish Veto: Why Erdogan Is Blocking Finland and Sweden's Path to NATO," Foreign Policy Research Institute, March 8, 2023; and John Solomou, "Why Erdogan, Infuriating the West, Blocks Sweden's and Finland's NATO Bid?," *The Print*, January 30, 2023. The possibility of Türkiye's expulsion from NATO is discussed in Aurel Sari, "Can Turkey Be Expelled from NATO? It's Legally Possible, Whether or Not Politically Prudent," *Just Security*, October 15, 2019. The F-16 deal is reported in Willem Marx, "The State Department Allows the Sale of F-16 Jets to Turkey to Move Forward," NPR, January 27, 2024.

Article Seven of the Treaty of the EU allows for the possibility of suspending a member country's rights (but not its obligations) if the country in question "seriously and persistently breaches the principles on which the EU is founded." See "Suspension Clause (Article 7 of the Treaty on European Union)," EUR-Lex, accessed March 2025, https://eur-lex.europa.eu/EN/legal-content/glossary/suspension-clause-article-7-of-the-treaty-on-european-union.html. The difficulties in expelling EU members are discussed in Alice Tidey, "EU Member States Can Leave, but Can the Bloc Kick One of Them Out?," Euronews, April 8, 2022. The blocking of EU aid to Ukraine is reported in Paul Taylor, "Despite the Wrecking Tactics of Viktor Orbán, the EU Will Find a Way to Get Aid to Ukraine," *The Guardian*, December 19, 2023.

Taiwan's Travails

Nuclear powers are listed in "Status of World Nuclear Forces," Federation of American Scientists, March 26, 2025, https://fas.org/initiative/status-world-nuclear-forces/. For details on Iran's nuclear weapons program, see Paul K. Kerr, *Iran and Nuclear Weapons Production* (Congressional Research Service, 2025), https://crsreports.congress.gov/product/pdf/IF/IF12106.

For a summary of China's economic history and its implications for US policy, see Wayne M. Morrison, *China's Economic Rise: History, Trends, Challenges, and Implications for the United States* (Congressional Research Service, 2019), https://crsreports.congress.gov/product/pdf/RL/RL33534.

Differing views among China's military are discussed in Tong Zhao, "How China's Echo Chamber Threatens Taiwan," *Foreign Affairs*, May 9, 2023; and Frederik Kelter, "Not All in China's Military View Taiwan, the West as Primary Threat," Al Jazeera, October 20, 2023. Xi's army purge is reported in Nectar Gan, "Xi Brought Down Powerful Rivals in the Military. Now He's Going After His Own Men," CNN, December 15, 2024.

Alternative perspectives on China's possible invasion of Taiwan are discussed in M. Mazza, "An Assessment of the 20th CCP Congress for US Policy Towards Taiwan," American Enterprise Institute, November 16, 2022, www.aei.org/articles/an-assessment-of-the-20th-ccp-congress-for-us-policy-towards-taiwan/; and "When It Comes to a War with Taiwan, Many Chinese Urge Caution," *The Economist*, June 19, 2023.

CSIS analysis on options for a Chinese blockade of Taiwan is at Bonny Lin, Brian Hart, Matthew P. Funaiole, Samantha Lu, and Truly Tinsley, *How China Could Blockade Taiwan* (Center for Strategic and International Studies, 2024), https://

features.csis.org/chinapower/china-blockade-taiwan/. RAND analysis on Chinese disinformation employed in Taiwan is at S. W. Harold, "How Would China Weaponize Disinformation Against Taiwan in a Cross-Strait Conflict?," RAND, April 15, 2024, www.rand.org/pubs/commentary/2024/04/how-would-china-weaponize -disinformation-against-taiwan.html.

Trump's quotes are reported in Seema Mody, "Trump Accuses Taiwan of Stealing U.S. Chip Industry. Here's What the Election Could Bring," CNBC, October 28, 2024; Didi Tang, "Trump Says Taiwan Should Pay More for Defense and Dodges Questions if He Would Defend the Island," Associated Press, July 17, 2024; and R. C. Bush and R. Hass, "How Would the Trump or Harris Administration Approach Taiwan?," Brookings Institution, October 3, 2024, www.brookings.edu/articles/how -would-the-trump-or-harris-administration-approach-taiwan/.

Republican opposition to a bill that included military aid to Israel and Ukraine is reported in Clare Foran, Ted Barrett, Morgan Rimmer, and Manu Raju, "Senate Republicans Block Bipartisan Border Deal and Foreign Aid Package Following Months of Negotiations," CNN, February 7, 2024.

6. New Technologies: Panacea or Peril?

The epigraph is taken from *Selected Poetry of Ogden Nash*, 346.

The video of the WEF session is available at "The Future of Money," World Economic Forum, June 27, 2023, video, YouTube, www.youtube.com/watch?v=gyAN VmHJB3c.

The story is reported at Karena Phan, "Video Doesn't Show World Economic Forum Speaker Calling for a Cashless Society," Associated Press, July 12, 2023, which also provides links to several of the video clips.

The discussion of the rates of adoption of new technologies is based on Azhar, *Exponential Age*.

The Digital Revolution in Finance

For more information on the India Stack, see its official website, accessed March 2025, https://indiastack.org/. Direct benefit transfers in India are described on its website, accessed March 2025, https://dbtbharat.gov.in/. Data on the proliferation of digital payments worldwide are available in the World Bank's Global Findex Database, accessed March 2025, www.worldbank.org/en/publication/globalfindex.

The original Bitcoin white paper is available at S. Nakamoto, "Bitcoin: A Peer-to-Peer Electronic Cash System," Bitcoin.org, March 2009, https://bitcoin.org /bitcoin.pdf. See also "Bitcoin," Libertarianism.org, accessed March 2025, www.lib ertarianism.org/topics/bitcoin. Bitcoin, blockchain technology, and other concepts discussed in this chapter, such as stablecoins and CBDCs, are explained in Prasad, *The Future of Money*.

For more on the use of blockchain in land record maintenance and government procurement, see "Land Records," Government of India, National Informatics Centre, accessed March 2025, https://blockchain.gov.in/Home/CaseStudy?Case

Study=LandRegistration; A. Sarkar, "Indian Town Adopts Avalanche Blockchain for Tamper-Proof Land Records," Cointelegraph, March 6, 2025, https://cointele graph.com/news/india-dantewada-land-records-avalanche-blockchain; and "Exploring Blockchain Technology for Government Transparency," World Economic Forum, accessed March 2025, www.weforum.org/publications/exploring-blockchain-tech nology-for-government-transparency-to-reduce-corruption/articles/.

Another example of a DAO is Maker DAO, which allows participants to create new units of currency using other cryptocurrencies as collateral. See MakerDAO's and ConstitutionDAO's official websites at, respectively, accessed March 2025, https:// makerdao.com/en/; and www.constitutiondao.com/. Ken Griffin's winning bid is discussed in Yun Li and Leslie Picker, "Citadel CEO Ken Griffin Pays $43.2 Million for Constitution Copy, Outbidding Crypto Group," CNBC, November 19, 2021.

For more details on the eCNY, see "E-CNY: Main Objectives, Guiding Principles and Inclusion Considerations," Bank for International Settlements, accessed April 14, 2025, www.bis.org/publ/bppdf/bispap123_e.pdf.

The Florida legislation on CBDC is noted in "Governor Ron DeSantis Announces Legislation to Protect Floridians from a Federally Controlled Central Bank Digital Currency and Surveillance State," Executive Office of Governor Ron DeSantis, March 20, 2024, www.flgov.com/eog/news/press/2023/governor-ron-desantis-an nounces-legislation-protect-floridians-federally-controlled.

For information about FedNow, see "FedNow® Service," Board of Governors of the Federal Reserve System, last updated July 20, 2023, www.federalreserve.gov/pay mentsystems/fednow_about.htm.

For details about the Thai transfer program, see Patpicha Tanakasempipat and Pathom Sangwongwanich, "Thailand Goes Ahead with Controversial $14 Billion Cash Handout to Prop Economy," *Time*, November 10, 2023; and A. Anantha Lakshmi, "Thailand Kicks off Bumper Cash Handouts to Boost Ailing Economy," *Financial Times*, September 29, 2024. The Bank of Thailand's work on CBDCs is described at "Central Bank Digital Currency," Bank of Thailand, accessed March 2025, www.bot.or.th/en/financial-innovation/digital-finance/central-bank-digital-cur rency.html. Also see the CBDC Tracker's page on Thailand at https://cbdctracker .hrf.org/currency/thailand; and Eswar Prasad, "Thailand May Tell Us a Great Deal about the Future of Money," *Financial Times*, August 6, 2024.

This discussion about privacy draws on Eswar Prasad, "Cryptocurrency Could Help Governments and Businesses Spy on Us," *Washington Post*, April 1, 2022.

Artificial Intelligence

A discussion of how AI is revolutionizing drug discovery is available at Dhruv Khullar, "How A.I. Teaches Machines to Discover Drugs," *New Yorker*, September 2, 2024.

For perspectives on AI's contribution to productivity growth and its impact on employment, see A. Singla, A. Sukharevsky, L. Yee, M. Chui, and B. Hall, "The State of AI: How Organizations Are Rewiring to Capture Value," McKinsey and Company, March 12, 2025, www.mckinsey.com/capabilities/quantumblack/our-insights /the-state-of-ai; M. Kinder, X. Briggs, M. Muro, S. Liu, "Generative AI, the American

Worker, and the Future of Work," Brookings Institution, October 10, 2024, www
.brookings.edu/articles/generative-ai-the-american-worker-and-the-future-of-work/; and
A. Klein, "Not All Robots Take Your Job, Some Become Your Co-Worker," Brookings Institution, October 30, 2019, www.brookings.edu/articles/not-all-robots-take
-your-job-some-become-your-co-worker/. One study that identifies the benefits of AI
for low-skill workers is available at E. Brynjolfsson, D. Li, and L. Raymond, "Generative AI at Work," November 18, 2024, https://danielle-li.github.io/assets/docs
/GenerativeAIatWork.pdf. For additional perspectives, see Autor, "Applying AI to
Rebuild Middle Class Jobs"; Acemoglu and Johnson, *Power and Progress*; and Deming, Ong, and Summers, "Technological Disruption in the Labor Market."

One study that shows how AI is transforming radiology is available at A. Bhan-
dari, "Revolutionizing Radiology with Artificial Intelligence," PubMed Central, October 29, 2024, https://pmc.ncbi.nlm.nih.gov/articles/PMC11521355/. The effect of
AI on India's tech outsourcing is reported in Megha Mandavia, "AI Is Coming for
India's Famous Tech Hub," *Wall Street Journal*, August 6, 2024.

An approach to reducing bias in AI models is described in A. Zewe, "Researchers
Reduce Bias in AI Models While Preserving or Improving Accuracy," *MIT News*,
December 11, 2024, https://news.mit.edu/2024/researchers-reduce-bias-ai-models
-while-preserving-improving-accuracy-1211.

For an explanation of deepfakes and their implications, see M. Somers, "Deepfakes, Explained," MIT Sloan School of Management, July 21, 2020, https://mit
sloan.mit.edu/ideas-made-to-matter/deepfakes-explained.

Information Technology

For an overview of the geopolitical and cyber threats posed by Russia, China, Iran,
and North Korea in the context of the 2024 US presidential election, see A. C. Rutay-
isire, "From Geopolitics to Cyber Threats," QuoIntelligence, October 18, 2024, https://
quointelligence.eu/2024/10/from-geopolitics-to-cyber-threats-2024-us-election/.

Guardrails

Google's dominance of search can be seen at "Search Engine Market Share in
2024," Oberlo, accessed April 14, 2025, www.oberlo.com/statistics/search-engine
-market-share.

See "Statement on the Approval of Spot Bitcoin Exchange-Traded Products,"
SEC, January 10, 2024, www.sec.gov/newsroom/speeches-statements/gensler-state
ment-spot-bitcoin-011023.

This discussion draws on Eswar Prasad, "Crypto Is Celebrating but Trump's
Boosterism Could End Badly," *Financial Times*, January 25, 2025. For Trump's shift-
ing views on Bitcoin, see Brian Bennett and Nik Popli, "Where Trump 2.0 Might
Look Very Different from Trump 1.0," *Time*, November 25, 2024.

The proposal for a US Bitcoin strategic reserve is reported here: Gertrude Chavez-
Dreyfuss and Lisa Pauline Mattackal, "How Would a US Bitcoin Strategic Reserve
Work?," Reuters, December 17, 2024. The issuance of the Trump and Melania meme

coins is discussed in Chandelis Duster, "What to Know About Trump Cryptocurrency Meme Coins," NPR, January 20, 2025.

For details about cryptocurrency usage in India, see "Cryptocurrencies: India," Statista, accessed March 2025, www.statista.com/outlook/fmo/digital-assets/cryptocurrencies/india. For details about the Indian government's regulation of cryptocurrencies, see "India's 2024 Regulatory Framework Unveiled," Impact and Policy Research Institute, September 9, 2024, www.impriindia.com/insights/crypto-india-regulatory-framework/.

Kreps, *Tech Titans*, discusses the tensions inherent in regulating new technologies.

The SEC's filing accusing FTX of fraud is available here: "SEC Charges Samuel Bankman-Fried with Defrauding Investors in Crypto Asset Trading Platform FTX," U.S Securities and Exchange Commission, December 13, 2022, www.sec.gov/newsroom/press-releases/2022-219. For a narrative of FTX's demise, see Sallee Ann Harrison, "A Timeline of the Collapse at FTX," Associated Press, May 8, 2024.

Dashed Dreams of Plenty

Ukraine's prewar share of wheat exports is noted in D. Ulybina and C. Rastogi, "Global Wheat Shipments Withstood the Shock of Russia's Invasion of Ukraine," *Trade Post* (blog), February 22, 2024, https://blogs.worldbank.org/en/trade/global-wheat-shipments-withstood-shock-russias-invasion-ukraine#. Restrictions on food exports and the implications for food security are discussed in K. Robinson, "How Russia's War in Ukraine Could Amplify Food Insecurity in the Mideast," Council on Foreign Relations, April 21, 2022, www.cfr.org/in-brief/how-russias-war-ukraine-could-amplify-food-insecurity-mideast; and "Rice Export Prices Highest in More than a Decade as India Restricts Trade," Foreign Agricultural Service, US Department of Agriculture, September 19, 2023, https://fas.usda.gov/data/rice-export-prices-highest-more-decade-india-restricts-trade.

The potential for expanding Africa's agricultural output is discussed in Susannah Savage, "Can Africa One Day Help Feed the World's Growing Population?," *Financial Times*, April 3, 2024.

7. Visions for the World

The epigraph comes from Camus, *The Rebel*, 208.

US opinion polls regarding government surveillance are discussed at H. Hartig and C. Doherty, "Two Decades Later, the Enduring Legacy of 9/11," Pew Research Center, September 2, 2021, www.pewresearch.org/politics/2021/09/02/two-decades-later-the-enduring-legacy-of-9-11/; and E. Goitein, "Rolling Back the Post-9/11 Surveillance State," Brennan Center for Justice, August 25, 2021, www.brennancenter.org/our-work/analysis-opinion/rolling-back-post-911-surveillance-state. See Trump's statements about immigrants at M. Waldman, "Fact-Checking Trump's Speech on Crime and Immigrants," Brennan Center for Justice, February 28, 2024, www.brennancenter.org/our-work/analysis-opinion/fact-checking-trumps-speech-crime-and-immigrants.

Developments in Rwanda are discussed in Declan Walsh, "From the Horror to the Envy of Africa: Rwanda's Leader Holds Tight Grip," *New York Times*, April 6, 2024.

The situation in El Salvador is described in Natalie Kitroeff, "He Cracked Down on Gangs and Rights. Now He's Set to Win a Landslide," *New York Times*, February 2, 2024; and Will Freeman and Lucas Perelló, "The Drop in Crime in El Salvador Is Stunning, but It Has a Dark Side," *New York Times*, February 8, 2024.

For an analysis of cooperation between authoritarian governments, see Christina Cottiero and Cassandra Emmons, *Understanding and Interrupting Authoritarian Collaboration* (International Foundation for Electoral Systems, 2024), www.ifes.org /publications/authoritarian-collaboration.

Economic Models

See Rajan and Zingales, *Saving Capitalism from the Capitalists*.

For more information about Mao Zedong's "Great Leap Forward," see C. D. Brown, "China's Great Leap Forward," Association for Asian Studies, 2012, www .asianstudies.org/publications/eaa/archives/chinas-great-leap-forward. For information on *swadeshi*, see N. Pai, "A Brief Economics History of Swadeshi," *Indian Public Policy Review* (July 2021), www.ippr.in/index.php/ippr/article/view/53.

China's saving rate is discussed in "Explaining Economic Growth and Savings Rates in China Following Its Demographic and Industrial Transformation," Federal Reserve Bank of Philadelphia, December 13, 2022, www.philadelphiafed.org/the -economy/explaining-economic-growth-and-savings-rate-in-china. For evidence on the share of Chinese bank loans issued to state-owned enterprises, see Yiming Cao, Raymond Fisman, Hui Lin, and Yongxiang Wang, *Why Do China's Banks Lend to Failing SOEs?* (Stanford Center on China's Economy and Institutions, 2024), https:// sccei.fsi.stanford.edu/china-briefs/why-do-chinas-banks-lend-failing-soes-effect -lending-targets-bad-debt-and-economic.

Prasad, "Has China's Growth Gone from Miracle to Malady?," analyzes China's GDP growth.

Press conference on August 13, 2015, translated by Yishuo (Cathy) Yang. The full transcript of the press conference, which was available in Chinese, is no longer available online. The press conference is alluded to here: Chi Hung Kwan, "The Yuan's Shift," RIETI, October 14, 2015, www.rieti.go.jp/en/china/15091001.html.

The case that government housing policies were the cause of the US financial crisis is made in N. Goodnow, "A Q&A with Peter Wallison on the 2008 Financial Crisis and Why It Might Happen Again," American Enterprise Institute, January 13, 2015, www.aei.org/economics/hidden-plain-sight-qa-peter-wallison-2008-financial -crisis-might-happen/.

For an analysis of the US banking turmoil in early 2023, see Tobias Adrian, Nassira Abbas, Silvia Ramirez, and Gonzalo Fernandez Dionis, *The US Banking Sector Since the March 2023 Turmoil: Navigating the Aftermath* (International Monetary Fund, 2024), www.imf.org/en/Publications/global-financial-stability-notes/Issues /2024/03/04/The-US-Banking-Sector-since-the-March-2023-Turmoil-Navigating -the-Aftermath-544809.

For a description of China's deposit insurance system, see "Officials Answered Questions on Regulations on Deposit Insurance," People's Bank of China, April 9, 2015, www.pbc.gov.cn/english/130721/2811497/index.html; and S. Desai, "A Regional Comparison of China's New Deposit Insurance System," Federal Reserve Bank of San Francisco, February 24, 2016, www.frbsf.org/research-and-insights/blog/sf-fed-blog/2016/02/24/regional-comparison-chinas-new-deposit-insurance-system/.

China's "dual circulation" policy is discussed in Kevin Yao, "What We Know About China's 'Dual Circulation' Economic Strategy," Reuters, September 9, 2020. For information on India's "Make in India" initiative, see "Major Initiatives," Prime Minister's Office, accessed March 2025, www.pmindia.gov.in/en/major_initiatives/make-in-india/. The CHIPS and Science Act is summarized at "Fact Sheet: CHIPS and Science Act Will Lower Costs, Create Jobs, Strengthen Supply Chains, and Counter China," The White House, August 9, 2022, https://bidenwhitehouse.archives.gov/briefing-room/statements-releases/2022/08/09/fact-sheet-chips-and-science-act-will-lower-costs-create-jobs-strengthen-supply-chains-and-counter-china/. For more on the Inflation Reduction Act and Europe's response to it, see C. Wessner and S. Khemka, "Getting Real on the Inflation Reduction Act," Center for Strategic and International Studies, March 7, 2023, www.csis.org/analysis/getting-real-inflation-reduction-act.

Jake Sullivan's remarks can be found at "Remarks by National Security Advisor Jake Sullivan on Renewing American Economic Leadership at the Brookings Institution," The White House, April 27, 2023, https://bidenwhitehouse.archives.gov/briefing-room/speeches-remarks/2023/04/27/remarks-by-national-security-advisor-jake-sullivan-on-renewing-american-economic-leadership-at-the-brookings-institution/; and Jake Sullivan, "The Sources of American Power," *Foreign Affairs*, October 24, 2023.

The full text of Macron's speech is available at "Emmanuel Macron: Europe—It Can Die. A New Paradigm at the Sorbonne," Groupe d'études géopolitiques, April 26, 2024, https://geopolitique.eu/en/2024/04/26/macron-europe-it-can-die-a-new-paradigm-at-the-sorbonne/.

For details on the Common Prosperity Policy, see A. C. Katy, "How to Understand China's Common Prosperity Policy," *China Briefing*, March 21, 2022, www.china-briefing.com/news/china-common-prosperity-what-does-it-mean-for-foreign-investors/.

Political Models

For reporting about the treatment of political dissidents in Singapore, see "Singapore: Authorities Given Broad New Powers to Police Protests," Amnesty International, April 4, 2017, www.amnesty.org/en/latest/press-release/2017/04/singapore-authorities-given-broad-new-powers-to-police-protests/; and Koh Ewe, "Scandals Test Singapore's 'Thin-Skinned' Approach to Public Criticism," *Time*, August 2, 2023.

For reporting on the elections in Russia, North Korea, and Iran, see Guy Faulconbridge and Andrew Osborn, "Putin Wins Russia Election in Landslide with No Serious Competition," Reuters, March 18, 2024; "Kim Jong Un Wins 100% of Votes in North Korea Election," NBC News, March 10, 2014; and "Hard-Line Judiciary Head Wins Iran's Presidency amid a Low Turnout," NPR, June 19, 2021.

Freedom, Accountability, and Legitimacy

See Prasad, *Gaining Currency*, Chapter 1, for a discussion of how the property of the entire family of a currency counterfeiter was once subject to confiscation. Also see Yao Lao, "Families That Hang Together," *China Daily*, May 17, 2004; and Maureen Fan, "In China, Children of Inmates Face Hard Time Themselves," *Washington Post*, October 13, 2006.

An update on the policy of limiting industrial activity around Beijing is reported in "Overgrown Beijing Slaps New Limits on Industry in Bid to Cut Smog," Reuters, July 25, 2014. The policy about driving restrictions in Beijing based on license plate numbers is available at "Notice: New Driving Restrictions Based on Last Digit to Be Implemented in Beijing," People's Government of Beijing Municipality, March 26, 2024, https://english.beijing.gov.cn/latest/news/202403/t20240326_3601791.html.

Chinese statistics and data blackouts are reported in Liyan Qi, "China's Fertility Rate Dropped Sharply, Study Shows," *Wall Street Journal*, August 19, 2023; Claire Fu, "China's Youth Unemployment Rate Is Back, and Better," *New York Times*, January 17, 2024; Daisuke Wakabayashi and Claire Fu, "A Crisis of Confidence Is Gripping China's Economy," *New York Times*, August 25, 2023; "New Rules Compel Leading China Financial Data Provider to Limit Offshore Access, Sources Tell Reuters," CNBC, May 4, 2023; and "Chinese Stock Investors Lose a Key Indicator to Gauge Sentiment," Bloomberg, August 18, 2024. See also Daisuke Wakabayashi and Claire Fu, "China's Censorship Dragnet Targets Critics of the Economy," *New York Times*, January 31, 2024; and Tom Hancock, "Did China's Economy Really Grow 5.2% in 2023? Not All Agree," Bloomberg UK, January 18, 2024.

The text of Modi's speech announcing the demonetization is available at "PM's Address to the Nation," Prime Minister's Office, November 8, 2016, www.pmindia.gov.in/en/news_updates/prime-ministers-address-to-the-nation/. For reporting on the impact of and public reactions to demonetization, see Geeta Anand, "Modi's Cash Ban Brings Pain, but Corruption-Weary India Grits Its Teeth," *New York Times*, January 2, 2017.

Trump's attitude toward and statements about paying taxes are reported in Steve Eder and Megan Twohey, "Donald Trump Acknowledges Not Paying Federal Income Taxes for Years," *New York Times*, October 10, 2016; Aaron Blake, "Donald Trump's Defenses of Not Paying Taxes Pretty Much Say It All," *Washington Post*, October 2, 2016; and Nolan D. McCaskill, "Trump Boasts About 'Brilliantly' Using the Tax Laws," *Politico*, October 3, 2016.

See Xi Jinping's slogan at Tania Branigan, "Xi Jinping Vows to Fight 'Tigers' and 'Flies' in Anti-Corruption Drive," *The Guardian*, January 22, 2013. The Bo Xilai arrest and its fallout are described in C. Li, "The Bo Xilai Crisis: A Curse or a Blessing for China?," Brookings Institution, April 18, 2012, www.brookings.edu/articles/the-bo-xilai-crisis-a-curse-or-a-blessing-for-china/; and Andrew Jacobs and Chris Buckley, "Chinese Official at Center of Scandal Is Found Guilty and Given a Life Term," *New York Times*, September 21, 2013.

The eventual impact of India's demonetization on corruption is discussed in Jeffrey Gettleman, "Modi's Cash Crackdown Failed, Indian Bank Data Shows," *New York Times*, August 30, 2018.

8. Reclaiming Order from Disorder

The epigraph comes from Calasso, *The Celestial Hunter*, 26.

The Uncertain Arc of History

See Fukuyama, *The End of History and the Last Man*.

For details about G20 cooperation during the global financial crisis, see G20 Research Group, *Declaration of the Summit on Financial Markets and the World Economy* (2008), https://g20.utoronto.ca/2008/2008declaration1115.html; and J. Furman and J. Zients, "The G-20's Role in Economic Progress Since 2009," The White House, September 2, 2016, https://obamawhitehouse.archives.gov/blog/2016/09/02/g-20s-role-economic-progress-2009.

Democracy and Free Markets

For details pertaining to the democracy summit, see "The 3rd Summit for Democracy," International IDEA, accessed March 2025, www.idea.int/events/3rd-summit-democracy. On the imposition of martial law and South Korea's history of coups and other episodes of martial law, see Foster Klug, "What to Know About South Korea's Short-Lived Period of Martial Law," Associated Press, December 12, 2024. President Yoon Suk Yeol's impeachment is reported in Hyung-Jin Kim and Kim Tong-Hyung, "South Korea's Parliament Votes to Impeach President Yoon Suk Yeol over His Martial Law Order," Associated Press, December 14, 2024.

For alternative perspectives on the Chinese economic and political systems, see Jin, *The New China Playbook*; and Li, *China's World View*.

The Role of the State

China's domestic stock market interventions are discussed in Tri Vi Dang, Wei Li, and Yongqin Wang, *What Are the Costs and Benefits of China's Domestic Stock Market Interventions?* (Stanford Center on China's Economy and Institutions, 2023), https://sccei.fsi.stanford.edu/china-briefs/what-are-costs-and-benefits-chinas-domestic-stock-market-interventions-0.

Institutions Rule—or Ought To

Conspiracy theories about FEMA are discussed in J. Cercone, "FEMA Conspiracy Theories Have Existed for Decades," WUSF, October 24, 2024.

Index

Eswar S. Prasad is the Tolani Senior Professor of Trade Policy at Cornell University and a senior fellow at the Brookings Institution. He is the author of *The Future of Money*, which was listed among the best books of the year by *The Economist*, *Financial Times*, *Foreign Affairs*, and *The Week*. Prasad lives in Arlington, Virginia, and Ithaca, New York.

TheDoomLoopBook.com